Readings in Social Studies

. . . .

ANCIENT TIMES

Upper Saddle River, New Jersey
Glenview, Illinois
Needham, Massachusetts

Acknowledgments

Grateful acknowledgment is made to the following for permission to reprint copyrighted material:

Enslow Publishers, Inc. "Cities of the Indus Valley" by Joyce Goldenstern from *Lost Cities.* Copyright © 1996 by Joyce Goldenstern.

Farrar, Straus & Giroux, Inc. From *Attar of the Ice Valley* by Leonard Wibberley. Copyright © 1968 by Leonard Wibberley. Reprinted by permission of Farrar, Straus & Giroux, Inc., LLC.

Free To Be Foundation, Inc. "Atalanta" by Betty Miles from *FREE TO BE...YOU AND ME.* Copyright © 1973 Free To Be Foundation, Inc.

Gaer & Associates "The Envious Buffalo: A Jataka Story" by Joseph Gaer from *The Fables of India.* Copyright © 1955 Joseph Gaer, renewed 1983 by Fay Gaer.

James Cross Giblin "The Great Walls of China" by James Cross Giblin from *Walls: Defense throughout History.* Copyright © 1984 by James Cross Giblin.

Golden Books, a division of Random House, Inc. "The Gorgon's Head" by Ann Terry White from *The Golden Treasury of Myths and Legends.* Copyright © 1950 by Golden Press Inc.

Grolier Publishing Company, an imprint of Scholastic "What Ancient Egypt Gave Us" by Geraldine Woods from *Science in Ancient Egypt.* Copyright © 1998 by Geraldine Woods.

Groundwood/Douglas & McIntyre Children's Books "The Friends of Kwan Ming" by Paul Yee from *Tales from Gold Mountain: Stories of the Chinese in the New World.* Copyright © 1989 by Paul Yee.

Harcourt, Inc. "The Monster Humbaba" by Bernarda Bryson from *Gilgamesh: Man's First Story.* Copyright © 1967 by Bernarda Bryson. Excerpt from *Aida* by Leontyne Price. Copyright © 1990 by Leontyne Price.

HarperCollins Publishers, Inc. "The Mysterious Hieroglyphs" by James Cross Giblin from T*he Riddle of the Rosetta Stone.* Copyright © 1990 by James Cross Giblin. "Mummy No. 1770" by Patricia Lauber from *Tales Mummies Tell.* Copyright © 1985 by Patricia Lauber. "To Agni (God of Fire)" from the *Rig Veda,* from *Poems from India,* selected by Daisy Aldan. Copyright © 1969 by Daisy Aldan. "The Egyptian Cinderella" by Shirley Climo from *The Egyptian Cinderella.* Copyright © 1989 by Shirley Climo.

Houghton Mifflin Company "The Life of a Bog" by James M. Deem from *Bodies From the Bog.* Copyright © 1997 by James M. Deem. From *The Bronze Bow* by Elizabeth George Speare. Copyright © 1961 and renewed 1989 by Elizabeth George Speare. "The First Gladiators" (Ch. II) and "Who Were the Gladiators?" (Ch. III) by Richard Watkins from *Gladiator.* Copyright © 1997 by Richard Watkins.

Kingfisher Books, Subsidiary of Groupe de la Cité "Nubia and the Kingdom of Kush," "Foundation of Rome," and "The Decline of the Roman Empire" by Mary Hazel Martell from *The Kingfisher Book of the Ancient World.* Copyright © 1995 by Larousse plc.

Alfred A. Knopf, Inc., a division of Random House, Inc. "Buddhism," "Judaism," & "Confucianism and Taoism" by Mary Pope Osborne from *One World, Many Religions: The Ways We Worship.* Copyright © 1996 by Mary Pope Osborne.

Acknowledgments continued on page 247

Contents

IV. Ancient India and China

Acknowledgments continued from copyright page

from *Walls: Defenses Throughout History.* Copyright © 1984 by James Cross Giblin.

Macmillan Publishing Co., A Division of Simon & Schuster, Inc. "Orpheus" by Alice Low from *Greek Gods and Heroes.* Copyright © 1985 by Macmillan Publishing Company.

Margaret K. McElderry Books, Simon & Schuster Children's Publishing Division "The Great Flood" by Geraldine McCaughrean from *God's People: Stories from The Old Testament.* Copyright © 1997 by Geraldine McCaughrean.

Oxford University Press, Inc. "The Race" by Debjani Chatterjee from *The Elephant-headed God and Other Hindu Tales.* Copyright © 1989 by Debjani Chatterjee.

Oxford University Press, Inc. "Scarlet on the Loom" by Rosemary Sutcliff from *Warrior Scarlet.* Copyright © 1958 Oxford University Press.

Oxford University Press, UK From *The Eagle of the Ninth* by Rosemary Sutcliff. Copyright © 1954 by Oxford University Press, England & Henry Z. Walck, Inc.

Penguin Books Ltd. From *Tao Te Ching (or The Way and Its Power)* by Lao Tzu. Copyright ©1963 by D.C. Lau. From "The Burning of Rome" by Tacitus from *The Annals of Imperial Rome.* Copyright © Michael Grant Publications Ltd., 1956, 1959, 1971.

Penguin Putnam, Inc., A Pearson Company From *The Boy of the Painted Cave* by Justin Denzel. Copyright © 1988 by Justin Denzel.

Peter Bedrick Books Inc. "Famous Women: Scholars and Artists" by Fiona Macdonald from *Women in Ancient Rome.* Copyright © 2000 by Fiona Macdonald.

Raintree/Steck-Vaughn Publishers, Division of Steck-Vaughn Company From *The Ancient Romans* by Anita Ganeri. Copyright © 2000 by Steck-Vaughn Company. "Early Rome" by Sean Sheehan and Pat Levy from *The Ancient World: Rome.* Copyright © 1999 by Steck-Vaughn Company.

Random House, Inc. "The Wooden Horse" by William Russell from *Classical Myths to Read Aloud.* Copyright © 1989 by William F. Russell.

Scholastic, Inc. "The Golden Apples" by Mary Pope Osborne from *Favorite Greek Myths.* Copyright © 1989 by Mary Pope Osborne. "The Sirens: A Greek Myth" by Bernard Evslin from *The Adventures of Ulysses.* © 1969 Scholastic.

Scott, Foresman and Company, a division of Pearson Education "Night Thoughts Aboard a Boat" by Tu Fu, "Ship of State" by Horace, "The Peach-Blossom Fountain" by T'ao Ch'ien from *Scott Foresman Database.*

Simon & Schuster, Inc. "Deborah" by Carol Armstrong from *Women of The Bible.*

The Atlantic Monthly Press, an imprint of Grove/Atlantic "I Built My House Near Where Others Dwell" by T'ao Ch'ien from *Anthology of Chinese Literature.* © 1965 by Grove Press Inc.

The Estate of Arthur Waley, c/o John Robinson From *The Analects of Confucius,* translated by Arthur Waley. Copyright © 1938 by George Allen and Unwin Ltd.

The Estate of Louis & Norma Untermeyer "Rama: The Bow That Could Not Be Bent," "Julius Caesar: The Ides of March," and "The Firebringer: Prometheus" by Louis Untermeyer from *The Firebringer and Other Great Stories.* Copyright © 1968 by Louis Untermeyer.

The Millbrook Press Inc. "In the Beginning" and "Babylonia" by Elaine Landau from *The Babylonians: The Cradle of Civilization.* Copyright © 1997 by Elaine Landau.

University of Chicago Press "The Mice That Set Elephants Free" and "The Brahman, The Thief, and the Ghost" by Arthur W. Ryder (translator) from the *Panchatantra.* Copyright 1952 by The University of Chicago; copyright renewed 1953 by Mary E. Ryder and Winifred Ryder. "The Death of Hektor" from Book XXII of the *Iliad* by Homer, from *Iliad of Homer,* translated by Richmond Lattimore. Copyright 1951, The University of Chicago.

University of Texas Press "I Love a Girl, But She Lives Over There" by John L. Foster from *Love Songs of the NEW Kingdom.* Copyright © 1974 by John L. Foster.

Viking Penguin, Inc., a division of Penguin Putnam, Inc. "Writing and Alphabets: Why Did People Begin Writing?" by Tiphaine Samoyault from *Alphabetical Order: How The Alphabet Began.* Copyright © 1996 Circonflexe. Translation copyright © Penguin Books USA Inc. 1998.

Note: Every effort has been made to locate the copyright owner of material reprinted in this book. Omissions brought to our attention will be corrected in subsequent printings.

Introduction

Literature creates its own vivid pictures of historical events. This anthology of fiction, nonfiction, poetry, and drama offers you a window into the thoughts, feelings, and dreams of people who lived in ancient times. You'll read literature from a variety of countries, cultures, and civilizations. As you read the literature in this collection, let it bring history to life for you and help you connect historical events to your own unique experiences.

Even the earliest history of the world includes stories that inspire, inform, and often amaze. This anthology of writing from and about ancient times provides literature that gives voice to the lives and dreams of people around the world whose lives were so different from, and yet in many ways so similar to, your own.

Early Human Societies

Life in the earliest human societies included challenges that twenty-first-century men and women can hardly imagine. Justin Denzel tells the moving story of a young boy who must hide his artistic talent from the members of his clan, who value only those skills that provide food and clothing. Then you will meet Attar, who becomes a man in a dangerous and thrilling encounter with a band of wolves, and Drem, who discovers that his future may not hold what he expects. In a fascinating informational piece, you will acquire unexpected facts about the historical evidence found in bogs, of all places.

Mesopotamia, Egypt, and Kush

From wandering nomads to settled tillers of the soil, early civilizations developed in a variety of ways. Aspects of life that we take for granted, from the alphabet to geometry, originated in the ancient world, as Tiphaine Samoyault and Geraldine Woods will tell you. The heroic saga of Gilgamesh, the story of the great flood, and a moving Egyptian poem about a young man separated from his beloved will remind you of how much you have in common with ancient peoples, while the intriguing story of Mummy No. 1770 will shed light on the fascinating sources that scientists and historians use to expand their knowledge.

Ancient Hebrews and Greeks

Myth and mystery have always fascinated human beings. A selection from the Hebrew Bible gives an account of the creation of the universe, while a selection from Homer's majestic epic about the Trojan War shows the dangers of careless curiosity. Two different versions of the story of Atalanta give you an opportunity to compare and contrast, and the cautionary tale of Narcissus will make you thoughtful the next time you look into a mirror.

Ancient India and China

Lost cities reappear and a Great Wall can be seen from space—it may sound like science fiction, but it is fact. In addition, India and China have their myths and legends as well as their philosophers. The insights of Confucius and the Tao Te Ching have relevance even in these modern times, and the compelling thoughts of poets reflect a world that is strangely familiar even though it was so long ago.

Ancient Rome

Roman centurions and gladiators are more than characters in movies, as you will learn from Rosemary Sutcliff and Richard Watkins. And women had an important role in the Roman empire, as they have had throughout human history. Great cities, cultures, and civilizations develop, progress, and decline, and Tacitus' account of the Great Fire of Rome will have you on the edge of your seat.

Since ancient times, literature has reflected and revealed the history of the world. Without the dimension of literature, history loses some of its richness and immediacy. The visions and inspirations of writers will always have power to move and to inform.

The literature in this anthology will enrich your reading in your social studies textbook and in your literature textbook with additional information, images, stories, and dramatic renditions from nonfiction, fiction, poetry, and drama.

Early Human Societies

The Firebringer: Prometheus

from The Firebringer and Other Great Stories

Louis Untermeyer

In his efforts to help humans, this mythical hero brings a terrible punishment upon himself.

THE LONG war between the fearful Titans[1] and the Olympian gods had finally come to an end with the defeat of the Titans. Zeus, leader of the gods, established his rule in heaven and imprisoned his enemies in Tartarus, a dark domain under the earth.

Not all the Titans had fought against the Olympians. One of those who had helped Zeus was Prometheus, on whom Zeus decided to bestow his favor.

"I have made men and women, three races of them," he told Prometheus. "They did not please me. One race did nothing but eat and drink; another planned only evil things; the third fought among themselves, had no reverence for the gods, and no respect for anything. Nevertheless, mankind should have one more chance, and this time it will be you, not I, who will make a new race. Make men and women out of clay, mix in any other element they may need, and let them work out their destiny. Use any material that is on earth. But one thing you must not do. You must not take anything from the heavens, nothing that belongs to the immortal gods. If you do, there will be a punishment too terrible to contemplate."

Prometheus obeyed. He scooped up some wet clay, and began to shape creatures resembling the gods. In their bodies he built characteristics of all the animals: the pride of the lion, the cleverness of the fox, the loyalty of the dog, the bravery of the bull. He gave them knowledge as well as instinct so they would know how to plow a field, plant seed, cultivate a crop, and reap a harvest. He taught them how to tame wild things, shear sheep, and milk cows. He showed them how to make tools out of stone and how to make weapons to protect themselves from the horns of deer and other beasts. He instructed

---

1. **Titans** a race of giant gods.

them how to exist in the wilderness, how to erect shelters and eventually, how to build houses.

But they were not happy. They shivered miserably through the winters; they sickened on uncooked food; they could not bake bread, bend cold iron, or melt metal. One thing was needed, and that one thing was forbidden: fire, the heavenly fire that belonged to the gods. For a while Prometheus hesitated. He remembered Zeus's threat and realized that anyone who took anything that belonged to the gods would suffer terribly. But men needed the gift of fire; they needed it not only for comfort but also for their future.

Prometheus knew what he had to do and how to do it. He took a long hollow reed, dried it, and filled the inside with pith.[2] He walked in and out of Olympus; none of the gods noticed what he was doing. He touched the gods' hearth-fire with his reed that looked like a walking stick, and a spark from the hearth caught on the pith which burned slowly like the wick of a candle. He brought this from Olympus, lit the first flame on earth, and taught men how to kindle fire whenever it was needed for warmth or for work, for cooking food, shaping metal tools, or creating things of beauty.

When Zeus saw smoke arising, he was furious. He thundered at Prometheus. "I warned you!" he stormed. "Because you dared to bring the gods' fire down to the earthlings you love so much, you shall never leave the earth again. You shall be chained to a rock on the highest peak of the bleak Caucasus. There you shall lie exposed to the heavens you violated. You shall be burned by the rays of the fiery sun and frozen by the icy winds of winter. You shall lie there sleepless and helpless, for no power will come to free you and no creature will hear you. Every day an eagle will tear your flesh and feed upon your liver, and every night the wound will heal so that the eagle can prey upon you again and again."

Prometheus was bound, fettered to the rock with chains of iron and manacles of brass. Years passed, the tortures continued, and Prometheus bore the cruelty of Zeus. He never cried out his agony, nor did he regret what he had done. From time to time Zeus sent a messenger to urge Prometheus to repent. Prometheus re-

---

2. **pith** n. soft, spongy tissue inside certain plant stems.

fused. Then said the messenger, "Zeus knows that you have some secret knowledge about the fate of the gods. If you will disclose the secret, Zeus will set you free."

Prometheus knew that one day Zeus would be dethroned by a son of his own, just as Zeus had overthrown his father. Prometheus knew who the mother would be, and Zeus needed to know the name of the mortal woman so he could guard against her offspring. But Prometheus refused to talk. He remained inflexible, suffering indescribable pain rather than help a tyrant who would not help mankind.

Finally he was freed, not by Zeus, but by Herakles—the Romans called him Hercules—who shot the eagle and restored Prometheus to liberty. Then he went back to work among men.

It was Prometheus (according to the ancients) who gave man humanity. From the Firebringer, mankind inherited his forethought, his fearless spirit as a fighter against tyranny, his courage and, most of all, his compassion for all people everywhere.

from The Boy of the Painted Cave

Justin Denzel

The challenges of life in this clan motivate hard work and skill. For one boy, the work of his heart conflicts with the necessary work of his hands.

Tao looked out across the valley with its endless waves of yellow grass rippling under the late afternoon sun. He could see the small band of hunters walking ahead, turning over logs and stones, searching for ground squirrels, moles and grubs.

Dirt matted their dark beards, burrs and stickers clung to their bearskin robes. They had been out three days, but the hunting was not good. Now they were returning home, tired, almost empty-handed.

The boy watched as the hunters disappeared over the brow of the hill. All day Tao had waited for this moment. With a rabbit in his hand and a leather pouch filled with moles and field mice dangling from his belt, he quickly hobbled over to the foot of a high embankment, where a smooth expanse of white sand had been washed down by the melting snows.

He looked around once again, took a deep breath and placed the rabbit on the ground. Then, with the point of his spear, he began tracing the shape of the rabbit in the sand.

He worked hurriedly, starting with the head, running the spear around the ears and along the back and stubby tail. When he came to the legs, his hand slipped, causing the spear to gouge a hole in the sand. He broke off a nearby willow branch and brushed away the drawing, then started over again. This time he worked carefully, guiding the spear along the natural curves of the animal's body. When it was finished, he stepped back, studying it for a moment. He shook his head. No, it did not look like a rabbit. It was too stiff, not real.

He felt a flush of anger and he shoved the rabbit aside. He looked over his shoulder again to be sure he was alone, then knelt down on the sand. With the fingers of his right hand he began to draw a picture of a bear. This he was sure he could do. Working from memory, he drew the huge head with its open mouth, showing the row of sharp teeth, the small round ears and the short snout.

As he worked, a warm feeling welled up in him. He forgot the hunters and the rabbit. He thought only of the big brown bears he had seen digging for roots in the marsh grass or scooping salmon out of the icy creeks down in the valley. He remembered their strong shoulders and shaggy brown coats, and for a moment the image became a living beast flowing from his mind, through his hand, directly onto the sand.

He finished his drawing by sketching in the high-arched back and sturdy legs. Then he stood up, brushing the sand from his knees. He looked down at the drawing, smiling broadly. It was good, he thought, the best he had ever done. Yet with time and practice he knew he could do better.

He did not remember when he first began making pictures. It must have been many summers ago when he lived with Kala. At first she was frightened of this. It was taboo[1] and she tried to stop him. Then she let him go. But he could draw only on the dirt floor within the skin hut, where he would not be seen.

Suddenly his thoughts were interrupted by a soft rustling sound. With a shuffling of his deerskin boots he stamped out the picture and dropped quietly into a patch of tall grass. He waited, his heart pounding. He knew he could be severely punished, even banished, if he were caught making images. Except for a chosen few it was a strong taboo and against the secret rites of the clan.

Yet he longed to be an image maker, to be a cave painter like old Graybeard. He knew it was a foolish hope, for he was born of no shaman,[2] he was the son of no chief or leader. He was only Tao, the boy with the bad foot. He did not even know his own father. His mother had died long before he could remember, and there was no elder to help him. Because of this, and because of his bad foot, he knew he could never become a Chosen One.

Whenever he saw the bison out on the plains, or the giant aurochs[3] and cave lions, he wanted to paint their pictures on the walls of the Secret Cavern, a magic place,

---

1. **taboo** (tə bo͞o′) *adj.* forbidden by tradition.
2. **shaman** (shä′ mən) *n.* priest or medicine man.
3. **aurochs** (ô′ räks) *n.* a shaggy, long-horned wild ox, now extinct.

far back in Big Cave, where only the Chosen Ones could go.

Often, at night, he lay in front of Kala's hut listening to the crackling fire and looking up at the sky. He saw pictures of deer and horses amongst the stars. By day the billowing clouds became herds of antelope or the lumbering shapes of the mountains-that-walk, the mammoths.

Always during the hunts, he lagged behind the other hunters to watch the giant vultures tracing lazy circles beneath the clouds or to catch a glimpse of a woolly rhino outlined against the horizon. Sometimes seeing these things made him lightheaded, almost bursting with joy, and he wanted others to see them as he did.

He knew that Garth and the other hunters did not understand this. Even Volt, the leader, looked upon him as an idler and a dreamer, unworthy of respect or manhood. He liked Garth best of all, because sometimes the big black-bearded man tried to help him. But when the other hunters came by, Garth often turned away and had other things to do.

Once again Tao heard the soft rustling sound in the grass. He waited, afraid to move. Then slowly he crept toward the sound, searching through the grass until he found a trail of pugmarks going around in circles. He gripped his spear tighter and fingered the leather pouch hanging from his belt. He was sure the scent of the dead mice had attracted a hungry animal and he had an uneasy feeling that he was being watched.

He waited silently, listening. Off in the distance he heard the harsh, scolding caw of a raven. That was all. He started walking again, along the foot of the cliffs, heading back for camp. He had only gone a few paces when the rustling noise came again.

This time he turned quickly, ready to defend himself. Then he saw it, peering at him through the shadows, a young wolf, its slitted eyes low and threatening.

Tao hunched down and raised his spear. If it was only one wolf it would be an easy target. He started to throw. Then he noticed the animal swaying back and forth on unsteady legs. Weak and half starved, its ribs showed through the scraggly patches of gray hair. Its yellow eyes looked up at Tao with a vacant stare. It was only half grown and Tao was sure it must have been deserted by the pack.

Slowly the boy lowered his spear. He could not bring himself to kill this helpless animal. Besides, such a scrawny beast would be a poor prize to take back to the clan.

Tao put out his hand, speaking softly to the frightened animal. "Come," he said, "I mean you no harm. You are hungry and I have food." He held up one of the dead field mice. But the young wolf backed away, a faint snarl curled on its lips, saliva dripping from its mouth. Tao slit the mouse open with his flint knife and dangled it in front of the wolf. Again the animal cringed and shied away, its thin legs trembling.

"Here," said Tao, "eat. You are hungry. Do not be afraid." With careful aim he tossed the mouse on the ground in front of the wolf.

The little animal came closer, slowly, one step at a time, its yellow eyes watching the boy intently. It nuzzled the dead mouse, pushing it around, licking at the oozing fluids. Yet it still refused to eat. Tao shook his head, puzzled.

It was growing dark now and he had to get back to the clan people with the rest of the field mice. He felt badly about leaving the little wolf, but he could not take him with him. He left the gutted mouse lying near the wolf's muzzle.

As he started to back away, the little animal looked up at him with pleading eyes. Tao shook his head sadly but there was little more he could do.

He made his way between the huge boulders that littered the foot of the cliffs. Born with a bad right foot, a foot that bent down and turned in slightly, Tao walked with a limp. However, by curling his foot around the shaft of his spear, he had learned to travel with greater ease and, when in a hurry, he could vault over the hills faster than a running man. Now, because of the darkness, he went slowly, picking his way through the weaving shadows.

He continued on through the oakwood forest until the fires of the little camp came into view. Here, in the clearing, a small group of skin huts was set up under the shelter of a massive rock overhang jutting out from the limestone cliffs. High above, Tao could see the great fire of the Endless Flame burning brightly, lighting up the entrance to Big Cave.

A white haze of smoke filled the clearing and flickering campfires lit up the darkness. Tao smelled the odor of cooking meat. Fat dropped from the spits, sizzling on the hot coals as the women grunted to each other and roasted the few ground squirrels and moles the hunters had brought back. Children sat on their haunches in front of the huts. They had been many months with little food, and their sunken eyes looked up at Tao. He knew his handful of field mice would not go far to ease their hunger.

He glanced quickly at Volt's bearskin hut in the center of the camp, hoping the big leader would not see him. Then he went directly to the edge of the clearing where two bison skin robes were lashed securely to a frame of cross poles, forming a ragged hut. He knelt down in front of it and called softly, "Kala."

The flap opened and an old woman peered out. Her square face was lined with wrinkles. Strings of gray hair hung down over her eyes, and she held a child in her arms. She smiled broadly, her big teeth yellow from chewing deer hide and spruce gum. "You are late," she said. "But you are safe."

Tao nodded and held out two of the mice. "We traveled far," he said. "But we did not get much."

The woman took the mice in her brawny hand and held them up by the tails. "I still have some dried grubs," she said, "and some roots. With these I can make a meal for the little one."

The little one was a girl child, an orphan from the winter famine. If it had not been for Kala, the elders would have taken her up among the boulders and left her for the hyenas. By caring for her, she had saved the child's life, much as she had done for Tao.

"Now you have another," said Tao, smiling, touching the old woman's shoulder.

The woman thought for a moment. "Three so far," she said. "You were the first."

Tao remembered it well. She had raised him as her own, when others had turned their backs because of his bad foot. He stayed with her for twelve summers, learning much from her wisdom and kindness.

"The sun is getting warmer," said Tao. "Soon the hunting will be good and there will be enough to eat." He said it even though he feared it might not be true. Perhaps

Graybeard would come and paint images in the Secret Cavern. If the spirits were pleased, great herds of horses, deer and bison would fill the plains and forests. The people would eat well and the clan would thrive. There would be many pelts with which to make new robes and boots, ivory and antlers to make needles, spears and knives.

Kala and Tao talked for a few more minutes. Then the woman listened and put her finger to her lips. "Go," she whispered, "before Volt comes." She went back into the hut and closed the flap, and for a moment Tao could hear her humming to the little one as she started the meal.

Tao went to the center of the camp near the large fire, to turn over the rest of his field mice. He was almost there when a dark shadow fell across his path. It was Volt, the leader. The big man planted himself in front of the boy. His sheepskin robe was singed and stained with spots of blackberry. He wore a necklace of bear claws. His dark beard was wild and unkempt.

Tao felt a sinking feeling in the pit of his stomach, but he stood firm. In the light of the fire he saw the man's left cheek gashed with livid scars that always turned his face into an ugly scowl.

The man pointed a fat, hairy finger at the boy and grunted. "Where have you been?"

Tao hesitated, at first not knowing what to say. "I stopped by the meadow."

The big man grumbled. "You are always late, always behind the others, dreaming, wasting time. You are a poor hunter when the people are hungry."

Tao saw the other hunters gathering around, attracted by the harsh words. Good, thought Tao, now he would tell them about the wolf dog. Wolf dogs were taboo, but he didn't have to tell them he tried to feed it. Maybe the others would listen. "I heard a noise in the high grass," said the boy eagerly. "I wondered what it was and I thought—"

Volt shook his head and interrupted gruffly, "Enough!" he shouted. "We do not need wondering, we do not need thinking or dreaming. *We need food.*"

The heat of anger flushed in Tao's cheeks. This man was like a mountain. He would listen to nothing. His words were always harsh and sullen. He would tell him no more. He handed Volt the pouchful of field mice.

The big man grunted again, glaring down at the boy. "And where is the rabbit?"

Tao's body stiffened. He had forgotten the rabbit.

Volt stepped closer, his eyes narrowing. "You ate the rabbit?"

The other hunters crowded around the boy.

"You ate the rabbit?" Volt repeated, his voice taut.

Tao shook his head, unable to speak. Garth, the black-bearded one, who was always with Volt, knocked him to the ground. Tao lay there in the firelight, looking up at the tight ring of spears.

"No," said Tao, trying to catch his breath. "I would not eat while others are hungry."

Volt brushed the back of his hand across his scarred cheek. "Then where is the rabbit?"

Tao squirmed, the sharp stones pressing against his shoulders. "I . . . I forgot the rabbit. I left it back in the meadow."

Garth looked down at him, frowning, shaking his head.

The men with the spears moved closer, Garth's shadow falling across Tao's face. He saw the dark anger in their eyes.

Volt pushed them aside. "Wait," he said, "there is a better way." He pointed off into the darkness where the tops of the oak trees were black against the purple night. "Go," he ordered, a sneering grin spreading across his face. "You say the rabbit is in the meadow. Go then, find your rabbit in the meadow and do not come back until you do. Maybe then you will learn to keep your mind on the hunting."

Tao got to his feet slowly, brushing himself off. He felt a bitter surge of anger, anger at himself for his own care-lessness, anger at these men who would not listen. As he walked out of the camp he saw one of the clan women reach into the fire and pull out a flaming willow torch. She handed it to him and, in the light, Tao saw that it was Kala. He wanted to speak, but she nodded slightly, her deep green eyes warning him to be quiet.

Slowly Tao made his way through the oak forest until he came to the foot of the cliffs bordering the grasslands. He held his torch high, limping across the dried-out streambed and around the scattered boulders.

Once or twice he was sure he heard something moving in the grass, but when he turned around all he saw was the dancing shadows of the stunted willow trees.

He was tired now and hunger gnawed at him. But first he had to find the rabbit. He followed the cliff until he came to the meadow, then looked around for the patch of sand. In the eery light of his torch, the darkness closed in and everything looked the same—the rocks, the bushes, the clumps of grass.

Finally he found the sand patch and the scuffed-out drawings he had made that afternoon. He poked his spear around in the torchlight and his heart sank. The rabbit was gone. In its place were the pugmarks of a large hyena.

Now he knew he could not go back to camp, not tonight, maybe not tomorrow, not until he had found another rabbit.

from Attar of the Ice Valley

Leonard Wibberley

Life presents challenges beyond our ability to imagine in this story of a young boy's passage into manhood.

1

Huru was squatted on his haunches[1] at the mouth of the cave, sorting over his stock of flints, which he kept in a bag made of the skin of a wild horse, an animal he and his people called *heys*. His supply of flints was low and he was glad that he had saved a number that he had at one time considered discarding because they were flawed. He put the better flints, the ones whose surface was smooth and had no niches or gulleys running through them, to one side on the ground in a line, each touching the other, and matched each against a finger of his hands. There were seven. He counted by quantity and not by units.

This done, he put the flawed flints in a line and did the same thing. He had to use all his fingers and his two thumbs for the count, plus four more fingers. That made fourteen, but Huru had no word for fourteen. All his fingers and thumbs and four fingers was his method of reckoning the number. He grunted, satisfied. By using both kinds of flints, he had enough, with careful manufacture, to see the tribe through until the sun had risen high enough in the sky for the snow to go from the ground. Then the tribe could journey again, hunting as it went, to the place where the flints were to be found, near the water that never froze, which was what Huru called the ocean.

Huru was alone in the cave except for two women who were looking after the babies, of whom there were five. These, the women and the babies, were far back in the cave both for safety and for warmth (the fires were always lit in the back of the cave) and also so that the crying of the babies would not attract the hunting dungoes, or wolves, of which he knew one pack was in the neighborhood.

---

1. haunch (hônch) *n.* the part of the body including the hip, buttock, and thickest part of the thigh.

Dungoes would not dare to attack when the men of the tribe were in the cave, but game was scarce now and the wolves were hungry. They might raid the cave when it had only one man to guard it. Two or three might corner him, for wolves hunted as a team, and then the others would dash to the rear of the cave and snatch one or more of the babies. It was a planned attack of this nature that Huru was afraid of, and it was for this reason that he had told the women to put the babies far in the back of the cave so that the fire would be between them and the wolves in case the pack decided to attack.

Huru was an old man but still very strong. There was no fat on him, only leathery muscles that moved about under his skin without any fat to soften their lines. His skin was loose and wrinkled. He had too much of it. Sometimes he looked at his hands and arms and was surprised at how they had changed. He could remember when there had been a little pad of fat between his thumb and forefinger and when the skin of his hand had been unwrinkled and elastic. That did not seem a long time ago. It seemed to Huru that he had become old very quickly.

The world beyond the mouth of the cave was utterly quiet. The valley below was covered with snow, which had drifted so deep in places that only the tops of spruce and fir trees showed above it. The ice wall at the top of the valley—which in summer was blue, green, and fiery red in the sun and around which soft mists appeared and disappeared—was now a vast precipice of snow with a blue fang or ridge of ice glittering through here and there where a scurry of wind had swept the snow away. The ice wall was too high to be climbed and in any case there was no object in climbing it. Above it nothing grew and no animals lived. Only the wind lived there, howling and moaning perpetually, and also certain invisible and powerful creatures that vented their fury at times by breaking off portions of the ice with a terrible noise and sending great masses tumbling down into the valley.

In the summer the valley was almost entirely cleared of snow. There were a number of tribes living in it and at peace. Each tribe consisted of only two or three families. When a tribe increased beyond that size, it broke up because it was impossible for a greater number to be fed by hunting and gathering of grasses, berries, roots, and bark. Each tribe-family moved off to fend for itself, but each recognized a relationship with the others. When there was big game to be hunted, they worked together.

The ice wall had not always been there. Huru could recall that in his childhood it had been possible to travel for several days before entering the area of mists and, beyond that, the place of the ice. How many days, he could not say. But then, a little while after he had first been allowed to accompany the men when they went hunting, the ice had begun to move down toward the valley. This movement was accompanied by mist and warmth and great noise. The noise had continued for weeks and months and, indeed, intermittently through the years as the furious spirits that controlled the ice wall and lived in the mists moved it around. Day and night there were crashes and sharp cracks and heavy rumblings that shook the earth, and the ice wall had moved slowly but irresistibly toward the valley.

Of course, as the ice wall came closer, it made the air colder, and the cold air froze the ground and also brought snow. So not only had the wall moved down on the valley but it had grown while it moved. This went on all the years that Huru was a boy, and through his manhood, and had ceased only with the approach of his old age, when the area available to him and his tribe had been cut to thirty miles, which were contained in the valley in which he lived. At the mouth of the valley was the sea, and into this flowed a big river that was fed by the ice wall.

Game in the valley was short not only because it was midwinter but because the people were increasing and the place was being hunted out. Huru the previous summer had seen only one small herd of heys and three of the big antlered deer called *glips*. The far end of the valley in his boyhood had swarmed with heys and glips and also goros, which were bison. He had not seen one of those in four years, and at the thought of a stew made of the entrails of the goro, with certain grasses and leaves added, old Huru's mouth watered with pleasure.

He was sitting all this time at the entrance of the cave, overlooking the full extent of the valley—the white waste with here and there a dark interruption where the top of a clump of trees struggled up through the snow. A tiny movement on the far side of the valley now caught his eye—a minute interruption of the serenity and the silence.

He stared in that direction, moving only his head, his body absolutely motionless so as not to betray his own presence, for he knew that although he was a hunter he was also one of the hunted. His hearing was in an instant more acute.

One who was not a hunter would have detected nothing in the white expanse of snow. But Huru saw a little flurry in the whiteness, a flinging up into the air of a few spurts of snow, and then detected a small dark figure that was betrayed only by its shadow on the snow. Across the valley came the sound of a kill—a high-pitched *hi hi hi hi hiyeee*. One of the women, fat, strong, and smelling very comfortingly of stale milk and warm skins, came swiftly to the mouth of the cave, and Huru, without taking his eyes off the dark dot in the distance, said, "It is Attar. He has made a kill."

From the bottom of the valley only a little farther to the north came a long-drawn howl, rising to a thin scream and then wavering away to nothing. That was the hunting call of the dungoes, who also knew from the cry of Attar that a kill had been made.

The two watching from the cave saw the dungoes, their white coats scarcely visible against the snow, move in a pack toward Attar. They went at a slow trot, their collective breath making a little mist in the air about them. They were cautious and determined and their leader, a little ahead of the pack, snapped at those who came abreast of him to keep them behind.

The dungoes always attacked like this—together, carefully, with determination and a plan. In fact, they were very much like men. Huru picked up several throwing sticks and put them carefully in the belt of skin that secured his cloak of skins around him. He took his stabbing spear and without a backward look went to the aid of Attar.

The women and the babies would be safe for a while, he reasoned, for the dungoes had found other prey in Attar.

2

Attar had killed a blue citti—a fox whose soft fur on the outside was silver but below was a deep blue. He had been stalking a much smaller animal, a snow rabbit, when he had come unexpectedly on the tracks of the citti. The citti had picked up the tracks of the rabbit too, and those of the citti were entirely fresh, for the snow had not yet begun to fuse in the footprints but was still powdery. The wind, the tiniest movement of the air, was from ahead, and soon, following the tracks, Attar could pick up the sharp and appetizing scent of the citti and, mixed with it, a whiff or two of the snow rabbit.

The tracks showed that neither suspected that it was being followed. The tracks meandered about, the snow rabbit stopping now and then to cock his long ears and listen, as was his habit. When he did so, the citti had stopped too, so Attar knew that the citti was in sight of his prey.

Attar eased himself over the top of a small round and saw citti and rabbit, the citti just about to pounce. He threw his throwing stick, which was armed at one end with a round flint, and hit the citti on the top of the skull. It collapsed in the snow, kicking, and the rabbit darted off in an explosion of snow.

Attar was not an old man like Huru but a boy. He had no hair on his face yet, and his voice had not begun to deepen. His hair was black and long, falling down past his shoulders. He had on a kind of cloak of fur, but it was the fur of rabbits, for, unlike Huru, Attar had not yet killed big game and so did not wear the skin of a wolf or a bear.

After he had killed the citti, Attar recovered his throwing stick and saw the dungoes slipping across the floor of the valley toward him. The leader had a black ear and a touch of black on the tip of his tail. Attar knew him well. He had seen him many times in the valley—indeed, they had often come across each other when hunting, stared at each other, and then gone their ways, neither sure that in combat he could win.

From the time Attar had first seen the black-eared dungo he had sensed that one day they would fight to the death. It seemed that this must be the day: the black-eared dungo was no longer alone but had his whole tribe with him. And Attar's tribe was dispersed at the southern end of the valley, looking for game.

Attar looked toward the cave whose safety he must gain, and saw Huru coming down the valley in his direction. He watched Huru for a few seconds and noted that he was moving not directly toward him but on a slant to the south. To give Huru time to reach him, then, that they might fight together, Attar must keep the wolf pack to the north so they would not get wind of Huru.

Attar slung the citti around his shoulders with its head and feet in front of him. He had, in addition to his throwing sticks, a stabbing spear, the head armed with a sharp knife of a certain green stone that came from another place. With this weapon he set out, walking obliquely toward the dungo pack, which changed direction a little to the north to cut him off.

Attar had listened many a night in the cave to tales of encounters with dungoes. He knew that one met alone would rarely attack. Even two or three would not attack a man. But when hunger drove them to collect in a pack the dungoes were dangerous to men. Yet, even then, they would attack only a solitary man or at best a small group.

"The difference between a man and a dungo is this," Huru had said. "The dungo is always afraid. He is as clever as a man, and faster, but he never loses his fear. Therefore, in fighting the dungo, be bold. And remember that he will always try to get behind and then spring on your back."

With this thought in mind, Attar had selected a sheer wall of blue ice rising from the side of the valley as the best place to make his stand. It lay a quarter of a mile away, but he could not go directly to it, for between him and the ice was a patch of soft snow that would not support his weight. He had to go east or west around this, and since west would take him to higher ground, he went that way.

The dungoes, led by Black Ear, were faster than he, however. The snow over which they were traveling was firm and they could trot where Attar had to wade along. He saw that he could not get to the ice wall in time, and there was no protection for his back nearer him. He would have to fight in the open, and that meant death. The dungoes were many and they could surround him and bring him down in a second. After the first leap he would be torn to pieces in a few moments—dismembered before his blood was frozen on the snow. He had seen a pack of dungoes destroy a deer as big as himself in such a fashion.

The dungoes were now very near, their green eyes gleaming, their tongues lolling out over their white fangs. They glanced nervously at one another and then at Attar, each anxious to get his share of the kill. This anxiety made them quarrelsome, and one snarled suddenly and, whirling, slashed at another with its fangs. The two fought, snapping and barking in the snow, and then separated, the fight ending as suddenly as it had begun. One of the dungoes was bleeding from the snout and its eye had been hurt.

Disabled, its sight partially gone, it slunk to the back of the pack, moving a paw across its injured eye in an effort to right the injury. One or two of the others watched the injured dungo and moved back with it. Then, without warning, they leaped on their fellow, fangs slashing, and bore him to the ground in a flurry of snow and fur. A fight broke out in another part of the pack, erupting as a result of sheer nerves and hunger. Black Ear growled, his fur bristling, and the fighting stopped.

The dungoes now ranged themselves around Attar, ringing him in, so that there was no chance at all of his gaining the protection of the ice cliff on the west side of the valley. Beyond the ring of his enemies Attar could see Huru coming, but Huru could not help him now. The dungoes encircled him completely, stretching toward him with their fierce heads and narrowed eyes, baring their teeth and snarling. They were waiting, driven by hunger yet held by fear, for Black Ear to make the first move, when they would leap for the kill.

Attar watched Black Ear closely; watched his lips tremble as he pulled them back to bare his fangs; watched the nervous twitch of his ears as he listened for any movement from the pack; watched his snout rise slowly in preparation for the sharp bark that would signal the attack. And then, just before that bark was given, Attar himself shouted and that shout of defiance cut off the bark of Black Ear, surprised him and left him for a moment unsure of himself. While he stood thus, shocked, with his snout still raised, exposing his throat, Attar hurled his throwing stick at Black Ear and the stick caught the dungo leader full in his outstretched neck so that he gave a yelp of surprise and pain and fell back in the snow on his hindquarters.

The rest of the pack cowered back immediately. Black Ear regained his feet and barked again, but more to give himself courage than to signal the onslaught. Attar took a quick step toward him, and Black Ear scurried back, snarling, and moved off to the side. He went only a few paces, his eyes on Attar, before he met soft snow and was in a moment buried in it to his withers. Attar feinted toward him again, and Black Ear, in sudden panic, plunged farther into the soft snow, yelping, snapping, struggling, and sinking deeper as he struggled. But he found firm ground and came bounding out, green eyes blazing. The others, seeing their leader so discomforted, slunk a little farther away.

The fear Attar had felt when he was first ringed around by the dungoes and in the open now left him. With a patch of soft snow nearby, he was no longer at so great a disadvantage. His courage returning, he began to mock the dungoes, for mocking was a means of combat, distracting the attention of the opponent from his attack.

"Ho, Black Ear," said Attar. "Are you really a leader and full grown? You seem like a cub to me, snapping and then slinking off. You are afraid. And you are right to be afraid. You are not equal to me, Four Feet. You stand low to the ground and I stand high. You must bite, but I can throw. Like that." And with these words Attar threw another of his stone-armed throwing sticks, not at Black Ear but at one of his pack who was slinking closer to the side. The stick caught the dungo on the skull between his eyes, for Attar had, since birth almost, practiced throwing things and was an expert. The dungo fell to the snow without a whimper, its skull fractured. The others scattered back like dust in the wind, and the dying dungo twitched and kicked, the snow flying about it, and then was still.

The others having slunk away, Attar quickly recovered his throwing stick, which lay by his victim. As he stooped, Black Ear leaped at him with a snarl. But his leap was spoiled by the take-off from the yielding snow. The dungo was a fraction of a second late, and Attar moved aside. The throwing stick was in his hand and he brought it down hard, like a club, on Black Ear's thick neck.

Black Ear yelped, lunged, and snapped at Attar and his fangs ripped the boy's shoulder but found no secure hold. Attar leaped backward and to the side, landing in the soft snow, where he lost his balance and fell on his back. The dungo was on him in a moment, terrible jaws snapping at his throat. But, in falling, Attar had raised his spear and the sharp point of stone went through Black Ear's shoulder.

The dungo, impaled on the spear, was not mortally hurt. But he could not move quickly. The shaft of the spear caught in the snow and hampered him and the sharp pain of his wound as he tried to leap away made him yelp. In falling back, Attar had lost his throwing stick and could not find it in the snow. He grabbed the end of the spear to pull it out and stab once more at Black Ear.

"Attar," cried Huru. "Here." The old hunter had come up. He threw a stick to the boy, who caught it in mid-air and in the same movement brought it down on Black Ear's head. In a few moments the dungo was dead and Huru, attacking from outside the ring, had frightened off the others. They gathered a little distance off, uncertain, snarling and baring their teeth, but afraid to attack without their leader.

Attar, excited by the battle and his victory, grabbed Black Ear by the forepaws and jerked him up. The dungo was longer than the boy, so even when Attar got the dungo's head level with his own his hindquarters were resting on the ground.

"See, dungoes," cried Attar, holding up his victim. "Attar has killed your chief. Learn fear of Attar. When Attar comes, run and hide." And again he gave his kill cry, which rang out high and clear over the whole valley.

"Now I do not wear the skins of little animals any more," said Attar. "I wear the skin of a dungo, for in one day I have killed two dungoes and this citti here."

Huru saw the wound from the fangs on Attar's shoulder. "Black Ear left his mark before he went to the Cave of the Great Bear," he said. "That is good. He drew blood and now his spirit can rest. Tonight we will honor him and his brother, and also the citti, so they can be happy in the Cave of the Great Bear and their spirits will not return to haunt us. It is important that this should be done."

Scarlet on the Loom

from Warrior Scarlet

Rosemary Sutcliff

In this story, Drem learns a painful truth when he overhears a conversation between his mother and his grandfather.

The old shepherd sitting with his face turned seaward and his broad-bladed spear across his knees, seemed as much a part of the downs as did the wind-stunted whitethorn trees along the bank behind him: a little man, dark and knotted and tough as a furze[1] root, with fine wrinkles round his eyes, under their jut of badger-grey brows, that told of a life-time of looking into the distance in sun and wind and rain. He was naked save for a sheepskin belted around his waist, and on the bare brown skin of his sides and shoulders showed the puckered silvery lines of more than one wolf-scar. Two great herd dogs lay beside him; one old and wise and grey-muzzled like himself, one young and gangling; and a boy of about nine summers old squatted at his feet, playing with the ears of the young one.

The boy also was half naked, but his kilt was of rough woollen stuff dyed with the red-brown crotal dye, and in all other ways he was as different from the old man as though they came from different worlds; the skin of his broad, hot-tempered face—of his whole body—freckle-dusted and fair, his hair the colour of polished copper, and his eyes grey with golden flecks in them; eyes that would seem when he was excited or angry to be all gold.

The boy stopped playing with the dog's ears, and laid his arm across his updrawn knees and his chin on his arm, gazing southward where the chalk fell in long, slow turf slopes and ridges, between willow and hazel choked combes,[2] into the forest and the Marsh Country far below, and the Marshes spread away and away to the shining bar of the Great Water on the edge of the world. Below him the turf of the steep combe-side was laced

---

1. **furze** (fŭrz) *n.* a prickly evergreen shrub or bush.
2. **combes** (ko͞oms) *n.* deep, narrow valleys.

with criss-cross sheep-tracks, and the faint formless cropping sounds of the flock at the bottom came up to him along the ground. Far off and lower down on the other side of the combe, he could see the tiny figures of Flann and his dogs, on watch also over the sheep. Flann whistled to one of the dogs, and the sound came clear across the combe, a tiny, shining arrow-point of sound in the great quietness. A little warm wind came up from the south, trailing the cloud shadows after it across the Marshes and up the slow-gathering slopes of the Chalk, thyme-scented and sea-scented and swaying the heads of the blue scabious flowers all one way. The shadow of a hawk swept across the turf below him, and the sun was hot on his head: the day was good.

Drem—the boy's name was Drem—heaved a small sigh of contentment. He liked it up here on the High Chalk with Doli and the others of the shepherd kind. Several times this summer and last, since his legs grew long enough for the journey, he had come up, and spent a night, or two nights, with the sheep. It was good. This time, he had been with Doli two nights already, sleeping in the shepherd's bothie by the dew-pond, and now he supposed it was time to be going home, because he had never been more than two nights away from home before; his mother was one to worry, and when she worried her hand was hard.

'It is good, up here,' he said by and by.

'Aye, it is good up here—when the sun shines and the wind blows soft without snow in it, and a man need not be away after a straying ewe, knee-deep in snow, and the wolves crying,' Doli said.

Drem screwed his head over his shoulder to grin at the old man. 'You need some of your own sheep medicine. Tell me more about the wolves. Tell me how you came by that long scar on your ribs.'

The old man shook his head, his gaze on the flock in the combe bottom. 'I have told you that story, aye, and more than once.'

'Tell it again.'

'Nay, it is hot, and I am in no mood to tell over again stories that I have told before.' Doli brought his gaze up out of the combe, and let it rest on the boy's face. Nothing else about him moved. He never moved without need. 'I have told you all that there is to tell about wolves and fights with wolves, and it is not good to talk of such things even in the summer. I have told you all the stories and the dreams that are of my people, save for those which may not be told. I have told you about Corn King, and Earth Mother; and I have told you how Tah-Nu, the Father of my people, in a land where the sun casts no shadows, dreamed a dream of the north, and how he hollowed out the trunk of a great tree and put into it his woman and his child and his hunting dog and a basket of barley seed, and paddled after the dream across the Great Water, and how he came to this land after many days, and sprang ashore and found that he had grown a shadow. Surely I am a great teller of stories, but even I must have rest. Maybe when you come again I shall have found in my head another story.'

Drem wriggled round, sticking a leg out sideways on the slope, to come face to face with the old man. He said, partly in the tone of a question, partly as one repeating a thing said before, 'And there was no one in the land before Tah-Nu, and no one after him except his children and his children's children, and his children's children's children, until we came?'

'Nay. Tah-Nu was the first, but there were others after him, before you came,' Doli said. 'There came giants as red-gold as you are, with great spears of bronze against which our flint spears were but brown-tufted rushes. So they set us to tend their herds, and sometimes they took our women to tend their fires and bear their sons; and in a while and a while and a while we became, in some sort, one people. *Then* you came, as it might be yesterday, and treated the children of the giants as they had treated us. Now we are all the Half People, Tah-Nu's children and the children of the giants alike, and we come at your call. But we who have yet the old blood strong in us, we the Little Dark People, we have the long memories, and we remember while we tend your sheep that once, when the long gravemounds yonder against the sky were new, Tah-Nu's children were the lords of the land.'

Drem nodded. 'Does it ache in your belly, when you remember that?' If you asked a thing like that of most of Doli's kind, they would only look at you sideways beneath their brows, and make you an answer that slid out from under your question like an eel from under a stone. But Doli was different.

The old shepherd shrugged, his gaze level enough on Drem's face; yet his answer slid a little, all the same. 'The wind from the east is a cold wind, and blood runs from a spear-thrust, and if a man be too long without food he will die. And all these things are bad; yet he would be a fool who spent his life grieving for such things.'

Drem waited, looking into Doli's face; but nothing more came, and the old man's face was shut as he gazed out over his sheep once more. It seemed that the time had come to be on his way again.

He gave a parting pull to the young dog's ears, drew his legs under him, and stood up. 'Now I go, if you will tell me no more stories.'

Doli looked up at him, mocking a little under his brows. 'It is a long trail back to the village, and a sad thing it would be if the evening stew was all of it eaten before you came.'

'As to that, my mother will keep something for me in the pot,' Drem said, with the assurance of the Lordly Ones of the world, for whom something is always kept in the pot. 'Nevertheless, I go now. Maybe I will come again before barley harvest. But if I do not, then surely I will come up and help with the droving when the time comes to bring the flock down at Samhain.'

'Come when you will. You have a way with the sheep; and it is in my heart that you would make none so ill a shepherd.'

Drem cocked up his head and laughed, rocking on his heels. 'Nay, I leave that to Tah-Nu's children. I shall be a warrior, after the way of my kind. Yet when I am a man I shall come up with my kind also, when the time comes to keep the Wolf Guard in the winter nights.'

'I will tell it to the Wolf-people, that they may grow afraid,' Doli said.

Drem flushed, still laughing. 'You laugh at me, and that is not good! But I will come back before barley harvest.'

He swung on a hard brown heel, and set off at a trot, following the curved bank of the great enclosure where the sheep were driven for shelter at night; and a short way beyond, on the crest of the hill, passed the turf-built bothie by the dew-pond, where Hunno, the brother of Flann, was swabbing a raw place on a sheep's back with elder-water to keep off the flies. He did not stop to talk to

Hunno, who was a surly little man with small round eyes like jet beads, but went on at a steady wolf-trot, heading for home.

Presently he struck the green Ridgeway that ran from the world's edge to the world's edge along the High Chalk, and followed it for a while, until another track came up from the seaward Marshes and crossed it; and then he turned inland. The sun was westering as he came dipping down into the steep combe that sheltered the home steading; and all the great, rounded, whale-backed masses of the downs were pooled and feathered with coolness, the shadows of a stunted whitethorn tree reaching across half a hillside, every rise and hollow of the land that did not show at all when the sun was high casting its own long, liquid shadow across the gold. The family cattle-ground in the head of the combe was already in shade, but farther down, where the combe broadened, the turf roofs of the steading[3]—drying up now in the summer heat—glowed tawny as a hound's coat in the sunlight, and the smoke from the house-place fire was blue as the fluttering haze of flower-heads in the flax plot as he trotted by.

He entered the steading garth[4] by way of a weak place he knew of in the thorn hedge, instead of going round to the gateway that faced towards the corn-land down the combe, and made his way between the byre[5] and the shelter where the two-ox plough was kept. Drustic must be out hunting, since there was no sign of him about the farm-land, and would scarcely be home by dusk; but his mother and the Grandfather would be there, and Blai. As he reached the back wall of the house-place and saw the familiar strip of warm darkness where the roof turf had been rolled back to let in more air and light, the idea suddenly woke in him that it would be fun to get in that way and drop on them like an earwig out of the thatch when they did not know that he was anywhere near.

The roof of the house-place came down to within elbow height of the ground all round, and the pitch was not very steep, but the sun-dried turf was slippery, and so it was not as easy to climb up as it looked. He managed it,

---

3. **steading** (sted′ iŋ) n. farmstead.
4. **garth** (gärth) n. an enclosed yard or garden.
5. **byre** (bīr) n. cow barn.

however, working his way up with infinite care until he could reach the edge of the opening, and after that it was easy. He drew himself up a little farther, then shifted his grip and slipped through between the rafters that showed in the gap, found a one-hand hold inside, and next instant, all without a sound—for few people could move more silently than Drem when he chose—was lying full length along the edge of the loft floor.

The half-loft in the crown of the roof was full of warm, crowding shadows through which the bar of fading sunlight from the gap in the roof fell like a golden sword. There was a warm smell of must and dust, and the sharper, aromatic tang of the dried herbs hanging in bundles from the rafters, and the animal smell of the skin rugs laid aside there until the winter. Spare farm tools were stacked deep under the eaves, and the raw, grey-brown bundles of wool from the last clip, and the wicker kists[6] in which the household kept their clothes and gear. Harness hung among the herbs, and a smoked bear ham; and there, too, were the two-handled crocks full of honey that kept the household in sweetness from one bee harvest to the next.

At the open side, almost in the smoke of the hearth fire that wreathed past on its way to the smoke hole, hung two shields: Drustic's shield that had been their father's, and the great bulls-hide buckler[7] with the bronze bosses that was the Grandfather's and would be Drem's one day.

But at the moment Drem had no interest to spare for the loft. Lying flat on his stomach and shielded from sight by the great roof-tree and the Grandfather's buckler, he was peering down over the edge into the main body of the house-place below. It was fun to see without being seen. Out of the fireglow and the fading sword of dusty gold, the great living-hut ran away on every side into brown shadows with a bloom of wood smoke on them, but where the light fell strongest near the doorway, his mother was working at her loom; a big upright loom, the warp threads held taut by a row of triangular clay weights at the bottom. He could hear the small rhythmical sounds as she passed the weaving-rod to and fro and combed up the woof between each row.

---

6. **kist** *n*. a chest or box.
7. **buckler** *n*. a small, round shield.

The warm, fatty smell of the evening stew came up to him from the bronze pot over the fire, and brought the warm water to his mouth, for he had not eaten since the morning bowl of stirabout with the shepherd kind. The Grandfather was sitting beside the fire as usual, on the folded skin of the bear that he had killed when the world was young; a man like a huge old brooding grey eagle that had once been golden.

On the other side of the hearth, the Women's side, Blai squatted on her heels, turning barley cakes with small, flinching hands in the hot ash. She was exactly beneath Drem, so that he thought how easy it would be to spit on her, like spitting on the back of a hare as it sunned itself on a far-down ledge of the old flint quarry north of the summer sheep-run. Blai was not his sister; her coming belonged to the time that he could only just remember, when a bronze-smith had come by from the Isles of the West, and his woman with him—a wild, dark creature with hair and eyes like the night. She had been sick already, and in the night she had died and left a new babe bleating in the fern against the wall. The bronze-smith had not seemed much interested, and two days later he had gone off along the track that led inland, leaving the babe behind him. 'What should I want with the creature?' he had said. 'Maybe I will come back one day.' But he never had come back. And now Blai was rising seven years old, black as her mother had been, in a house where everyone else was red-gold like flame, and somehow never quite belonging to them. Blai believed that one day the bronze-smith would come back: 'One day, one day my father will come for me!' seemed to be her talisman against all ills, the faith that she clung to as something of her own. But of course he never would come back; everybody knew that except Blai. Blai was stupid.

Drem decided not to spit on her after all, because that would betray his presence in the loft, and turned his attention back to his mother. The cloth on the loom had grown a little since he saw it last, though not much, because there was so much else to do; a piece of fine chequered wool, blue and violet and flaming red. There was red wool on his mother's weaving-rod now, the true burning Warrior Scarlet that was the very colour of courage itself. No woman might wear that colour, nor might the Half People who came and went at the Tribe's call. It was for the Men's side. One day, when he had passed through the Boy's House, and slain his wolf single-handed, and become a man and a warrior of the Tribe, with his Grandfather's shield to carry, his mother would weave scarlet on the loom for him.

The Grandfather raised his great grey-gold head from watching bygone battles in the fire, and turned his gaze on the woman at the loom. 'It grows slowly, that piece of cloth,' he said, in a voice that came mumbling and rattling up from the depth of his great frame. 'When it is finished, let you use it to re-line my good beaver-skin cloak. The old lining is worn to shreds.'

Drem's mother looked over her shoulder, showing a tired face in which the beautiful bones stood out so sharply that it looked as though you could cut your hand on it. 'I had thought to use this piece for Drustic; he also needs a new cloak, for his old one does not keep out the wind and the rain.'

'Drustic is young, and the wind blows less cold for him. He can wait. Let you set up the loom for him next time.'

'Next time and next time and next time,' Drem's mother said quietly. 'Sometimes I wish that I had been born to the Men's side; sometimes I grow weary of the spinning and the weaving and the grinding corn.'

The Grandfather spat into the fire. 'By right there should be three son's wives to weave and grind for me!'

'Then there should be three sons for them to weave for also,' Drem's mother said with a spurt of tired and angry laughter, thrusting back a bright wisp of hair that had strayed as her hair was always straying from the blue linen net in which it was gathered, and looked round again. 'Or would you have them all widows?'

Drem knew his mother in this mood; it came when she was very tired; and he began to feel that it would not be a good idea to play his earwig-out-of-the-thatch trick, after all.

The Grandfather drew his brows together, and glared. 'Aiee! A hard thing it is that I grow old, and of all my three sons there is not one left, and that the wife of my youngest son should taunt me with it! A hard thing it is that I should have but one grandson to carry my spear after me; I who have been among the greatest warriors of the Tribe.'

('The Old One grows forgetful,' Drem thought. 'He has lived so long with old battles that his mind grows dim; and he has forgotten Drustic.')

His mother turned again from her weaving, with a fierceness that struck him even at that moment as odd. 'Two grandsons there are at the hearth fire! Have you forgotten?'

It was then that the Grandfather said the thing that altered the whole world for Drem, so that it could never return to being quite the same as before.

'Nay then, I have not forgotten. I grow old but I can still count the tally of my ten fingers. Two grandsons there are at the hearth fire; but a grandson at the hearth fire is not a grandson among the spear-warriors of the Tribe. Is it likely, think you, that the young one will ever win his way into the Men's side, with a spear-arm that he cannot use?'

There was a sudden silence. Drem's mother had turned back to her loom, but she was not weaving. The Grandfather sat and glowered. And in the warm shadows of the loft above them, the small boy lay on his stomach, staring down at them with dilated eyes, and feeling all at once cold and sick. Only Blai went on turning barley cakes among the hot ashes, her small wan face telling as little as usual of what she thought or felt.

Then Drem's mother said, 'Talore the Hunter is one of the great ones of the Men's side to this day.'

'Talore the Hunter was a man and a warrior before ever he lost a hand to the cattle raiders,' the Grandfather said, deep and grumbling, and he eyed her with a kind of disgusted triumph. 'Na na, it is in my mind that the boy must go to the Half People when the time comes. He is often enough away with Doli and the sheep as it is; maybe he will make a shepherd.' He spat again. 'Lord of the Sun! That I should have a grandson herding sheep! I, who have been such a warrior as men speak of round the fire for a hundred winters!'

'If the child fails, then he must go to the Half People,' Drem's mother said, and her voice sounded tight in her throat. 'But it may be that he will not fail. He is your own grandson, and not lightly turned from the things he sets his mind to.'

'So. But it is not his mind alone that must be set.' The Grandfather flared his nostrils in a derisive snort. 'Say then that he comes through his years in the Boy's House and slays his wolf at the end of them, and the time comes for him to receive his weapons; there must be two warriors, let you remember, and one of them not kin to him, to bring each New Spear before the Clan. And who shall I find, think you—or Drustic if I have gone beyond the Sunset—to stand for a one-armed champion?'

'It is six summers before that question need be answered—and must I then answer it this evening?' Drem's mother cried. 'If he fails, then let him go to the Half People as I say, and let you be thankful that there is Drustic to carry your spear after you!' She gave a swift exclamation and turned from the loom towards the open pottery lamp that hung from the roof-tree just below Drem's hiding-place. 'The light fades, and if I am to finish this stripe before Drustic is home to be fed, I must have the lamp.'

Quick as a lizard, Drem darted back into the shadows.

'Surely there is a rat in the roof. I heard it scamper.' He heard her voice, dry and hard, behind him as he slid out through the opening in the roof. He dropped silently to the ground, driven by an odd panic fear of anyone knowing that he had overheard what passed in the house-place, because somehow—he could not have said why—that would make it quite unbearable.

The little stilt-legged hut where the seed corn was stored seemed to offer refuge and he dived under it and crouched there, breathing hard as though he had been running.

The sun was gone, but a golden after-glow was spread behind the Chalk, and there was still light to see by. And crouching there among the timbers that upheld the floor, he looked at his right arm, as though he had never seen it before: his spear arm that he could not use, the Grandfather had said. It was thinner than his left, and somehow brittle looking, as though it might snap like a dry stick. He felt it exploringly with his left hand. It was queer, like something that did not quite belong to him. He had always known, of course—when he thought about it at all—that he could not use that arm, but it hadn't seemed important. He held things in his teeth and he held things between his knees, and he managed well enough without it. Certainly he had never for a moment thought of it coming between him and his Warrior Scarlet.

But he thought now, crouching under the floor of the corn store and staring straight before him with eyes that did not see the golden after-glow fading behind the Chalk. Never to take his proud place among the Men's side with the others of his kind; to lose the world he knew, and go out into the world of the Half People, the Dark People, the Flint People, whose homes, half underground, were the little green hummocks in the hidden combes of the Chalk; who came and went at the Tribesmen's call, though they never owned the Tribesmen as their masters; to be cut off, all his life, from his own kind . . . He was only nine years old, he could not yet understand all that it would mean; but he understood enough—more than enough. He crouched there for a long time, whispering over and over to himself, 'I *will* be a warrior of the Tribe. Let you say what you like, Old Man! I will show you—I will *show* you'—lashing up anger within himself, for a shield against fear.

When he went back to the house-place it was almost dark. Drustic had returned from the hunting trail, and the newly paunched carcass of a roe hind was hanging from the birch tree beside the door, out of reach of the dogs who were fighting over the offal, the white of her under-belly faintly luminous in the dusk, where the blood had not fouled it. He went in through the fore porch, where the ponies were stabled in winter. The apron of skins over the inner doorway was drawn back, and the tawny glow of the lamp and the low fire came to meet him on the threshold as he checked, blinking. The evening meal was over, and the Grandfather, it seemed, had returned to his watching of old battles in the fire. Drustic, with a half-made bow-stave across his knee and a glue-pot beside him, was busy on the great hunting bow that he was building for himself, while on the Women's side of the hearth their mother sat spinning. She looked up as Drem appeared. 'Cubbling! Here is a time to be coming home! When it drew to sunset I said, "He will not come now until tomorrow."'

'I would have been home by sunset, but—I stopped on the way. There were things to look at and I stopped on the way,' Drem said. But he could not meet his mother's

eyes. Keeping his head down, he went to squat beside
Drustic, holding out his hand. 'I will hold it steady while
you put on the binding.'

But Drustic hated anyone else to meddle in a thing
that he was making. He looked up slowly—all his move-
ments were slow and deliberate—and said quite kindly,
'Na, I can manage well enough. Let you learn to shaft a
spear; that is the thing for you to do.'

Drem snatched his hand back as though it had been
stung. You needed two hands for a bow, but you could
learn to use a spear with one. That was another thing
that he had not really thought about.

And at the same moment, his mother called to him.
'See, there is some stew left. Let you come round here
and take your bowl. You are not a man already, that you
should eat on the Men's side of the hearth.'

Drem came at her call, and took the black pottery bowl
of stewed mutton that she held out to him, and squatted
down in the fern. As he did so, he caught sight of Blai
squatting far back in the shadows, picking the furze
prickles and bits of dirt from a lapful of raw wool, and
watching him as she worked. And he realized that Blai
also had heard what the Grandfather had said. So he
turned his shoulder on her, hunching it in a way that
was meant to show her that she mattered so little that he
had not noticed that she was there at all.

And somehow in doing that—he overset the bowl.

It was such a small thing, a thing that might have
happened to anyone. But to Drem, coming so close on
the heels of what had gone before, it was overwhelming.
The words that the Grandfather had said, Drustic's re-
fusal to let him help with the bow—they were things that
came from outside; and a thing that came from outside
could be in some sort shut out; it could be defied and
snarled against. But this was different; this came from
inside himself; there was no defence against it, and it let
in all the rest.

Dismay and something that was almost terror swept
over him as the warm stew splashed across his knee and
into the fern. The Grandfather grunted; a grunt that said
as plainly as words could do, 'See now, did I not say so?'
And his mother caught up the bowl, crying in exasperation and something under the exasperation that was as

though he had hurt her, 'Oh, you clumsy one! You grow more clumsy every day! Can you never look what you are about?'

Black misery rushed up into Drem's breast, so that it was as though his heart were bursting because there was more misery in it than it could hold. He raised a white, desperate face to his mother's, and shook his head. Then he scrambled to his feet and bolted for the doorway.

'Where are you going?—Come back, cub!' his mother called after him; and he called back mumbling that he was not hungry, that he would come again in a while, and stumbled out through the fore porch into the summer night.

The gateway of the steading was closed, as always after dark, by an uprooted thorn bush, and he went out through the weak place that had let him in earlier that evening before the blow fell that changed the world, and making his way round the steading hedge, started down the chalk-cut driftway between the lower corn-plots and the half-wild fruit trees that were his mother's care.

He had no clear idea what he was doing or where he was going, or why. Blindly, instinctively, he turned to the wilderness, like any small desperately hurt animal seeking solitude from its own kind and the dark and a hole to crawl into.

The Life of a Bog

from Bodies from the Bog

James M. Deem

Wet, mossy areas yield unexpected and precious information about human life thousands of years ago, as this selection shows.

Early people of Europe believed that watery places were quite special. They thought they could communicate with the supernatural world there—gods and goddesses and even their dead ancestors. Sometimes they deposited weapons, tools, jewelry, and other objects in these wetlands to please or thank their gods. And sometimes they placed sacrificed human bodies there.

Although some ancient objects have been found on the bottom of European rivers and lakes, some have also been unearthed by farmers and peat cutters who were working in peat-filled soil.

Peat is found in waterlogged areas called fens and bogs. It is a soil that is composed of partially decayed dead plants which have piled on top of each other for thousands of years. Fens are created when shallow lakes lose their water supply and become stagnant pools. Reeds growing around the edge die and begin to fill in the pool. Because the pool is waterlogged, the reeds decay slowly and over time build up layers of fen peat.

Bogs are created if sphagnum moss begins to grow in a fen. This moss which lives on rainwater builds up its own layers of peat on top of the fen peat. A thin layer of moss and other hardy plants live on top of the bog, like a bumpy floating carpet, dotted with occasional pools of water. Underneath it lies the bog peat, which is 90 percent water. When something is placed into the bog, an object or a body, it is immersed in watery peat.

Although fen peat and bog peat preserve objects equally well, they differ in their preservation of human remains. Fen peat, for example, allows bacteria to thrive. This in turn promotes the decay of a body placed in fen peat.

Bog peat produces quite different results. Scientists discovered that sphagnan, a substance in sphagnum moss, prevents the growth of microbes. When a body is placed in bog peat, sphagnan prevents bacteria from growing and the body can become mummified. Even wooden objects placed into a peat bog are preserved from rot for the same reason. However, any material made from a plant product (such as linen cloth) will decay over time and disappear without a trace. That may explain why Tollund Man[1] was discovered wearing only a leather cap and belt. His linen clothing may simply have deteriorated in the bog.

Scientists have also learned that sphagnan tans a body, turning it into a kind of leather. But unlike normal leather with its brownish tint, many bog bodies develop a much darker "black coffee" color. In a few unusual cases, the internal organs of a bog body have become tanned while the skin has decayed. At least one scientist, T. J. Painter, believes that this happened when the person had been the victim of a fire—perhaps burned at the stake as a witch.

But a body cannot be preserved in a peat bog unless one final condition is met: it would have to be placed in the soggy bog almost immediately after death and remain covered with bog water. This avoids two problems. First, scavenging animals will not smell the scent of the body and attack it. Second, the body will not come into contact with oxygen, assuring its preservation. This process shows how remarkable bog bodies truly are.

Whether bodies become skeletons in fen peat or mummies in bog peat, scientists refer to both as "bog bodies." But not all bog mummies are preserved equally well, even when the bacteria are thwarted and the skin is tanned. Some, like Tollund Man and Grauballe Man,[2] have been so well preserved that, at a glance, they look quite lifelike. However, despite their outward appearance, many of their internal organs are decayed and their bones decalcified. Parts of some bog mummies have decayed, perhaps because of their position in the peat; the side facing down is often preserved better. Other bog bodies have been so flattened by the peat pressing

---

1. **Tollund Man** a body found in a peat bog in 1950; the man is believed to have died about 400 B.C.
2. **Grauballe Man** a body found in a peat bog in 1952; the man is believed to have died about 55 B.C.

against them that they are much harder to study, for there is nothing to examine except skin and hair.

Whatever their condition, they provide scientists with valuable information about persons who lived and died long ago.

The Magic of Sphagnum Moss

Early European civilizations knew that sphagnum moss had special qualities. By 1200 B.C., wounds were treated with bandages made from dried sphagnum moss. Even during World War I, such bandages were used on the European battlefield when cotton bandages were in short supply. And bog water from sphagnum peat bogs was taken by sailors on long sea voyages because it stayed fresher much longer than spring or well water. Even in gardening, sphagnum peat moss never becomes moldy or bug-infested.

Mesopotamia, Egypt, and Kush

The Great Flood

Retold by Geraldine McCaughrean

This traditional story from the Old Testament Bible recounts the experiences of Noah and his family. Stories like this one reflect ancient peoples' awareness that the waters that supported their civilizations could also destroy them.

As time passed, the family of Adam grew larger and larger. His children had children, their grandchildren had grandchildren. The number of people on Earth grew with every generation. But although there were more people, they were no better than Cain or wiser than Eve.[1]

Only one man was better. Noah was a good man. God and he were like friends. So God said to his friend, "Noah! The world has become a sordid, wicked place and I'm sorry I ever made it. I will wash it clean with a flood. So build a wooden ship—an ark—and daub the planks with pitch outside and in, to keep out water. Build it three stories high, and take aboard your wife and three sons—oh, and their wives, too. Then find every kind of animal—a male and a female of every bird and beast— and load them on, too. Why should they die for people's sins? Don't forget provisions, mind! Plenty of food for yourselves and the animals!"

Noah did exactly as he was told, whether or not his neighbors jeered and pointed and called him a madman, pelting him with pebbles and abuse. He set about building—right there, in the middle of dry land. He and his family went aboard, but it was seven days more before the rain came.

Then, in out of the wet came all the birds and beasts on Earth—two by two, as lightning tore the heavens open like a ripsaw and let fall the rain in torrents.

The rising water shifted, then lifted the ark, bumping it across the gro nd before setting it fully afloat. Standing at the rail, Noah saw the fields silvered over, his mud house crumbling, whole cities filled to the brim with water, and everyone—every wicked living soul—run,

---

1. **Cain . . . Eve** In the Bible, Cain, son of Adam and Eve, killed his brother Abel. Eve had earlier been tricked into disobeying God.

wade, swim, scream, then sink in the mud-brown Flood. Noah, his family, his zoo—and God—watched it happen.

When, after forty days and forty nights, the rain finally stopped, water masked the face of the Earth. Nothing broke the surface—not a rock, not a tree. Then a wind sprang up; the water steamed. The ark ran aground on the peak of Mount Ararat.[2]

Noah freed a raven to fly away in search of something to eat, somewhere to perch. But the raven only flew up and down, up and down, finding nowhere, nothing. Noah freed a dove, but she came back exhausted. A week later, Noah sent the dove out again. And again she came back to the ark. But to Noah's delight, there was a leaf from an olive tree in her beak. Now Noah knew that the water really was dropping. After another week, Noah's dove did not come back at all: She had found somewhere better than the ark to roost. So Noah opened up the ark and everyone climbed out: Noah, his family, and all the animals.

"Have children—lots of children!" God told the little family. "People the world all over again! But I promise you—no more floods, never again such destruction." And He wrote His oath in the sky, in the shining arc of a rainbow, His everlasting promise of pity.

---

2. Mount Ararat (ar′ ə rat′) mountain in Turkey, known in modern times as Agri Dagi.

Writing and Alphabets
from Alphabetical Order:
How the Alphabet Began

Tiphaine Samoyault

*As long ago as 3400 B.C., some forms of writing existed.
But the alphabet as we know it today developed gradually
over time, as this selection shows.*

Why Did People Begin Writing?

Alphabets didn't just appear. The earliest writing started
long before alphabets, when people began to connect
meaning with natural or manmade markings. We have
found forms of writing from as far back as around 3400
B.C. in Mesopotamia and China.

In almost every civilization, the earliest writing was
connected to religion and magic. Priests were always
looking for signs from the gods—literally. They looked on
tortoise shells or inside animal livers, and they found
them! Perhaps a squiggle or a circle—anything that
looked like a distinctive mark—could be seen as a message from a god, which had to be interpreted. Ultimately,
these interesting shapes and patterns or "divinations"
may have been the inspiration for developing written language. In fact, the name of one early writing system,
"hieroglyphics," means "priest-writing." But writing was
quickly put to use for financial life and daily activities as
well.

Ideograms and pictograms were some of the earliest
writing systems. These systems do not use an alphabet:
they use pictures and symbols and represent more com-
plicated ideas by combining signs.

The oldest known writing system is called **cuneiform**.
It was invented by the Sumerians, who lived in
Mesopotamia (part of modern-day Iraq) more than 5,000
years ago.

What were the conditions in Mesopotamia that gave its
citizens a need for writing? It is helpful to look at the
whole picture. Mesopotamia was a civilization rich in certain raw materials. They had plenty of corn, vegetables,
meat, leather, and especially clay. But they were almost

entirely lacking wood, stone, and metal, which were needed to maintain a successful society. Mesopotamia needed to trade with other cultures, to acquire the things they lacked in exchange for what they had too much of. In order to keep track of what they traded, they started marking symbols for numbers and items in clay tablets, which then hardened. We call the system "cuneiform," meaning "wedge-shaped," because when a stick or reed was pressed into the clay to make the mark, it left a triangular shape.

Cuneiform was not in any particular language. The symbol for an object could be understood by different cultures as whatever their particular word for that object was. From the Sumerians, cuneiform writing spread to Akkadians, Babylonians, and Assyrians, and eventually became the writing system of the entire Middle East. Hieroglyphics, the writing system used in ancient Egypt, appeared about 3200 B.C., or maybe even earlier. This system was very different from the one used in Mesopotamia—it was a mixture of pictorial signs, which stood for individual things, and sound signs, which represented sounds.

Sound signs, which make up a true alphabet, offer some advantages. Being able to write any word using a small set of alphabetic letters was much more convenient than having a different sign for every single word. Since the letters in a word have no visual connection to the word they represent, phonetic writing is abstract, unlike the concrete pictorial writing. Looking at a word no longer meant seeing a picture and identifying a thing or an idea. Now it meant making connections between symbols and sounds.

The Monster Humbaba

from Gilgamesh: Man's First Story

Bernarda Bryson

This selection from Gilgamesh has all the ingredients of a national epic—the larger-than-life hero, the supernatural overtones, the serious tone, and the elevated language. Like all epics, this one serves to preserve and transmit a national culture to future generations.

Perfect was the friendship of Gilgamesh and Enkidu. The wild man asked only to be the servant of the King, but Gilgamesh called him "my younger brother," and Ninsun, the queen looked upon him almost as a son. Everywhere, they went together and everywhere they were admired. They took part in feats of strength and daring, winning all prizes and all praise. And in all this Enkidu was content.

Not so, Gilgamesh. On one occasion he said to his friend, "Day and night I dream of a great enterprise. Whenever I close my eyes, voices come to me and say: 'Arouse yourself, Gilgamesh, there are great things to be done!'"

Enkidu's mind was full of foreboding.

"You and I, Enkidu, we will climb the mountain and destroy the monster Humbaba!"

Enkidu's eyes filled with tears and he turned away.

"Why should you cry, O Enkidu? Are you not the bravest of men? Are you no longer my friend and brother whom I admire more than anyone at all?"

Enkidu spoke: "I knew the presence of Humbaba even when I was a wild man on the steppes and in the forest. I could hear the sighing of his voice rise over the sound of thunder and high winds. I could hear the beating of his heart and feel the heat of his breath at a distance of five-hundred shar. I do not fear beast or mortal man, O Gilgamesh, but Humbaba is not mortal; he is the appointed servant of the gods, the guardian of the wild cows and the cedar forest. Whoever comes near him will grow weak. He will become paralyzed and will fail."

"The monster is an everlasting evil," said Gilgamesh. "It oppresses the people. Day and night it spreads fires and spews its ashes over the town. It is hated by great

Shamash,[1] constantly obscuring his face. O Enkidu, shall my life be as an empty wind? What am I, if I turn aside from the things I want to do? I am nothing, only someone waiting for death! But if I do this thing, O Enkidu, even though I should fail, then they will say, 'Gilgamesh died a hero's death! He died defending his people.' I will have made an everlasting name for myself and my life will not be as an empty wind!"

Still Enkidu turned away.

Gilgamesh then called in the armorers, the makers of spears and shields and axes. They cast for him swords of bronze inlaid with silver and gold. They made powerful long-bows and arrows tipped with stone, and most beautiful of all, a spear with a handle of lapis lazuli[2] and gold inset with many glittering jewels.

Gilgamesh called Enkidu and laid the weapons before him, hoping to tempt him with their beauty. And still Enkidu said no.

Gilgamesh was downcast. "My brother has grown soft and timid. He no longer loves daring; he has forgotten adventure; I will go alone!"

The elders of Uruk, who had long ago forgotten their hatred of the King, now came to him: "O Gilgamesh, do not undertake this thing. You are young; your heart has carried you away. Settle down, O King; take a bride to yourself; let your life be tranquil!"

Gilgamesh laughed. "Save your wise counsel for my friend, Enkidu. He'll listen. You waste your words on me, good fathers!"

The elders came in secret to Enkidu. "If the King stubbornly insists on doing this thing, risking danger and defying the gods, then Enkidu you must accompany him!"

"Indeed, you must go ahead of him," a second elder said, "for it is known that whoever first enters the cedar gate will be the first killed."

"Besides, it is you who know the way, Enkidu. It is you who have trodden the road!"

"May Shamash stand beside you!"

"May he open the path for you!"

---

1. **Shamash** the sun god.
2. **lapis lazuli** (lap' is laz' yo͞o lī) a blue, semi-precious stone.

Enkidu went to Gilgamesh. "My head is bowed, O King. I am your brother and your servant; wherever you will go, I will go."

Tears came into the eyes of Gilgamesh; his faith in Enkidu was restored. "Now, my brother, we will go to Ninsun; we will tell our plan and ask her to petition the gods for our success!"

Pale as she was, Ninsun turned more pale. But since she could not dissuade her son, she merely kissed him, giving him her blessing. To Enkidu she said, "Even though you are not my son, O Enkidu, you are like a son to me, and I shall petition the gods for you as for Gilgamesh. But remember, please, that as a man protects his own person, so must he guard the life of his companion!"

The people of Uruk walked with the two friends through the streets admiring their weapons and praising their bold plan: "Praise be to Gilgamesh who dares everything! Praise be to Enkidu who will safeguard his companion!" But Harim the priestess mourned, "May your feet carry you back safely to the city, Enkidu!" And thus they set out.

Ninsun dressed herself in her finest garments. She attached the golden pendants to her ears and set the divine tiara upon her head. She anointed herself with perfumes and carried in her hand an incense that would carry its pleasant odors into the sky. Mounting with stately grace to the roof of her palace, she raised her voice to its highest pitch and called out, "O Shamash, listen to me!" Then waiting a little for her voice to reach the ears of the god, she went on: "O Shamash, why have you given my son Gilgamesh such a restless heart? Why have you made him so eager for adventure? Now he has gone up to fight with the indestructible monster Humbaba. Why have you sent him, O Shamash, to wipe out the evil that you abhor? It is all your plan! It is you who have planted the idea in his head! May you not sleep, O Shamash, until Gilgamesh and his friend Enkidu return to Uruk. If they fail, may you never sleep again!"

Ninsun extinguished the small blaze from under the incense and descended from the roof of the palace.

Gilgamesh and Enkidu walked toward the mountain of the cedar forest. At a distance of twenty double-hours they sat down beside the path and ate a small amount of food. At a distance of thirty double-hours, they lay down to sleep, covering themselves with their garments. On the following day they walked a distance of fifty double-hours. Within three days' time, they covered a distance that it would have taken ordinary men some fifteen days to cover. They reached the mountain and saw before them a towering and magnificent gate of cedar wood.

"Here," said Gilgamesh, "we must pour meal upon the earth, for that will gain us the goodwill of the gods; it will persuade them to reveal their purpose in our dreams!"

They poured meal on the ground and lay down to sleep. After some time Gilgamesh wakened his friend. "Enkidu, I have had a dream; it went like this: We were standing in a deep gorge beside a mountain. Compared to it, we were the size of flies! Before our very eyes the mountain collapsed; it fell in a heap!"

"The meaning of that seems very clear," said Enkidu. "It means that Humbaba is the mountain and that he will fall before us!"

They closed their eyes again and slept. After some time, Gilgamesh again awakened his friend. "I've had another dream, Enkidu. I saw the same mountain this time, and again it fell, but it fell on me. However, as I lay struggling, a beautiful personage appeared. He took me by my feet and dragged me out from under the mountain. Now I wonder what this means? Is it that you will rescue me from the monster, or will someone else come along?"

They pondered a little and went back to sleep. Next Enkidu wakened his brother, Gilgamesh. "Has a cold shower passed over us? Did the lightning strike fires, and was there a rain of ashes?"

"The earth is dry and clean," said Gilgamesh, "you must have dreamed!" But since neither of them could understand the meaning of this dream, they fell asleep again, and soon the day came.

They approached the magnificent gate. "Let's open it, Enkidu! Let's be on our way!"

For a last time, Enkidu tried to persuade his friend to turn back.

But since the King would not listen, it was he who went first and placed his hand against the gate to push it open. Enkidu was thrown backward with such violence that he fell to the earth. He rose to his feet. "Gilgamesh, wait! My hand is paralyzed!"

"Put it on my arm, Enkidu! It will take strength from my arm because I am not afraid."

When the two friends threw their weight against the gate, however, it swung inward.

They walked up the mountainside through the sacred trees. And these became closer and thicker until the sky was blotted out. They could hear the giant heartbeat of Humbaba and smell the smoke from his lungs.

To show his daring, Gilgamesh cut one of the cedar trees. The blows of his axe rang out, and from afar the terrible Humbaba heard the sound.

With a crashing of timbers and a rolling of loose stones, Humbaba came down upon them. His face loomed among the tree tops, creased and grooved like some ancient rock. The breath he breathed withered the boughs of cedar and set small fires everywhere.

Enkidu's fears now vanished and the two heroes stood side by side as the monster advanced. He loomed over them, his arms swinging out like the masts of a ship. He was almost upon them when suddenly the friends stepped apart. The giant demon lurched through the trees, stumbled, and fell flat. He rose to his feet bellowing like a bull and charged upon Enkidu. But the King brought down his axe on the toe of Humbaba so that he whirled about roaring with pain. He grasped Gilgamesh by his flowing hair, swung him round and round as if to hurl him through the treetops, but now Enkidu saw his giant ribs exposed and he thrust his sword into the monster's side. Liquid fire gushed from the wound and ran in small streams down the mountainside. Gilgamesh fell to the earth and lay still, trying to breathe. But meanwhile Humbaba grasped the horns of Enkidu and began to flail his body against a tree. Surely the wild man would have died, but now Gilgamesh roused himself. He lanced into the air his long spear with its handle of lapis lazuli and gold. The spear caught Humbaba in the throat and remained there poised and glittering among the fires that had ignited everywhere.

The giant loosened his hold on Enkidu; he cried out. The earth reverberated with the sound, and distant mountains shook.

Gilgamesh felt pity in his heart. He withdrew his sword and put down his axe, while the monster Humbaba crept toward him grovelling and wailing for help. Now Enkidu perceived that the monster drew in a long breath in order to spew forth his last weapon—the searing fire that would consume the King. He leaped on the demon and with many sword thrusts released the fire, so that it bubbled harmlessly among the stones.

Humbaba was dead; the two heroes, black with soot and dirt, were still alive. They hugged each other; they leaped about; and singing and shouting, they descended the mountainside. Gentle rains fell around them and the land was forever free from the curse of the giant Humbaba.

from The Babylonians

Elaine Landau

The development of civilizations like ours was a many-stepped process. To find enough food to support life, groups had to wander, following and hunting herds of animals. Later, as this selection shows, a large change came when groups who tilled the soil could settle in one area. These groups could farm to provide food for themselves.

IN THE BEGINNING

Thousands of years ago there were no cities, countries, or governments as we know them today. Instead, small bands of people roamed the Earth living off the land. They were hunters and gatherers who were always on the move in search of wild game and fish as well as fruits and nuts to eat. These individuals didn't think of themselves as having a homeland. They were nomadic, or wandering, groups guided in their travels by the need to find food to survive.

No one knows precisely how or why things changed. What made some people trade the freedom to follow the animal herds for the strenuous task of tilling the soil? Although there are no definite answers, a number of theories have been suggested.

Historians note that at first just a few people may have separated from the wandering band. These were probably the weaker or smaller individuals who might have found it difficult to keep up with the rest. In addition, those who had been scorned or were unhappy with the group for some reason may have started to drop out as well.

It is also thought that women possibly played an important role in families settling down. Giving birth to and caring for young children while on the go must have been extremely difficult. Once women realized that remaining in one place would be best for both their offspring (children) and families, they may have been a powerful force behind this change of lifestyle.

There are numerous other unanswered questions as well. For example, when did the process of growing one's own food or planting and harvesting crops begin? Did a specific incident or change in the environment spur it on? Could some gathered seeds stored outdoors have accidentally taken root and become the first crop field? Or did the first "crops" spring up after some seeds left in a rubbish heap sprouted?

Naturally, this change didn't occur all at once. First, small groups of people settled down together, forming early villages that eventually grew into towns and cities. As these communities continued over the years, they changed. Societies complete with a written language, a code of law, and advanced technologies developed.

One of the places this first occurred was an area in what is now the Middle East known as Mesopotamia—a land between where the Tigris and Euphrates rivers empty into the Persian Gulf. There on a hot, dry, windswept plain, now referred to as a "cradle of civilization," some of the earliest cultures arose. Among these was Assyria, an area on the upper Tigris River in northern Mesopotamia. Another important region known as Sumer occupied 10,000 square miles (26,000 square kilometers) in southern Mesopotamia. Sumer later became Babylonia—a third accomplished Mesopotamian civilization.

The borders between these ancient areas were not always precisely drawn. Wars, political takeovers, and population shifts all served to intermingle the various peoples in the vicinity. Yet these three cultures remain distinct for their important contributions to the world. Ancient Mesopotamians invented the wheel, studied the stars and other heavenly bodies, and achieved important developments in mathematics, medicine, and architecture. They built cities, made advances in art and literature, and were the first people to develop a legal code.

For many years little was known about ancient Mesopotamia. Rain, floods, shifting sands, and other natural occurrences had erased its narrow, winding streets, and its courtyards, religious towers, and magnificent palaces. But by the mid-nineteenth century, archaeologists unearthed the clay tablets, pottery, tools, and building ruins of the Mesopotamians. To accomplish this, archaeological teams dug through huge mounds of soil, stripping away numerous layers of earth. Photographers took pictures of any articles found, while archaeologists interpreted when and how the various items were used.

Specialists in ancient languages translated the writings on clay tablets, providing even more information on societies of the past. These clues enabled them to piece together a fascinating picture of the extremely advanced and industrious peoples who once inhabited this "cradle of civilization."

BABYLONIA

Picture a magnificent city in the ancient Near East, a center of life filled with stunning temples, towers, and palaces. Airy courtyards dot the landscape—there's even a lush green garden overflowing with plants and trees in this desert haven. Beauty and color seem to greet your eye at every turn. Bright yellow, red, and white wall tiles are used to create images of dragons and rows of lions on city walls and gates.

Yet this city is more than just dazzling to see. It is also a cultural center where painting, sculpture, literature, and music thrive. Scientists also live here, anxious to advance their studies and research. This city is not an imaginary paradise. It's Babylon, the capital of the ancient land of Babylonia.

While Babylonia was among the earliest advanced civilizations, its capital city of Babylon wasn't always as majestic as it eventually became. In about 3000 B.C., Babylon was just one of many loosely connected city-states ruled by the Amorites, a group of desert people descended from nomadic Syrian and Arabian tribes. The various city-states existed in an uneasy alliance. Any family or cultural ties between the different Amorite sheikhs, or rulers, did little to rein in their lust for power and possessions. At times, petty jealousies and conflicts between the Amorite city-states erupted into full-scale battles. The victor usually considered his success a step toward gaining control of the entire region.

Hammurabi was sixth in a line of Amorite sheikhs ruling the city-state of Babylon. When he took the throne in 1750 B.C. his work was cut out for him. As the sheikh of Babylon, Hammurabi found himself surrounded by dangerously cunning rival city-states. These included Larsa—a powerful Amorite city-state that already dominated a number of city-states to the south of Babylon. Another of Babylon's powerful rivals was Mari, which lay to the northwest in what today is Syria. But Hammurabi was particularly concerned about two especially warlike city-states to the north known as Eshnunna and Assur.

Being a skilled statesman and militarist, Hammurabi knew he would have to wait and fortify his position before launching a strike. So for the first twenty-five years of his forty-two-year reign, he entered into a number of advantageous alliances with other city-states. These relationships served to both keep enemies at a safe distance as well as enhance his own city-state of Babylon through favorable trade agreements.

However, Hammurabi never hesitated to break these ties when it benefited him to do so. Following his thirtieth year as Babylon's sheikh, he ordered a surprise attack on the city-state of Larsa. Hammurabi emerged as its conqueror as well as head of most of central and southern Mesopotamia. Within three years Hammurabi also destroyed the rival city-state of Mari. This victory allowed him to seize control of western Mesopotamia, which Mari had long dominated.

At that point, Hammurabi needed only to overtake the north to secure all of Mesopotamia. But the brilliant military strategist knew that this might prove extremely difficult. Much of northern Mesopotamia was controlled by Assyria, a country of fierce warriors that placed great emphasis on military might. Yet, during Hammurabi's reign, Assyrian strength had declined somewhat and this once fearsome power had become increasingly dependent on its alliance with the northern Mesopotamian city-state of Eshnunna. After Hammurabi attacked and conquered Eshnunna, the Assyrians had no choice but to accept his rule. Like the rest of Mesopotamia, they were at least temporarily under his control.

Hammurabi had realized his goal of ruling a united Mesopotamia with Babylon as its capital city. Having brought Babylon to a new level of greatness, the whole area came to be known as Babylonia. Proud of his achievement, Hammurabi proclaimed that Babylonia was "supreme in the world." He described his position and that of Babylonia as being "as firm as those of heaven and earth." And during his lifetime, this appeared to be true.

What Ancient Egypt Gave Us

from Science in Ancient Egypt

Geraldine Woods

*Twenty-four hour days, the pyramids, even geometry—
all these originated in Egypt, as this selection explains.*

In Egypt the past is alive. The majestic pyramids are survivors of ancient times, as is the simple shaduf[1] a farmer
dips for water and the mud bricks that villagers set to
bake in the sun. It is still possible to find flat looms, sun
clocks, papyrus, and faience[2] made in the 5,000-year-old
way. These are only the obvious traces of the past. Many
other achievements of the early Egyptians also appear in
our modern world.

What is the most important contribution ancient Egypt
has made to modern times? It may be time itself. Our
sun-based calendar came to us from Egypt by way of
Julius Caesar, who brought it to Rome about 2,050 years
ago. So did our 24-hour days, although our winter and
summer hours are always the same length.

The Egyptians also laid the foundations of geometry, a
type of advanced math, with their formulas for calculat-
ing area and volume and their study of angles. Their
practical engineering math was passed along to the
Greeks when Alexander the Great conquered Egypt about
2,330 years ago. The Greeks extended this knowledge
into the theories of math taught to schoolchildren today.

The scientific study of medicine also began in ancient
Egypt. Their physicians handed down knowledge of
anatomy, drugs, and surgery to later cultures. They also
passed along an attitude. The ancient doctors were
taught to observe, examine, diagnose, and prescribe
treatment, just as doctors do today.

As pioneers in irrigation and agriculture, the ancient
Egyptians were the first to build canals and reservoirs, to
use a plow, to keep cattle, sheep, oxen, goats, and
donkeys.

---

1. **shaduf** (shä do͞of′) *n.* a long pole with a bucket on one end and a weight on the
other end.
2. **faience** (fī′əns) *n.* glazed pottery or tiles.

The form and craftsmanship of the pyramids probably inspired architects of later eras. The Egyptians invented many techniques for handling stone, and they were the first to use it in monumental structures. Until the Egyptians worked with this material, no one else in the world had even laid a slab of stone on top of two columns.

Recently an underground tomb containing almost 100 rooms was discovered. It will take decades to explore the tomb completely, and no one knows what wonders will be found. Yet even if no scientific artifacts appear, the Egyptians' achievements stand out. Their ideas and tools have been passed down through more than 100 centuries to shape modern science and modern civilization.

Nubia and the Kingdom of Kush (2000 B.C.–A.D. 400)

from The Kingfisher Book of the Ancient World

Hazel Mary Martell

This selection shows Egyptian civilization reaching beyond its own borders around 2000 B.C.

Nubia was on the Nile River, just south of Egypt. Although it was surrounded by desert, the land alongside the river was kept fertile by the annual floods. Tomb paintings from Egypt show that the Nubians were black Africans, and written references often describe them as tall and strong.

Egyptian civilization reached Nubia by about 2000 B.C., which was also when the kingdom of Kush was starting to develop there. Its capital was at Napata, just below the fourth cataract on the Nile. Soon trade was flourishing, with the Nubians supplying Egypt with gold, ivory, exotic animals, and fruits. Nubians also joined the Egyptian army as mercenaries.

By the 1400s B.C., an Egyptian viceroy ruled over Nubia. As Egypt's power declined toward the end of the New Kingdom period, however, that of Kush began to increase.

By around 750 B.C., the Kushite army defeated the Egyptians at Memphis, and the Kushite rulers founded the 25th dynasty of pharaohs. It lasted until 663 B.C., when the Egyptians were conquered by the Assyrians and the Kushite rulers returned to the lands of Nubia and their capital at Napata.

Ironworking Brings Wealth

In about 600 B.C., they changed their capital to Meroë, farther south on the Nile. Knowledge of ironworking had spread from Egypt, and because Meroë was surrounded by deposits of iron ore, it quickly grew in size and wealth. By 500 B.C. it had grown into a city of mud-brick houses built around cemeteries of pyramid-like tombs, which in turn were built around a complex of royal temples. The most important one at this time was dedicated to Amun, the chief Egyptian god, but later ones were dedicated to the Nubians' own gods, such as Marduk.

Meroë had trade links with the Mediterranean via the Nile, while camel trains brought goods from Arabia overland from Red Sea ports.

As Egyptian influence declined, the Nubians used an alphabetical script in place of hieroglyphs. It has been deciphered, but the language has not yet been translated.

Nubia and Kush remained independent, even after Egypt was conquered by the Romans in 30 B.C., but by A.D. 400 their power was waning.

I Love a Girl, but She Lives Over There

Translated by John L. Foster

The annual flooding of the Nile River was essential to the development of Egyptian civilization—but in this poem, it separates two people in love.

I love a girl, but she lives over there
     on the too far side of the River.
A whole Nile at floodstage[1] rages between,
     and a crocodile hunched on the sand
Keeps motionless guard at the crossing.
     Still I go down to the water,
Stride out into the waves—
     how is it
5   Desire can soar in the wrench of this current,
     rough water be tame as my fields?
Why she loves me!   she loves me!   hers is the love
     anchors the shifting toeholds;
My charming girl whispered water magic
     (crocodile sits spellbound)—   O my love,
Where are you, whose hand
     is so small yet has mastered the River?
—There, over there! already waiting,
     right in the path of my burning eyes!
10   The only one dear to my heart,
     and she crowns the shore like a queen!

---

1. Nile at floodstage The Nile river, which flows through Egypt, floods once every year.

The Mysterious Hieroglyphs
from The Riddle of the Rosetta Stone

James Cross Giblin

As this selection shows, cracking the code of an ancient language took a special discovery—the Rosetta Stone.

The scene: The Egyptian Sculpture Gallery of the British Museum in London. The time: Now.

Near the entrance to the long, high-ceilinged room stand two magnificent granite statues of Pharaoh Amenophis III, who ruled Egypt about 1400 B.C. Farther on is a colossal head of Pharaoh Ramesses II dating back to 1250 B.C. And beyond it, resting on a simple base, is a slab of black basalt, a volcanic rock.

Next to the statues and the head, the slab seems unimpressive at first glance. It is roughly the size of a tabletop—three feet nine inches long, two feet four and a half inches wide, and eleven inches thick. But many experts would say that this rather small piece of rock was more valuable than any of the larger objects in the room. For it is the famed Rosetta Stone, which gave nineteenth-century scholars their first key to the secrets of ancient Egypt.

What makes this stone so special? Step closer, and you'll see. Spotlights pick out markings carved into the surface of the stone, and close up you can tell that these marks are writing. At the top are fourteen lines of hiero-glyphs—pictures of animals, birds, and geometric shapes. Below them you can make out thirty-two lines written in an unfamiliar script. And below that, at the bottom of the slab, are fifty-four more lines written in the letters of the Greek alphabet.

Before the Rosetta Stone was discovered in 1799, no one knew how to read Egyptian hieroglyphic writing. Its meaning had been lost for almost 1400 years. But countless visitors to Egypt over the centuries had tried to decipher the mysterious symbols. This is the story of their attempts, and of how the Rosetta Stone finally enabled scholars to unlock the Egyptian past.

The story begins in the seventh century A.D., when Greek scholars visiting Egypt first called the symbols "hieroglyphs." They gave them that name, which means "sacred carvings" in Greek, because they found so many of them on the walls of Egyptian tombs and temples.

As the Greeks sailed up the Nile River to the ancient cities of Memphis and Thebes, they asked native after native what the hieroglyphs meant. Not even the oldest Egyptians could tell them, for the language expressed in the hieroglyphs had already been dead for several hundred years. It had been replaced by Coptic, the language spoken by Christian Egyptians. And Coptic, in turn, was replaced by Arabic after the Arabs conquered Egypt in A.D. 642. By the time the visitors from Greece arrived, no living Egyptian knew how to read the hieroglyphic writing of his ancestors.

Frustrated in their attempts to get someone to translate the hieroglyphs for them, the Greeks decided on their own that the symbols must be a kind of picture writing. Some thought the pictures were mystical devices used in ancient religious rites, whose meaning was known only to long-dead Egyptian priests.

Others stumbled on the correct definitions of a few hieroglyphs. No one knows exactly where the Greeks obtained this information. Some think it came from craftsmen who made good-luck charms based on ancient Egyptian designs and still knew what those symbols meant.

However they obtained it, the Greeks couldn't resist adding their own original "explanations" to the definitions. For example, a Greek writer named Horapollo said correctly that the picture of a goose stood for the word "son." But then he explained that this was because geese took special care of their young, which was completely inaccurate. He wrote that the image of a rabbit meant "open" because a rabbit's eyes never close—an equally false statement.

Horapollo offered an even more unlikely explanation of a hieroglyph drawn in the form of a vulture. First, he said that it stood for the word "mother," which happened to be correct. Then his imagination took over, and he claimed that the hieroglyph also meant "a sight, or boundaries, or foreknowledge." He went on to explain why.

"The vulture means a mother since there is no male in this species of animal," Horapollo wrote. (Of course this was untrue!) "It stands for sight since of all animals the vulture has the keenest vision. It means boundaries because, when a war is about to break out, the vulture limits the place in which it will be fought by hovering over the area for seven days. And it stands for foreknowledge because, in flying over the battlefield, the vulture looks forward to the corpses the slaughter will provide it for food."

The writings of Horapollo circulated widely throughout Europe and influenced the study of hieroglyphs for centuries to come. No one questioned the Greek writer's explanations. Instead, European scholars accepted them as truths and put forward their own mistaken interpretations of the mysterious symbols.

Some of these scholars made otherwise significant contributions to the world's knowledge of ancient Egypt. A German priest of the 1600s, Athanasius Kircher, wrote the first grammar and vocabulary of Coptic, the language of Christian Egypt. These books were to prove of great value when the hieroglyphs were eventually deciphered.

But Kircher's ideas about the hieroglyphs themselves were even farther off the mark than those of Horapollo. Looking at a certain group of symbols—which actually stood for the name of a pharaoh—Kircher let his imagination run wild. Without any evidence to support him, he said that the hieroglyphs meant "The blessings of the god Osiris are to be procured by means of sacred ceremonies, in order that the benefits of the river Nile may be obtained."

From 1650 onward, Kircher produced several volumes of such nonsense. It earned him a reputation for being an expert on the hieroglyphs—a reputation that lasted, unfortunately, long after his death in 1680.

A few genuine advances in understanding the hieroglyphs were made during the 1700s. The French scholar C. J. de Guignes observed that groups of hieroglyphs in Egyptian texts were often enclosed by an oval outline, which he called a *cartouche*. "Cartouche" is a French word that originally meant a cartridge, and the line around the hieroglyphs had a similar shape. De Guignes guessed rightly that the cartouches in hieroglyphic inscriptions were intended to draw attention to important names, probably the names of Egyptian rulers.

Along with such insights, de Guignes advanced other ideas about the hieroglyphs that were as silly as any that had been proposed by Kircher or Horapollo. After comparing some Egyptian hieroglyphs with examples of Chinese picture writing, de Guignes announced that settlers from Egypt must have colonized China in ancient times. English students of the 1700s went the Frenchman one better. They declared that it had happened the other way around: The ancient Egyptians had come from China!

None of these theories brought scholars any closer to a true understanding of the hieroglyphs. As the 1700s came to an end, their meaning was as much of a mystery as ever.

Travelers to Egypt gazed in awe upon the pyramids. But because they could not decipher the hieroglyphs, neither they nor the natives had any idea when the gigantic structures were built, or how. The travelers saw the ruins of ancient cities and palaces. But they did not know who had lived in them, or what their lives were like.

All the secrets of ancient Egypt—its history, its literature, its religious beliefs—remained hidden behind the lines of the mysterious hieroglyphs. And it looked as if they might stay there forever. Then, in 1798, something happened that seemed at first to have nothing to do with the puzzle of the hieroglyphs. The French general Napoleon Bonaparte invaded Egypt with an army of 38,000 soldiers.

France was at war with England, and Napoleon's main goal was to occupy Egypt and then attack British-held India. But like many Europeans of the time, Napoleon was also interested in learning more about Egypt itself. So, along with the soldiers, Napoleon brought with him to Egypt a party of 167 scholars and scientists. Their assignment: to study every aspect of the country and its history.

What neither Napoleon nor the scholars could guess was that their most important discovery would be an odd-shaped black slab with three different kinds of writing on it.

Aïda

As told by Leontyne Price

Leontyne Price, who wrote this story version of the well-known opera Aïda, *is famous for acting and singing the part of its main character, Aïda.*

Long ago, in the faraway land of Ethiopia, there lived a Princess named Aïda. She was fair as the sunrise and gentle as starlight touching a flower. Her father, the great King Amonasro, loved her dearly.

It was a time of terrible fear and danger in Ethiopia, for the kingdom was at war with its neighbor, Egypt. Both countries raided each other's lands, killing or enslaving their enemies.

For the safety of his people, King Amonasro set strict boundaries at the borders of his country, and no Ethiopian was allowed beyond them.

The Princess Aïda was young and, locked within the palace, she grew restless. So, one morning, Aïda and her trusted friends disobeyed the King's command. They disguised themselves and slipped away from the palace guards.

It was a glorious day of freedom, out in the gentle breezes and lush green fields of their beautiful country. But Aïda wandered farther than she should have. Off on her own, enjoying the warm sun and fresh country air, she did not hear her friends in the distance when they shouted, "Aïda! Beware! Come back!"

Once again, Egyptian soldiers had invaded Ethiopia, crossing the south edge of the River Nile. Now they marched toward Aïda.

When she finally did hear her friends' warning, it was too late. Soldiers seized her. Bound with ropes and chains, Aïda, the Royal Princess of Ethiopia, was carried off to Egypt as a slave.

Aïda had learned her royal lessons well. She revealed to no one that she was the daughter of King Amonasro of Ethiopia. But her beauty and noble bearing attracted great attention. So sparkling and unusual was she that the all-powerful Pharaoh, the ruler of Egypt, chose her from among thousands of captured slaves to be his gift—

a personal handmaiden—to his only daughter, the
Princess Amneris.

It was easy for Aïda to perform the duties of a servant,
for she remembered what her own handmaidens had
done. The Egyptian Princess Amneris was fascinated, for
Aïda was different from any slave she had ever seen. She
wanted her new handmaiden to be her closest companion.

Even with the special privileges granted to one so close
to the Royal Princess, Aïda felt nothing but despair. All
her life she had been the beloved daughter of Ethiopia's
King, and now she was a slave to her father's enemy. She
knew there was no hope of seeing Ethiopia again.

There was one source of light in her life, however. For
Radames, the handsome young captain of the Egyptian
Army, had fallen in love with the gentle, beautiful slave
the moment he saw her. She, too, had fallen for Radames,
despite his position as an enemy of her homeland.

They met often, in secret, by the Temple of Isis, and in
the joy of their moments together, Radames confided his
dreams to Aïda.

"I will lead the Egyptian Army to victory," he told her,
"and when I return, our countries will be united, and you
will become my bride and reign as the Queen of your
people. It will not be long, I promise."

The day finally came when the Pharaoh was to hold
court and announce the new leader of the war against
Ethiopia.

Amid the majestic columns of a great hall in the
palace, Egypt's High Priest, Ramfis, confided to Radames:
"There are rumors that the Ethiopians plan to attack.
Prepare yourself, for the Goddess Isis has chosen, and
the great honor of leadership may be bestowed upon
you."

All his life, Radames had dreamed of this day. If he became the new leader, he could return triumphant to free
Aïda and marry her. "Ah, heavenly Aïda," he thought. "I
could finally enthrone you in your native land."

Radames was deep in thought when Princess Amneris
stepped from the shadows. She, too, was in love with the
handsome leader, but she suspected he loved another.

Aïda suddenly appeared.

Oh, how Radames's eyes filled with passion! And when Amneris saw the look that passed between them, she was seized with suspicion and jealousy. Could Radames prefer a *slave* to the Princess of Egypt? It was intolerable! But her fury was interrupted by trumpets heralding the arrival of the Pharaoh.

A messenger came forward to give his report.

"Mighty Pharaoh, the Ethiopians have attacked. They are led by the fierce warrior King Amonasro, who has invaded Egypt!"

A thunder of anger broke out in court, and upon hearing her father's name, Aïda quietly cried out in fear.

The Pharaoh rose, and the crowd grew still.

"Radames will lead our army," he cried. "It is the decree of the Goddess Isis. Death to the Ethiopians! Victory to Egypt!" he shouted. "Return victorious, Radames!" he commanded.

"Return victorious! Return victorious!" the throng shouted, and Aïda, too, was stirred by the cry. In spite of herself, she also began to shout, "Return victorious! Return victorious!" as the court led the soldiers off to battle. Aïda was now left alone.

"Return victorious!" she called after Radames, but as her own voice echoed in the great hall, she suddenly realized she was asking for the death of her father, her mother, her friends, and all those she cherished. Yet how could she pray for the death of the man she loved?

Aïda was shocked. Her heart was torn between Radames and her loyalty to her father and Ethiopia. She fell to her knees and prayed.

"Oh, great gods of my youth!" she cried. "Pity me!"

That night, the halls of the temple rang as the priestesses chanted the sacred consecration[1] song. The High Priest, Ramfis, led prayers to Phtha,[2] the creator of life and mightiest Egyptian god, as he gave the great hero the sacred sword of Egypt.

"Let the sword of Radames be the strength of our nation! Let his bravery in battle crush the Ethiopians! Protect our land," they prayed, "and make Radames the most magnificent warrior of all."

---

1. **consecration** (kän si krā´ shən) *n.* a blessing ceremony.
2. **Phtha** (ftah)

"Praise to Phtha! Praise to Phtha!" the Egyptians chanted, and the priestesses danced a sacred dance to please the great god and ensure death to their enemies.

With Radames gone, time passed slowly for Aïda. But soon the prayers of the priests were granted. A special day dawned for Egypt—a day of ceremony and grandeur, of pomp and pageantry. The Ethiopians had been defeated at last.

Amneris sat before her mirror. Surrounded by slaves and adorned in her most beautiful gown and jewels, she was pleased with her reflection. Surely today when Radames returned, he would be struck by her radiance. Yet despite her vanity, she secretly burned with jealousy to think that Aïda, a mere handmaiden, might truly be loved by Radames.

So Amneris decided to test her privileged slave. And when gentle Aïda entered the royal chambers, Amneris sobbed, pretending great grief.

"Oh, Aïda, Aïda!" she cried in a shaking voice. "Egypt has lost its finest warrior. Radames has been killed in battle!"

Immediately Aïda wept with the pain of one whose heart has been broken forever. There was no longer any doubt in Amneris's mind.

"It is all a lie!" she shouted. "Radames was not killed. He lives!"

Aïda's tears of sorrow turned to tears of joy.

Overcome with fury, Amneris hurled Aïda to the floor. "How dare you, a lowly slave, love the same man loved by the Princess of Egypt?"

But Aïda, too, was a Princess. She rose proudly. She was about to tell Amneris the truth, but she stopped herself. Instead, with great difficulty, she asked to be forgiven.

"Have mercy on me," she begged. "Your power is unquestioned—you have all that a person could want. But what do I have to live for? My love of Radames, and that alone."

Aïda's plea only fueled Amneris's rage. She stormed out of the chamber, leaving Aïda to fear the worst.

Flags flew, and the entire city gathered to see the grand spectacle of the victory parade led by the Pharaoh, the Princess, and the High Priest. Trumpets blared, and dancing girls threw rose petals to form a welcoming carpet before the magnificent chariot of Radames.

The handsome warrior dismounted and knelt before the royal throne. When Amneris placed a laurel wreath[3] on his head, the crowd was wild with joy.

"Hail to the conqueror!" they roared. "Hail to Radames!"

The Pharaoh proclaimed, "Radames, you are my greatest soldier. As a reward, whatever you wish shall be yours."

When Radames rose, he saw Aïda. Amneris saw the look of love on his face, and she was consumed with jealousy. Yet he dared not ask for Aïda's hand, not at that moment in public court.

"Mighty Pharaoh," he said instead, "I ask that you allow me to call forth our prisoners of war."

The Pharaoh granted Radames's request, and the Ethiopians were led into the square in chains. One tall, proud man stood out above the rest. Aïda gasped. It was her father!

The crowd was shocked to see her run and embrace him, but he whispered to her, "Do not betray that I am King."

Amonasro addressed the Pharaoh. "I am Aïda's father, and I have faithfully fought for my sovereign[4] who died in battle. I am prepared to die for him and my country, but I beseech you to have mercy on those who have been defeated."

With outstretched arms, Aïda joined the Ethiopians. "Let the prisoners go free," she begged Radames and the Pharaoh.

So moved by her appeal, the Egyptian people joined in, and their cries urged the Pharaoh to allow the captured soldiers to be released.

"No!" the High Priest, Ramfis, cried. "The Ethiopians are still a threat and should be put to death."

"Their freedom is my wish," Radames told the Pharaoh.

---

3. **laurel** (lôr'əl) **wreath** a crown of shiny flat leaves used to crown a winner.
4. **sovereign** (säv'rən) *n.* a king or ruler.

"Unchain the Ethiopians!" the Pharaoh ordered. "But you, Aïda's father, must remain my prisoner as a pledge of your people's good faith."

An even greater reward was now to be bestowed upon Egypt's greatest warrior. The Pharaoh led Amneris to Radames.

"My daughter will be your bride," he proclaimed, joining their hands. "One day, you shall be Pharaoh, and together you will rule."

Radames was horrified. He dared not refuse the Pharaoh. He bowed and pretended gratitude, but his heart was filled with sorrow. Amneris looked scornfully at her handmaiden.

Aïda wept in her father's arms as the triumphant Egyptian Princess held Radames's hand and led him to the palace.

"Do not lose faith," Amonasro whispered to his daughter. "Ethiopia will soon avenge our conquerors."

It was the eve of the great wedding, and a full moon shone on the dark waters of the River Nile beside the Temple of Isis. By boat, the High Priest, Ramfis, brought Amneris to the temple. There she was to pray that her marriage be blessed. Little did she know that Radames had sent a message to Aïda, who was waiting to meet him nearby.

Aïda sadly watched the moonlit river and longed with all her heart and soul to return to her beloved homeland. Suddenly she heard Radames approach. But when the man came closer, she was stunned to see that it was her father, King Amonasro.

"Listen carefully, Aïda," he said sternly. "My plan will bring both you and Radames back to Ethiopia. Our soldiers stand ready to attack when I signal. There is a secret, unguarded road, but only Radames knows it. It is your duty as the Princess of Ethiopia to make him reveal this path."

"Father!" she cried. "I *cannot* betray Radames!"

With anger and disdain King Amonasro forced her to her knees. "You are no longer my daughter! You are nothing more than a lowly slave of the Egyptians and a betrayer of your country! Have you forgotten your loved ones who were slaughtered without mercy by these, your enemies?"

"You are wrong! I am *not* and will *never* be a slave to anyone. I am the Princess of Ethiopia, and I have never forgotten my royal blood. My duty to you and to my country will always be first in my heart!"

Even as she swore to obey his command, she cried inside for what her father and her dear country would cost her. Amonasro embraced her to give her courage, and he hid in the bushes to listen.

When Radames finally came, he was breathless with love. But Aïda turned on him scornfully.

"How could you betray me and marry Amneris as your reward?"

"Aïda, you have always been my love. My passion for you is deeper than the Nile, deeper than life itself," Radames told her.

"Then show me," Aïda demanded. "You have betrayed me. And if you truly love me, you will leave Egypt tonight and flee with me to Ethiopia. Only there will we find happiness and peace."

Radames was torn. The thought of leaving Egypt was unbearable, but the thought of living without Aïda was even more painful. At last, after much persuasion, he agreed to flee.

"The roads are heavily guarded by your soldiers. How will we escape?" she asked.

"All the roads are guarded except one," he told her. "The Gorges of Napata."

"The Gorges of Napata!" a voice rang out. Amonasro sprang from his hiding place. He was ready to attack with his army.

Radames could not believe it. "You, Aïda's father, are King of Ethiopia?" He was overcome. "I have sacrificed my country for my love of you!" he cried to Aïda.

"Come with us now," Amonasro told Radames. "You and Aïda will reign happily in Ethiopia."

But as the King took Radames's hand to lead him away, a shout rang out in the darkness. "Traitor!"

It was Amneris. She and the High Priest had come from the temple and had overheard the plot.

"Traitor!" she screamed again.

Amonasro leapt to kill Amneris with his dagger, but Radames ran between them to shield her.

"Go quickly!" he warned Aïda and Amonasro, and the King ran, dragging Aïda with him.

Radames stood before Amneris and the High Priest. He did not try to escape. Instead, he threw down his sword. "I surrender!" he cried. "I am your prisoner!"

The treason of Radames shocked and infuriated all of Egypt. Guards locked him in the deepest dungeon in the palace. Soon his trial would begin, and he would be sentenced to a horrible death.

Amneris was in a state of grief. Her love for Radames had not diminished. Deep in her heart, she knew he had not meant to betray his country. Her own jealousy had made the mighty warrior a prisoner. She longed to beg her father, the Pharaoh, to release him, but she knew Radames still loved Aïda. She also knew soldiers had killed Amonasro, but Aïda had escaped and was still alive—somewhere.

In desperation, Amneris commanded the guards to bring Radames to her. She humbled herself and pleaded with him to forget Aïda.

"I will find a way to set you free, free to marry me and share the throne of Egypt," she said. "But you must never see Aïda again."

Radames refused. "You are Princess of Egypt, my country; and you have all that anyone could ask for. Yet I will always love Aïda, and there will never be room in my heart for anyone else."

The more Amneris begged him, the more strongly he refused.

When the priests came to take Radames, Amneris was in a rage of anger and jealousy, and she made no attempt to stop them. But when he left, she fell to the ground in tears, cringing as she heard the priests loudly accuse Radames of betrayal.

"Traitor! Traitor!" the High Priest, Ramfis, shouted again and again, but Radames never uttered a word to defend himself. Louder and louder the cruel accusations were hurled at him.

Amneris prayed to Isis and the other gods of Egypt to show mercy and save the man she loved, but the gods were silent.

The tribunal[5] of priests pronounced Radames guilty of treason and sentenced him to be buried alive.

---

5. **tribunal** (trī byoo′ nəl) *n.* a court that passes judgment.

As the priests passed from the trial, Amneris flung herself before the High Priest. She insulted him and threatened revenge, but her cries were in vain.

"Radames, the traitor, will die," he said coldly.

Only the priests and guards were allowed to watch Radames walk into the deepest vault below. They sealed the last opening, shutting out all light and the last breath of fresh air. Alone, waiting quietly for death, Radames thought only of Aïda. He would never see her sparkling eyes and gentle smile again.

Suddenly, in the darkness, he heard Aïda's voice. At first, Radames thought it was a dream. But no—she had escaped and was hiding in the vault, waiting for him.

"Aïda, my love, you are too young and too beautiful to die."

Radames pushed in vain, trying to open the vault.

But Aïda gently placed her arms around him. With a tender kiss, she told him to stop.

"Remember, we will never be separated again. For eternity, we will be together."

And with all the love in the world, they held each other close—so close—as if they would never part.

Above their tomb, dressed in black, Princess Amneris prayed to the gods to forgive her and to grant heavenly rest to Radames, her love.

The gods granted her wish, but not as she hoped. For as she prayed to the gods and wept, a peaceful death had come to the Ethiopian Princess Aïda and Radames, the greatest warrior of Egypt. Finally they were together—forever in each other's arms.

The Egyptian Cinderella

Shirley Climo

There are more than nine hundred versions of this classic story—the oldest has been traced back more than a thousand years to China. But for all the differences between the stories, the poor girl always manages to escape her unhappy life, marry the prince, and live happily ever after, as Rhodopis does in The Egyptian Cinderella.

Long ago, in the land of Egypt, where the green Nile River widens to meet the blue sea, there lived a maiden called Rhodopis.[1] When she was still a small child, Rhodopis had been stolen by pirates. She was snatched from her home in Greece, taken across the sea to Egypt, and there sold as a slave.

Like the Egyptian servant girls, Rhodopis went to the water's edge each day to wash clothes or to gather the reeds that grew along the riverbank. But Rhodopis looked different from the Egyptian girls. Their eyes were brown and hers were green. Their hair hung straight to their shoulders, while the breeze blew hers into tangles. Their skin glowed like copper, but her pale skin burned red beneath the sun. That was how she got her name, for Rhodopis meant "rosy-cheeked" in Greek.

"Rosy Rhodopis!" scoffed the servant girls, hissing her name between their teeth.

Rhodopis pretended not to hear, but she blushed rosier than ever.

Although her master was kind, he was old and liked to doze beneath a fig tree. He seldom heard the servant girls tease Rhodopis. He never saw them ordering her about.

"Hurry, Rhodopis!" they would shout at her. "The geese are in the garden, eating up the onions!"

"Mend my robe!"

"I'm hungry, Rhodopis! Bake the bread!"

Rhodopis always hurried to do their bidding, for the Egyptian girls were household servants and she was only a slave.

---

1. **Rhodopis** (rō dō′ pəs)

Rhodopis found friends among the animals instead. Birds ate crumbs from her hands. She coaxed a monkey to sit upon her shoulder and charmed a hippopotamus with her songs. It would raise its huge head from the muddy water and prick its small ears to listen.

Sometimes, when her chores were done and the day had cooled, Rhodopis would dance for her animal companions. She twirled so lightly that her tiny bare feet scarcely touched the ground. One evening her master awakened to see her dance.

"No goddess is more nimble!" he called out. "Such a gift deserves reward." He tugged his chin whiskers, thinking, and then declared, "You shall go barefoot no longer."

Her master ordered a pair of dainty slippers made especially for Rhodopis. The soles were of real leather, and the toes were gilded with rose-red gold. Now when Rhodopis danced, her feet sparkled like fireflies.

The rose-red slippers set Rhodopis more apart than ever. The Egyptian servant girls were jealous, for they wore clumsy sandals woven from papyrus.[2] Out of spite they found new tasks for her to do, keeping Rhodopis so busy that she was too tired to dance at night.

One evening, Kipa, who was chief among the servant girls, announced, "Tomorrow we sail for Memphis to see the Pharaoh. His Majesty is going to hold court for all his subjects."

"There will be musicians and dancing," said another servant girl, eyeing the rose-red slippers.

"There will be feasting," added a third.

"Poor Rhodopis! You must stay behind." Kipa jeered. "You have linen to wash and grain to grind and the garden to weed."

The next morning, just as Ra the Sun was climbing into the sky, Rhodopis followed the servant girls to the riverbank. Kipa wore a necklace of blue beads. Bracelets jingled on the wrists of the second. The third had tied a many-colored sash about her waist. Although Rhodopis wore a plain tunic, on her feet were the rose-red slippers. Perhaps they will let me come along to see the Pharaoh after all, she thought. But the three servant girls poled

---

2. **papyrus** (pə pī′ rəs) *n.* a tall water plant that grows in the Nile region.

their raft around the bend in the river without giving Rhodopis a backward glance.

Rhodopis sighed, and turned to the basket piled high with dirty clothes. "Wash the linen, weed the garden, grind the grain." She slapped the wooden paddle against the cloth in time to her song.

The hippopotamus, tired of so dull a tune, pushed out of the reeds and splashed into the river.

"Shame!" cried Rhodopis, shaking her paddle. "You splattered mud on my beautiful slippers!"

She polished the shoes on the hem of her tunic until the rosy glow glittered in the sun. Then she carefully put them on the bank behind her.

"Wash the linen, weed the garden . . ." Rhodopis began again, when suddenly a shadow fell on the water. Rhodopis jumped up. A great falcon, the symbol of the god Horus, circled in the sky with wings spread so wide that they blotted out the sun.

"Greetings to you, Proud Horus," Rhodopis murmured. She bowed her head and felt a rush of air on the back of her neck.

When Rhodopis dared to lift her eyes, she saw the falcon soar away. Dangling from his talons was one of her beautiful slippers. "Stop!" she pleaded. "Come back!"

But the bird did not heed her. He flew toward the sun until he was no more than a dark speck against the gold.

Rhodopis bit her tongue. One shoe was worse than none at all. Now she'd have to dance like a stork, hopping about on one foot and even the monkey would laugh. Rhodopis tucked the slipper into her tunic and returned to her laundry, salting the river with her tears.

After Rhodopis had lost sight of the falcon, the mighty bird followed the course of the Nile to the city of Memphis, to the square where the Pharaoh was holding court. There the falcon watched and waited.

The Pharaoh's name was Amasis. On his head he wore the red-and-white crown of the Two Egypts. The double crown was heavy and pinched his ears. He preferred driving his chariot fast as the wind to sitting on the throne. Amasis yawned.

At that very moment, the falcon dropped the rose-red slipper into his lap.

The slipper was so bright that Amasis thought it was a scrap of the sun. Then he saw the falcon wheeling overhead.

"The god Horus sends me a sign!" exclaimed the Pharaoh. He picked up the rose-red slipper. "Every maiden in Egypt must try this shoe! She whose foot it fits shall be my queen. That is the will of the gods."

Amasis dismissed the court, called for his chariot, and began his search at once.

When the Egyptian servant girls arrived to Memphis, they found the throne empty and the streets deserted.

They were so angry on their return that even seeing Rhodopis without her rose-red slipper did not please them. "Slaves are better off barefoot," snapped Kipa.

The Pharaoh journeyed to distant cities. He tracked the desert where pyramids tower over the sand, and he climbed the steep cliffs where falcons nest. The rose-red slipper was always in his hand. Wherever he went, women and girls, rich or poor, flocked to try on the slipper. But none could fit into so small a shoe.

The longer Amasis searched, the more determined he became to marry the maiden who had lost the tiny slipper. He summoned his royal barge and vowed to visit every landing along the Nile. The barge was hung with sails of silk. Trumpets blared and oarsmen rowed to the beat of gongs. The din was so dreadful that, when the barge rounded the bend in the river, Rhodopis fled in alarm. But the servant girls ran to the water's edge.

"Now we will see the Pharaoh!" cried Kipa.

Amasis held up the rose-red slipper. "Whoever can wear this shoe shall be my queen."

The servant girls knew that shoe, and knew its owner, too. Yet they clapped their hands over their mouths and said nothing. If one of them could wear it . . .

First Kipa, then the others, tried to put on the slipper. Each cramped her foot and curled her toes and squeezed until tears ran down her cheeks. Still her heel hung over.

"Enough!" said Amasis wearily. He would have set sail again had he not chanced to see Rhodopis peering through the rushes.

"Come!" he commanded. "You must try this rose-red slipper."

The servant girls gawked openmouthed as the Pharaoh kneeled before Rhodopis. He slipped the tiny shoe on her foot with ease. Then Rhodopis pulled its mate from the folds of her tunic.

"Behold!" cried Amasis. "In all this land there is none so fit to be queen!"

"But Rhodopis is a slave!" protested one of the servant girls.

Kipa sniffed. "She is not even Egyptian."

"She is the most Egyptian of all," the Pharaoh declared. "For her eyes are as green as the Nile, her hair as feathery as papyrus, and her skin the pink of a lotus flower."

The Pharaoh led Rhodopis to the royal barge, and with every step, her rose-red slippers winked and sparkled in the sun.

Mummy No. 1770

Patricia Lauber

*In this essay, identifying the faceless and nameless
mummy no. 1770 is a challenge for scientist-detectives.*

Museums have a limited number of mummies. Every
time one is unwrapped, the number grows smaller, and
so autopsies[1] are not often performed. But sometimes a
museum has a mummy that is not important to its collection. This is a mummy it does not want to display and
a mummy about which almost nothing is known. As it
happened, the Manchester Museum had just such a
mummy. Its wrappings were in poor condition and no
one knew what period it dated from, where it was found,
or who the dead person was. The mummy was known
only by its museum number, 1770. This was the mummy
the museum made available to a team of scientists who
wanted to use modern techniques to study the wrappings
and body in detail.

It was also a mummy with a mystery. X-rays taken
years earlier had shown the mummy was that of a young
person. The lower parts of the legs were missing, and
close to the leg bones was a rounded object. The x-rays
did not reveal what it was, but its shape suggested
a baby's head. Was this the mummy of a mother
and child? Had the mother died shortly after giving
birth? Was she perhaps an unwed-mother who had
been punished with a violent death? Those were questions the scientists wondered about as they began their
work.

After new x-rays were taken, the unwrapping began.
Insect remains found in the bandages were carefully removed for later study. As pieces of cloth were lifted away,
the lower part of the mask came into view. Beneath it
were the bare bones of the neck and skull. These were in
small pieces, but even so, once the pieces had been
cleaned it was possible to see that the left side of the
nose had been damaged by the iron hook the embalmers
had used to remove the brain. The team was surprised to

---

1. **autopsies** (ô′ täp sēz) *n.* examinations and dissections of dead bodies to find
the causes of death or physical damage from disease.

see red and blue paint on the skull bones. How and why had the bones been exposed?

Gently removing more cloth, the scientists found the mummy's arms were crossed on the chest and the hands had gold fingertip covers. The inner organs had been removed and the space filled with bandages and mud. The organs themselves were missing.

A small, hard object that had appeared in the x-rays proved to be a Guinea worm, a parasite[2] that is taken in with drinking water. Within a human host, the young forms of Guinea worm develop into adults. The adults mate, and the male dies. The female, which may grow three feet long, wanders through the tissues under the skin. She generally comes to rest in the legs or feet of the host. There blisters form. They burst on contact with fresh water. The female's eggs are released into the water, and the life cycle starts again. If invaded by bacteria, the blisters may form dangerous sores.

When the Manchester team unwrapped the legs of mummy 1770, they found, as the x-rays had shown, that both legs had been amputated, the left below the knee and the right above the knee. The mummy's right leg had been lengthened with a piece of wood to make it the same length as the left. The wood had been splinted to the leg bone. This meant there could not have been much, if any, flesh on the bone when the splinting was done. The feet were artificial and had gold toenail covers. The right foot was made of reeds and mud, with the ends of the reeds serving as toes. The left foot was simply a mass of reeds and mud.

By now the scientists could see that there was not even a trace of a baby. The rounded shape that had shown in the x-rays was actually a pair of beautiful slippers that had been placed on the soles of the feet.

In one way mummy 1770 was disappointing—it was very poorly preserved. No one could even be certain of its sex, although members of the team came to feel that the young person had been a girl and spoke of the mummy as female. Very little skin, muscle, or soft tissue were left, and the bones of the skull and lower trunk were broken. The scientists could not tell when the fractures had

---

2. parasite (par′ ə sīt) *n.* organism, often harmful, that gets food or protection from another living thing without giving anything back.

occurred. In a living person, tissue called callus forms at the place where a bone is broken. It holds the bone together until the fracture heals. Callus in a recently dead person shows that the fracture occurred during life. But callus thick enough to last thousands of years would take several weeks to form. So if there is no callus in a mummy—and there was none in 1770—there was no way to tell whether the fracture occurred after death or shortly before. The scientists suspected, however, that the bones were broken after death. The damaged mask and the lack of jewelry and charms spoke of tomb robbers and rough handling.

In other ways, mummy 1770 was both interesting and puzzling. The evidence indicated that the body had been in a state of considerable decay when the embalmers worked on it. The wooden leg was attached to bone. All the internal organs were missing and so was the left kneecap, which suggested that the ligaments holding it in place had rotted away. The red and blue paint on the skull bones was a sign that the hair and scalp had been missing.

Why had the body decayed? Why were the legs amputated? The scientific team could think of various explanations.

One had to do with the Guinea worm. Perhaps infections had cut off the flow of blood to the legs and feet. In an effort to save the girl's life, doctors had amputated her legs, but the patient died. But if that was the case, why hadn't she been promptly embalmed?

Or perhaps the legs had been cut off in an accident, such as the collapse of a building. If the girl had been buried in rubble and not found for some time, that might explain the decay.

Or suppose the girl had drowned in the Nile, where decay would set in quickly. The body might have been attacked by a hippopotamus. Although hippos are plant eaters, they are likely to attack floating objects that appear threatening. One bite from a hippo could easily cut off a pair of legs.

A crocodile was another possibility, because it would certainly attack a floating body. The problem with this idea was that crocodiles do not usually bite through bones. They are much more likely to grasp an arm or a leg in their huge jaws and shake it until it tears loose. On the other hand, a crocodile attack might explain why the embalmers went to so much trouble over a body that was hauled out of the Nile—why they made a face and chest mask, lengthened a leg, made artificial feet, applied gold covers to the fingers and toes. The ancient Egyptians, believing that crocodiles were earthly forms of gods, considered anyone who became food for them to be sacred.

As things turned out, there was another explanation for the state of the body and it took everyone by surprise. When the carbon-14 dating[3] was completed, it showed that the mummy was far older than its wrappings. The wrappings dated to a time when the Romans ruled Egypt, around A.D. 260. The mummy's bones dated to around 1000 B.C. This meant that 1770 was a mummy that had been wrapped twice. It had been preserved and wrapped after the girl died, then rewrapped more than a thousand years later. Now some pieces of the puzzle began to fall into place.

There was no need to explain why the corpse had decayed, because it hadn't. Rather, it was the mummy that had been damaged by water and then had decayed. The soft tissues of the body were probably missing because they had stuck to the original wrappings.

The way the second embalmers had prepared the body made clear that they did not know whether they were dealing with a male or a female. This meant they did not know the mummy's identity. But the trouble they took shows that they thought they were dealing with someone of importance. The tomb from which the mummy came must have led them to that conclusion. At times in ancient Egypt royal mummies were moved to new tombs. If they had been damaged, they were repaired at the time of the move. Quite possibly 1770 was a person of royal or noble birth whose mummy was damaged when a tomb was flooded.

X-rays had shown that the mummy's wisdom teeth had not yet grown in, and so the girl must have been less than 20 years old. The dentist on the team now examined the roots of the second molars. Their stage of development told him that 1770 had been 13 to 14 years old. He was surprised to see that the teeth showed no sign of

---

3. **carbon-14 dating** method for figuring out approximate age by measuring the radioactive carbon-14 that is left in a fossil or other once-living thing.

being worn down by sand.[4] He also found that two teeth in the upper jaw were oddly placed. A space between them near the gum formed a trap for food particles. Usually such a trap leads to infection, which damages the bone of the jaw. But this had not happened to 1770. The lack of wear and damage suggested that her diet was soft, perhaps mostly liquid. Or she may have swallowed food without trying to chew it much. Most likely she had not been very healthy.

She must also have breathed mainly through her mouth. The badly formed bones in the inner part of her nose would have made it almost impossible to breathe any other way. If a person always breathes through the mouth, the gums around the upper front teeth become irritated and the bone behind them pitted. Pits in the bones of 1770's mouth showed that she had indeed breathed through her mouth.

By this time the Manchester team had learned a great deal about 1770. She was a young person who had lived a short life with considerable suffering. She had had to breathe through her mouth, had sore gums, ate only liquid or soft food, and had been infected by Guinea worms, which cause fever and an itching rash as well as blisters. Finally, by means still not clear, she had lost her legs around the time she died.

One final step remained to be taken—to find out what 1770 had looked like. The skull had broken into about 30 pieces, some of them very small and fragile. The pieces lay in a jumbled heap and were mixed with mud and bandages. Once the pieces of bone had been cleaned, one member of the team made casts of them in plastic. When the plastic pieces were fitted together, much of the left side of the skull was still missing. A plaster cast was made to fill out the basic shape of the head. Now small pegs were placed in the plastic skull and cut to precise lengths. Each showed how thick the soft tissues of the face would be on a 13-year-old person. The face was then built up with modeling clay. First it took on a general human appearance. Then it took on an appearance of its own, shaped by the underlying bones. This model was used to cast the head in wax, so that

---

4. teeth showed no sign . . . sand Food eaten by Egyptians usually contained some sand that blew in by accident. The sand ground down their teeth.

changes could be made if more was learned about 1770. The wax head was painted, given glass eyes, a wig, and eyelashes. And there at last was 1770—an attractive teenager, perhaps of royal or noble birth, who had laughed, cried, and lived 3,000 years ago.

Ancient Hebrews
and Greeks

Judaism

from One World, Many Religions

Mary Pope Osborne

This story of one of the world's major religions begins with a shepherd and his wife.

> *"Hear, O Israel: The Lord Our God,*
> *The Lord Is One."*

—Old Testament: Deuteronomy 6:4

The story of Judaism begins with a shepherd named Abraham and his wife, Sarah. They lived almost four thousand years ago in the ancient land of Ur, in what is now Iraq. At that time, the people of Ur worshiped many gods, including gods of fire, water, and the sky.

According to a Jewish legend, Abraham began to wonder which of these gods was the one true God. One day, when the sun was shining, Abraham decided the sun must be God. When the sun went down and the moon rose in the sky, he decided the moon was God. But when the moon vanished the next morning, Abraham decided there must be a power even greater than the sun or the moon—greater than all living things. He thought this great invisible power must be the one true God.

In time, this one true God spoke to Abraham and made a covenant, or agreement, with him. God promised to bless Abraham and Sarah and lead them to a far-away land called Canaan. In return, Abraham promised that he and his family would always be faithful to God.

From then on, Abraham and his descendants believed in only one God, a God who enters every human life in a personal way. This was a stunning new idea—one that made Judaism different from all other religions of the time.

After Abraham and Sarah reached Canaan, their son Isaac had a son named Jacob, who would later be called Israel. As the centuries passed, Abraham's descendants came to be called the Israelites. The Israelites eventually left Canaan because of a shortage of food. About five hundred years after Abraham's death, they were living in Egypt. At first the Egyptians treated them well, but the Israelites grew too numerous, and the Egyptian ruler forced them into slavery.

According to Jewish history, one day God spoke to an Israelite named Moses. God told Moses that he should lead the Israelites out of Egypt and back to the "Promised Land" of Canaan—the land God had promised to Abraham long ago.

Moses went to the Egyptian king and asked him to free the Israelite slaves. When the king said no, God caused ten terrible plagues to happen to the Egyptians, including a hailstorm, an infestation of locusts, and, worst of all, the death of every firstborn son. Finally, the king begged Moses to lead his people away.

The Israelites began to leave Egypt. But the king changed his mind and sent his soldiers after them to bring them back. The soldiers caught up with the Israelites at the Red Sea. The Israelites were trapped—water in front of them, soldiers behind.

Moses climbed up on a rock and prayed to God for help. Then he stretched his hand over the waters, and they parted. The Israelites crossed safely to the other side, and the waters returned, drowning the soldiers. At last, the Israelites were free from slavery. For the next forty years, they wandered in the desert, learning how to be a free people under the leadership of Moses and God.

During that time, God gave ten laws to Moses to give to the Israelites. These laws, called the Ten Commandments, were carved on stone tablets. They told the Israelites how they should behave in their daily lives.

Moses died before his people reached the Promised Land. But after his death, the Israelites carried the stone tablets bearing the Ten Commandments into Canaan. And there they built a great nation.

The Ten Commandments became the core of Judaism's holy book, which the Jews call the *Tanach*, or Bible. The first five books of the Bible are called the Torah, which means "teaching." Many Jewish people believe that God gave these five books directly to Moses.

The Torah includes some of humanity's greatest stories. It tells us that God created the world in six days, then rested on the seventh. It tells the stories of Adam and Eve in the Garden of Eden; of their son Cain killing his brother, Abel; of Noah and the ark. The Torah tells Jews how they should live their lives, and it tells the history of their people.

The Torah is the most important object in every synagogue, or Jewish meeting place of worship. It is handwritten in Hebrew, the ancient language of the Jews, on long scrolls of parchment paper. During worship services led by a rabbi—the spiritual leader of the synagogue—worshipers read out loud from the Torah.

THE TEN COMMANDMENTS

Thou shalt have no other gods before me.

Thou shalt not make thyself a graven image.

Thou shalt not take the name of the Lord thy God in vain.

Remember the Sabbath day, to keep it holy.

Honor thy father and thy mother.

Thou shalt not murder.

Thou shalt not commit adultery.

Thou shalt not steal.

Thou shalt not bear false witness against thy neighbor.

Thou shalt not covet.

The Creation and the Fall

Genesis 1–3

King James Version

These first three chapters of the Hebrew Bible are an account of the creation of the universe, including the stars, the sun, the moon, and the Earth.

Chapter 1

1 In the beginning God created the heaven and the earth.

2 And the earth was without form, and void;[1] and darkness was upon the face of the deep. And the Spirit of God moved upon the face of the waters.

3 And God said, "Let there be light": and there was light.

4 And God saw the light, that it was good: and God divided the light from the darkness.

5 And God called the light Day, and the darkness he called Night. And the evening and the morning were the first day.

6 And God said, "Let there be a firmament[2] in the midst of the waters, and let it divide the waters from the waters."

7 And God made the firmament, and divided the waters which were under the firmament from the waters which were above the firmament: and it was so.

8 And God called the firmament Heaven. And the evening and the morning were the second day.

9 And God said, "Let the waters under the heaven be gathered together unto one place, and let the dry land appear": and it was so.

10 And God called the dry land Earth; and the gathering together of the waters called he Seas: and God saw that it was good.

11 And God said, "Let the earth bring forth grass, the herb yielding seed, and the fruit tree yielding fruit after

---

1. void (void) *adj.* vacant or empty.
2. firmament (furm′ ə mənt) *n.* the sky, viewed poetically as a solid arch or vault.

his kind, whose seed is in itself, upon the earth": and it was so.

12 And the earth brought forth grass, and herb yielding seed after his kind, and the tree yielding fruit, whose seed was in itself, after his kind: and God saw that it was good.

13 And the evening and the morning were the third day.

14 And God said, "Let there be lights in the firmament of the heaven to divide the day from the night; and let them be for signs, and for seasons, and for days, and years:

15 "And let them be for lights in the firmament of the heaven to give light upon the earth": and it was so.

16 And God made two great lights; the greater light to rule the day, and the lesser light to rule the night: he made the stars also.

17 And God set them in the firmament of the heaven to give light upon the earth,

18 And to rule over the day and over the night, and to divide the light from the darkness: and God saw that it was good.

19 And the evening and the morning were the fourth day.

20 And God said, "Let the waters bring forth abundantly the moving creature that hath life, and fowl that may fly above the earth in the open firmament of heaven."

21 And God created great whales, and every living creature that moveth, which the waters brought forth abundantly, after their kind, and every winged fowl after his kind: and God saw that it was good.

22 And God blessed them, saying, "Be fruitful and multiply, and fill the waters in the seas, and let fowl multiply in the earth."

23 And the evening and the morning were the fifth day.

24 And God said, "Let the earth bring forth the living creature after his kind, cattle, and creeping thing, and beast of the earth after his kind": and it was so.

25 And God made the beast of the earth after his kind, and cattle after their kind, and every thing that creepeth upon the earth after his kind: and God saw that it was good.

26 And God said, "Let us make man in our image, after our likeness: and let them have dominion[3] over the fish of the sea, and over the fowl of the air, and over the cattle, and over all the earth, and over every creeping thing that creepeth upon the earth."

27 So God created man in his own image, in the image of God created he him; male and female created he them.

28 And God blessed them, and God said unto them, "Be fruitful, and multiply, and replenish[4] the earth, and subdue[5] it: and have dominion over the fish of the sea, and over the fowl of the air, and over every living thing that moveth upon the earth."

29 And God said, "Behold, I have given you every herb bearing seed, which is upon the face of all the earth, and every tree, in the which is the fruit of a tree yielding seed; to you it shall be for meat."

30 "And to every beast of the earth, and to every fowl of the air, and to every thing that creepeth upon the earth, wherein there is life, I have given every green herb for meat": and it was so.

31 And God saw every thing that he had made, and, behold, it was very good. And the evening and the morning were the sixth day.

Chapter 2

1 Thus the heavens and the earth were finished, and all the host of them.

2 And on the seventh day God ended his work which he had made; and he rested on the seventh day from all his work which he had made.

3 And God blessed the seventh day, and sanctified it: because that in it he had rested from all his work which God created and made.

4 These are the generations of the heavens and of the earth when they were created, in the day that the Lord God made the earth and the heavens.

5 And every plant of the field before it was in the earth, and every herb of the field before it grew: for the Lord God had not caused it to rain upon the earth, and there was not a man to till the ground.

---

3. dominion (də min′ yən) *n.* rule or power to rule.
4. replenish (ri plen′ ish) *v.* make full or complete again.
5. subdue (səb do͞o′) *v.* conquer or master.

6 But there went up a mist from the earth, and watered the whole face of the ground.

7 And the Lord God formed man of the dust of the ground,[6] and breathed into his nostrils the breath of life; and man became a living soul.

8 And the Lord God planted a garden eastward in Eden; and there he put the man whom he had formed.

9 And out of the ground made the Lord God to grow every tree that is pleasant to the sight, and good for food; the tree of life also in the midst of the garden, and the tree of knowledge of good and evil.

10 And a river went out of Eden to water the garden; and from thence it was parted, and became into four heads.

11 The name of the first is Pison: that is it which compasseth the whole land of Havilah, where there is gold;

12 And the gold of that land is good: there is bdellium[7] and onyx stone.

13 And the name of the second river is Gihon: the same is it that compasseth the whole land of Ethiopia.

14 And the name of the third river is Hiddekel: that is it which goeth toward the east of Assyria. And the fourth river is Euphrates.[8]

15 And the Lord God took the man, and put him into the garden of Eden to dress it and to keep it.

16 And the Lord God commanded the man, saying, "Of every tree of the garden thou mayest freely eat:"

17 "But of the tree of knowledge of good and evil, thou shalt not eat of it: for in the day that thou eatest thereof thou shalt surely die."

18 And the Lord God said, "It is not good that the man should be alone; I will make him an help meet for him."

19 And out of the ground the Lord God formed every beast of the field, and every fowl of the air; and brought them unto Adam to see what he would call them: and whatsoever Adam called every living creature, that was the name thereof.

---

6. **And the Lord God . . . ground** the name Adam is said to come from the Hebrew word 'adhāmāh, meaning "earth."

7. **bdellium** (del' ē əm) a deep-red gem.

8. **Assyria . . . Euphrates** (yōō frāt' ēz) Assyria was an ancient empire in southwestern Asia; the Euphrates River flows from East Central Turkey generally southward through Syria and Iraq.

20 And Adam gave names to all cattle, and to the fowl of the air, and to every beast of the field; but for Adam there was not found an help meet for him.

21 And the Lord God caused a deep sleep to fall upon Adam, and he slept: and he took one of his ribs, and closed up the flesh instead thereof;

22 And the rib, which the Lord God had taken from man, made he a woman, and brought her unto the man.

23 And Adam said, "This is now bone of my bones, and flesh of my flesh: she shall be called Woman, because she was taken out of Man."

24 Therefore shall a man leave his father and his mother, and shall cleave unto his wife: and they shall be one flesh.

25 And they were both naked, the man and his wife, and were not ashamed.

Chapter 3

1 Now the serpent was more subtil[9] than any beast of the field which the Lord God had made. And he said unto the woman, "Yea, hath God said, 'Ye shall not eat of every tree of the garden'?"

2 And the woman said unto the serpent, "We may eat of the fruit of the trees of the garden:

3 "But of the fruit of the tree which is in the midst of the garden, God hath said, 'Ye shall not eat of it, neither shall ye touch it, lest ye die.'"

4 And the serpent said unto the woman, "Ye shall not surely die:"

5 "For God doth know that in the day ye eat thereof, then your eyes shall be opened and ye shall be as gods, knowing good and evil."

6 And when the woman saw that the tree was good for food, and that it was pleasant to the eyes, and a tree to be desired to make one wise, she took of the fruit thereof, and did eat, and gave also unto her husband with her; and he did eat.

7 And the eyes of them both were opened, and they knew that they were naked; and they sewed fig leaves together, and made themselves aprons.

---

9. subtil, old-fashioned spelling for **subtle** (sut′ 'l) *adj.* crafty, sly, and clever.

8 And they heard the voice of the Lord God walking in the garden in the cool of the day: and Adam and his wife hid themselves from the presence of the Lord God amongst the trees of the garden.

9 And the Lord God called unto Adam, and said unto him, "Where art thou?"

10 And he said, "I heard thy voice in the garden, and I was afraid, because I was naked; and I hid myself."

11 And he said, "Who told thee that thou wast naked? Hast thou eaten of the tree, whereof I commanded thee that thou shouldest not eat?"

12 And the man said, "The woman whom thou gavest to be with me, she gave me of the tree, and I did eat."

13 And the Lord God said unto the woman, "What is this that thou hast done?" And the woman said, "The serpent beguiled[10] me, and I did eat."

14 And the Lord God said unto the serpent, "Because thou has done this, thou art cursed above all cattle and above every beast of the field; upon thy belly shalt thou go, and dust shalt thou eat all the days of thy life:

15 "And I will put enmity[11] between thee and the woman, and between thy seed[12] and her seed; it shall bruise thy head, and thou shalt bruise his heel."

16 Unto the woman he said, "I will greatly multiply thy sorrow and thy conception; in sorrow thou shalt bring forth children; and thy desire shall be to thy husband, and he shall rule over thee."

17 And unto Adam he said, "Because thou hast hearkened unto the voice of thy wife, and hast eaten of the tree, of which I commanded thee, saying 'Thou shalt not eat of it': cursed is the ground for thy sake; in sorrow shalt thou eat of it all the days of thy life;

18 "Thorns also and thistles shall it bring forth to thee; and thou shalt eat the herb of the field;

19 "In the sweat of thy face shalt thou eat bread, till thou return unto the ground; for out of it wast thou taken: for dust thou art, and unto dust shalt thou return."

20 And Adam called his wife's name Eve; because she was the mother of all living.[13]

---

10. beguiled (bē gīld') v. tricked, deceived.
11. enmity (en' mə tē) n. hostility, the bitter attitude of an enemy.
12. seed descendants.
13. Mother . . . living *Hawwāh*, the Hebrew word translated as Eve, is derived from another Hebrew word meaning "alive" or "a living thing."

21 Unto Adam also and to his wife did the Lord God make coats of skins, and clothed them.

22 And the Lord God said, "Behold, the man is become as one of us, to know good and evil: and now, lest he put forth his hand, and take also of the tree of life, and eat, and live for ever":

23 Therefore the Lord God sent him forth from the garden of Eden, to till the ground from whence he was taken.

24 So he drove out the man; and he placed at the east of the garden of Eden Cherubims[14] and a flaming sword which turned every way to keep the way of the tree of life.

---

14. Cherubims (cher′ ə bimz) winged heavenly beings that support the throne of God or act as guardian spirits.

Deborah

from Women of the Bible

Carole Armstrong

Women have always had an important role to play in the history of the world. Here a woman is a powerful judge.

> *"Awake, awake, Deborah! Awake, awake, utter a song."*

(Judges 5:12)

Deborah was a great judge of Israel, the only woman ever to have held such a position. Many people flocked to hear her wise words as she delivered her judgments on Mount Ephraim, sitting under a palm tree, the tree of life and a symbol of hope.

At this time, the Israelites were ruled by the Canaanites who were led by a general called Sisera. He was a powerful man and for twenty years he had oppressed the Israelites. Eventually the Israelite leaders came to Deborah in the hope that she could rescue them from their plight. Knowing that she could rely on God's help, Deborah immediately summoned Barak, military commander of the Israelites, and ordered him to gather together ten thousand men. She reminded him of God's command to lead his people to Mount Tabor and fight Sisera's army. Barak was afraid—Sisera had nine hundred chariots of iron and an army that far outnumbered his. "If thou wilt go with me," he told Deborah, "then I will go." Deborah agreed, for she had God's promise that the Israelites would win: "I will draw unto thee Sisera, with his chariots and his multitude; and I will deliver him into thine hand," she assured Barak, and before long, the Israelites defeated Sisera's army.

Sisera was forced to escape on foot and took refuge in the tent of a friend called Heber. Jael, Heber's wife, pretended to welcome the General, but secretly she sympathized with the Israelites. When he feel asleep, she brutally killed him with a blow to his head.

From that day, the Israelites were free from oppression. Deborah composed a beautiful song of triumph and praise to God, as it was with His help that the Israelites had overthrown the Canaanites.

Solimena, a Neapolitan artist, painted Deborah sitting on her throne, commanding Barak to go into battle. Above Barak's head is a winged figure holding a palm leaf of victory and a laurel wreath which symbolizes triumph and eternity.

The Death of Hektor

from Book XXII *of the* Iliad

Homer

Translated by Richmond Lattimore

In this selection from Homer's epic Iliad, *we feel for
Achilleus, who has lost his friend, but we also feel for
Andromache when she loses her husband. The gods
take both sides and interfere with the humans in ways
that seem both helpful and unfair.*

At the climax of the *Iliad*, Hektor, greatest of the Trojan warriors, has slain Patroklos, best friend of Achilleus.
Filled with rage, Achilleus, greatest of the Greek warriors,
returns to battle to avenge his friend's death. Aided by
the god Apollo, all of the Trojans but Hektor flee to safety
within the city walls. Hektor must make a decision
whether to stay and fight Achilleus.

> Deeply troubled he [Hektor] spoke to his own
>   great-hearted spirit:
> "Ah me! If I go now inside the wall and the
>   gateway,
> Poulydamas[1] will be first to put a reproach[2] upon
>   me,
> since he tried to make me lead the Trojans inside
>   the city
> on that accursed night when brilliant Achilleus
>   rose up,
> and I would not obey him, but that would have
>   been far better.
> Now, since by my own recklessness I have ruined
>   my people,
> I feel shame before the Trojans and the Trojan
>   women with trailing

5

---

1. Poulydamas (pôl ə däm′ əs) fighter and seer who frequently opposed his
brother Hektor's reckless strategy.
2. reproach (ri prōch′) *n.* an expression of blame.

robes, that someone who is less of a man than I
will say of me:

10 'Hektor believed in his own strength and ruined
his people.'

Thus they will speak; and as for me, it would be
much better

at that time, to go against Achilleus, and slay
him, and come back,

or else be killed by him in glory in front of the
city.

Or if again I set down my shield massive in the
middle

15 and my ponderous helm, and lean my spear up
against the rampart

and go out as I am to meet Achilleus the
blameless

and promise to give back Helen, and with her all
her possessions,

all those things that once in the hollow ships
Alexandros

brought back to Troy, and these were the
beginning of the quarrel;

20 to give these to Atreus' sons to take away, and for
the Achaians

also to divide up all that is hidden within the city,

and take an oath thereafter for the Trojans in
conclave[3]

not to hide anything away, but distribute all of it,

as much as the lovely citadel keeps guarded
within it;

25 yet still, why does the heart within me debate on
these things?

I might go up to him, and he take no pity upon
me

nor respect my position, but kill me naked so, as
if I were

a woman, once I stripped my armor from me.
There is no

way any more from a tree or a rock to talk to him
gently

30 whispering like a young man and a young girl, in
the way

---

3. **conclave** (kän klāv') *n*. private or secret meeting.

a young man and a young maiden whisper
    together.
Better to bring on the fight with him as soon as it
    may be.
We shall see to which one the Olympian grants
    the glory."
       So he pondered, waiting, but Achilleus
       was closing upon him

35   in the likeness of the lord of battles, the helm-
    shining warrior,
and shaking from above his shoulder the
    dangerous Pelian[4]
ash spear, while the bronze that closed about him
    was shining
like the flare of blazing fire or the sun in its
    rising.
And the shivers took hold of Hektor when he saw
    him, and he could no longer

40   stand his ground there, but left the gates behind,
    and fled, frightened,
and Peleus' son went after him in the confidence
    of his quick feet.
As when a hawk in the mountains who moves
    lightest of things flying
makes his effortless swoop for a trembling dove,
    but she slips away
from beneath and flies and he shrill screaming
    close after her

45   plunges for her again and again, heart furious to
    take her;
so Achilleus went straight for him in fury, but
    Hektor
fled away under the Trojan wall and moved his
    knees rapidly.
They raced along by the watching point and the
    windy fig tree
always away from under the wall and along the
    wagon-way

50   and came to the two sweet-running well springs.
    There there are double
springs of water that jet up, the springs of
    whirling Skamandros.

---

4. Pelian (Pel' ē ən) *adj.* belonging to Peleus, Achilleus' father.

One of these runs hot water and the steam on all sides

of it rises as if from a fire that was burning inside it

But the other in the summer-time runs water that is like hail

55   or chill snow or ice that forms from water. Beside these

in this place, and close to them, are the washing-hollows

of stone, and magnificent, where the wives of the Trojans and their lovely

daughters washed the clothes to shining, in the old days

when there was peace, before the coming of the sons of the Achaians.

60   They ran beside these, one escaping, the other after him.

It was a great man who fled, but far better he who pursued him

rapidly, since here was no festal[5] beast, no ox-hide

they strove for, for these are prizes that are given men for their running.

No, they ran for the life of Hektor, breaker of horses.

65   As when about the turnposts racing single-foot horses

run at full speed, when a great prize is laid up for their winning,

a tripod or a woman, in games for a man's funeral,

so these two swept whirling about the city of Priam

in the speed of their feet, while all the gods were looking upon them.

70   First to speak among them was the father of gods and mortals;

"Ah me, this a man beloved whom now my eyes watch

being chased around the wall; my heart is mourning for Hektor

who has burned in my honor many thigh pieces of oxen

---

5. festal (fes′ təl) *adj.* of a joyous celebration.

on the peaks of Ida[6] with all her folds, or again on
the uttermost

75   part of the citadel, but now the brilliant Achilleus
drives him in speed of his feet around the city of
Priam.

Come then, you immortals, take thought and take
counsel, whether

to rescue this man or whether to make him, for
all his valor

go down under the hands of Achilleus, the son of
Peleus."

80   Then in answer the goddess gray-eyed
Athene spoke to him:

"Father of the shining bolt, dark misted, what is
this you said?

Do you wish to bring back a man who is mortal,
one long since

doomed by his destiny, from ill-sounding death
and release him?

Do it, then; but not all the rest of us gods shall
approve you."

85   Then Zeus the gatherer of the clouds spoke to her
in answer:

"Tritogeneia,[7] dear daughter, do not lose heart; for
I say this

not in outright anger, and my meaning toward
you is kindly.

Act as your purpose would have you do, and hold
back no longer."

       So he spoke, and stirred on Athene, who
was eager before this,

90   and she went in a flash of speed down the
pinnacles of Olympos.

But swift Achilleus kept unremittingly[8] after
Hektor,

chasing him, as a dog in the mountains who has
flushed from his covert[9]

a deer's fawn follows him through the folding
ways and the valleys,

---

6. Ida (ī də) *n.* mountain near the site of Troy.
7. Tritogeneia (trī tō jen′ ē ə) another name for Athene, who was born near Lake
Tritonis in a part of Africa.
8. unremittingly (un ri mit′ iŋ lē) *adv.* persistently.
9. covert (kuv′ ərt) *n.* a hiding place.

and though the fawn crouched down under a
  bush and be hidden
95 he keeps running and noses him out until he
  comes on him;
so Hektor could not lose himself from swift-footed
  Peleion.
If ever he made a dash right on for the gates of
  Dardanos
to get quickly under the strong-built bastion,
  endeavoring
that they from above with missiles thrown might
  somehow defend him,
100 each time Achilleus would get in front and force
  him to turn back
into the plain, and himself kept his flying course
  next the city.
As in a dream a man is not able to follow one who
  runs
from him, nor can the runner escape, nor the
  other pursue him,
so he could not run him down in his speed, nor
  the other get clear.
105 How then could Hektor have escaped the death
  spirits, had not
Apollo, for this last and uttermost time, stood by
  him
close, and driven strength into him, and made his
  knees light?
But brilliant Achilleus kept shaking his head at
  his own people
and would not let them throw their bitter
  projectiles[10] at Hektor
110 for fear the thrower might win the glory, and
  himself come second.
But when for the fourth time they had come
  around to the well springs
then the Father balanced his golden scales, and
  in them
he set two fateful portions of death, which lays
  men prostrate;[11]

---

10. **projectiles** (prō jek′ təlz) *n.* objects designed to be thrown forward.
11. **prostrate** (präs′ trāt) *adj.* flat; face downward; completely overcome.

one for Achilleus, and one for Hektor, breaker of
    horses,
115 and balanced it by the middle; and Hektor's
    death-day was heavier
and dragged downward toward death, and
    Phoibos Apollo forsook[12] him.
But the goddess gray-eyed Athene came now to
    Peleion
and stood close beside him and addressed him in
    winged words: "Beloved"
of Zeus, shining Achilleus, I am hopeful now that
    you and I
120 will take back great glory to the ships of the
    Achaians, after
we have killed Hektor, for all his slakeless[13] fury
    for battle.
Now there is no way for him to get clear away
    from us,
not though Apollo who strikes from afar should
    be willing to undergo
much, and wallow[14] before our father Zeus of the
    aegis.
125 Stand you here then and get your wind again,
    while I go
to this man and persuade him to stand up to you
    in combat."
        So spoke Athene, and he was glad at heart,
            and obeyed her,
and stopped, and stood leaning on his bronze-
    barbed ash spear. Meanwhile
Athene left him there, and caught up with
    brilliant Hektor,
130 and likened herself in form and weariless voice to
    Deïphobos.[15]
She came now and stood close to him and
    addressed him in winged words:
"Dear brother, indeed swift-footed Achilleus is
    using you roughly
and chasing you on swift feet around the city of
    Priam.

---

12. **forsook** (fôr so͞ok′) v. abandoned.
13. **slakeless** (slāk′ ləs) adj. unable to be satisfied or lessened.
14. **wallow** (wäl′ ō) v. move heavily and clumsily.
15. **Deïphobos** (dā′ i fō′ bōs) son of Priam; powerful Trojan fighter.

Come on, then; let us stand fast against him and
beat him back from us."
135   Then tall Hektor of the shining helm
answered her: "Deïphobos,
before now you were dearest to me by far of my
brothers,
of all those who were sons of Priam and Hekabe,
and now
I am minded all the more within my heart to
honor you,
you who dared for my sake, when your eyes saw
me, to come forth
140   from the fortifications, while the others stand fast
inside them."
Then in turn the goddess gray-eyed Athene
answered him:
"My brother, it is true our father and the lady our
mother, taking
my knees in turn, and my companions about me,
entreated
that I stay within, such was the terror upon all of
them.
145   But the heart within me was worn away by hard
sorrow for you.
But now let us go straight on the fight hard, let
there be no sparing
of our spears, so that we can find out whether
Achilleus
will kill us both and carry our bloody war spoils
back
to the hollow ships, or will himself go down under
your spear."
150   So Athene spoke and led him on by
beguilement.[16]
Now as the two in their advance were come close
together,
first of the two to speak was tall helm-glittering
Hektor:
"Son of Peleus, I will no longer run from you, as
before this
I fled three times around the great city of Priam,
and dared not

---

16. beguilement (bē gīl′ mənt) *n.* trickery; deceit.

155   stand to your onfall. But now my spirit in turn has driven me
to stand and face you. I must take you now, or I must be taken.
Come then, shall we swear before the gods? For these are the highest
who shall be witnesses and watch over our agreements.
Brutal as you are I will not defile you, if Zeus grants
160   to me that I can wear you out, and take the life from you.
But after I have stripped your glorious armor, Achilleus,
I will give your corpse back to the Achaians. Do you do likewise."
        Then looking darkly at him swift-footed Achilleus answered:
"Hektor, argue me no agreements. I cannot forgive you.
165   As there are no trustworthy oaths between men and lions,
nor wolves and lambs have spirit that can be brought to agreement
but forever these hold feelings of hate for each other,
so there can be no love between you and me, nor shall there be
oaths between us, but one or the other must fall before then
170   to glut with his blood Ares the god who fights under the shield's guard.
Remember every valor of yours, for now the need comes
hardest upon you to be a spearman and a bold warrior.
There shall be no more escape for you, but Pallas Athene
will kill you soon by my spear. You will pay in a lump for all those
175   sorrows of my companions you killed in your spear's fury."
        So he spoke, and balanced the spear far shadowed, and threw it;

but glorious Hektor kept his eyes on him, and avoided it,
for he dropped, watchful, to his knee, and the bronze spear flew over his shoulder
and stuck in the ground, but Pallas Athene snatched it, and gave it
180 back to Achilleus, unseen by Hektor shepherd of the people.
But now Hektor spoke out to the blameless son of Peleus:
"You missed; and it was not, o Achilleus like the immortals,
from Zeus that you knew my destiny; but you thought so; or rather
you are someone clever in speech and spoke to swindle me,
185 to make me afraid of you and forget my valor and war strength.
You will not stick your spear in my back as I run away from you
but drive it into my chest as I storm straight in against you;
if the god gives you that; and now look out for my brazen
spear. I wish it might be taken full length in your body.
190 And indeed the war would be a lighter thing for the Trojans
if you were dead, seeing that you are their greatest affliction."
So he spoke, and balanced the spear far shadowed, and threw it,
and struck the middle of Peleïdes' shield, nor missed it,
but the spear was driven far back from the shield, and Hektor was angered
195 because his swift weapon had been loosed from his hand in a vain[17] cast.
He stood discouraged, and had no other ash spear; but lifting
his voice he called aloud on Deïphobos of the pale shield,

---

17. vain (vān) *adj.* ineffective; fruitless; unprofitable.

and asked him for a long spear, but Deïphobos
   was not near him.
And Hektor knew the truth inside his heart, and
   spoke aloud:
200   "No use. Here at last the gods have summoned
   me deathward.
I thought Deïphobos the hero was here close
   beside me,
but he is behind the wall and it was Athene
   cheating me,
and now evil death is close to me, and no longer
   far away,
and there is no way out. So it must long since
   have been pleasing
205   to Zeus, and Zeus' son who strikes from afar, this
   way; though before this
they defended me gladly. But now my death is
   upon me.
Let me at least not die without a struggle,
   inglorious,
but do some big thing first, that men to come
   shall know of it."
      So he spoke, and pulling out the sharp
      sword that was slung
210   at the hollow of his side, huge and heavy, and
   gathering
himself together, he made his swoop, like a high-
   flown eagle
who launches himself out of the murk of the
   clouds on the flat land
to catch away a tender lamb or a shivering hare;
   so
Hektor made his swoop, swinging his sharp
   sword, and Achilleus
215   charged, the heart within him loaded with savage
   fury.
In front of his chest the beautiful elaborate great
   shield
covered him, and with the glittering helm with
   four horns
he nodded; the lovely golden fringes were shaken
   about it
which Hephaistos had driven close along the horn
   of the helmet.

220 And as a star moves among stars in the night's
      darkening,
    Hesper, who is the fairest star who stands in the
      sky, such
    was the shining from the pointed spear Achilleus
      was shaking
    in his right hand with evil intention toward
      brilliant Hektor.
    He was eyeing Hektor's splendid body, to see
      where it might best
225 give way, but all the rest of the skin was held in
      the armor,
    brazen and splendid, he stripped when he cut
      down the strength of Patroklos;
    yet showed where the collar-bones hold the neck
      from the shoulders,
    the throat, where death of the soul comes most
      swiftly; in this place
    brilliant Achilleus drove the spear as he came on
      in fury,
230 and clean through the soft part of the neck the
      spearpoint was driven.
    Yet the ash spear heavy with bronze did not sever
      the windpipe,
    so that Hektor could still make exchange of words
      spoken.
    But he dropped in the dust, and brilliant
      Achilleus vaunted above him:
    "Hektor, surely you thought as you killed
      Patroklos you would be
235 safe, and since I was far away you thought
      nothing of me,
    o fool, for an avenger[18] was left, far greater than
      he was,
    behind him and away by the hollow ships. And it
      was I;
    and I have broken your strength; on you the dogs
      and the vultures
    shall feed and foully rip you; the Achaians will
      bury Patroklos."
240   In his weakness Hektor of the shining helm
      spoke to him:

---

18. avenger (ə ven′ jər) *n.* one who takes revenge, especially on behalf of another.

"I entreat you, by your life, by your knees, by your parents,
do not let the dogs feed on me by the ships of the Achaians,
but take yourself the bronze and gold that are there in abundance,
those gifts that my father and the lady my mother will give you,
245 and give my body to be taken home again, so that the Trojans
and the wives of the Trojans may give me in death my rite of burning."[19]
    But looking darkly at him swift-footed Achilleus answered:
"No more entreating of me, you dog, by knees or parents.
I wish only that my spirit and fury would drive me
250 to hack your meat away and eat it raw for the things that
you have done to me. So there is no one who can hold the dogs off
from your head, not if they bring here and set before me ten times
and twenty times the ransom, and promise more in addition,
not if Priam son of Dardanos should offer to weigh out
255 your bulk in gold; not even so shall the lady your mother
who herself bore you lay you on the death-bed and mourn you:
no, but the dogs and the birds will have you all for their feasting."
    Then, dying, Hektor of the shining helmet spoke to him:
"I know you well as I look upon you, I know that I could not
260 persuade you, since indeed in your breast is a heart of iron.
Be careful now; for I might be made into the gods' curse

---

19. rite of burning proper funeral ritual of burning the dead body.

upon you, on that day when Paris and Phoibos
Apollo
destroy you in the Skaian gates, for all your
valor."
He spoke, and as he spoke the end of death
closed in upon him,
265   and the soul fluttering free of the limbs went
down into Death's house
mourning her destiny, leaving youth and
manhood behind her.
Now though he was a dead man brilliant
Achilleus spoke to him:
"Die: and I will take my own death at whatever
time
Zeus and the rest of the immortals choose to
accomplish it."
270   He spoke, and pulled the brazen spear from
the body, and laid it
on one side, and stripped away from the
shoulders the bloody
armor. And the other sons of the Achaians came
running about him,
and gazed upon the stature and on the imposing
beauty
of Hektor; and none stood beside him who did not
stab him;
275   and thus they would speak one to another, each
looking at his neighbor:
"See now, Hektor is much softer to handle than
he was
when he set the ships ablaze with the burning
firebrand."
So as they stood beside him they would
speak, and stab him.
But now, when he had despoiled[20] the body,
swift-footed brilliant
280   Achilleus stood among the Achaians and
addressed them in winged words:
"Friends, who are leaders of the Argives and keep
their counsel:

---

20. despoiled (dē spoild´) v. deprived of value and honor.

since the gods have granted me the killing of this
    man
who has done us much damage, such as not all
    the others together
have done, come, let us go in armor about the city

285   to see if we can find out what purpose is in the
    Trojans,
whether they will abandon their high city, now
    that this man
has fallen, or are minded to stay, though Hektor
    lives no longer.
Yet still, why does the heart within me debate on
    these things?
There is a dead man who lies by the ships,
    unwept, unburied:

290   Patroklos: and I will not forget him, never so long
    as
I remain among the living and my knees have
    their spring beneath me.
And though the dead forget the dead in the house
    of Hades,
even there I shall still remember my beloved
    companion.
But now, you young men of the Achaians, let us
    go back, singing

295   a victory song, to our hollow ships; and
        take this with us.
We have won ourselves enormous fame; we have
    killed the great Hektor
whom the Trojans glorified as if he were a god in
    their city."
        He spoke, and now thought of shameful
        treatment for glorious Hektor.
In both of his feet at the back he made holes by
    the tendons

300   in the space between ankle and heel, and drew
    thongs of ox-hide through them,
and fastened them to the chariot so as to let the
    head drag,
and mounted the chariot, and lifted the glorious
    armor inside it,
then whipped the horses to a run, and they
    winged their way unreluctant.

A cloud of dust rose where Hektor was dragged, his dark hair was falling

305 about him, and all that head that was once so handsome was tumbled

in the dust; since by this time Zeus had given him over

to his enemies, to be defiled in the land of his fathers.

So all his head was dragged in the dust; and now his mother

tore out her hair, and threw the shining veil far from her

310 and raised a great wail as she looked upon her son; and his father

beloved groaned pitifully, and all his people about him

were taken with wailing and lamentation all through the city.

It was most like what would have happened, if all lowering

Ilion had been burning top to bottom in fire.

315 His people could scarcely keep the old man in his impatience

from storming out of the Dardanian gates; he implored[21] them

all, and wallowed in the muck before them calling on each man

and naming him by his name: "Give way, dear friends,

and let me alone though you care for me, leave me to go out

320 from the city and make my way to the ships of the Achaians.

I must be suppliant to this man, who is harsh and violent,

and he might have respect for my age and take pity upon it

since I am old, and his father also is old, as I am

Peleus, who begot and reared him to be an affliction

325 on the Trojans. He has given us most sorrow, beyond all others,

---

21. implored (im plord') v. asked or begged earnestly.

such is the number of my flowering sons he has
    cut down.
But for all of these I mourn not so much, in spite
    of my sorrow,
as for one, Hektor, and the sharp grief for him will
    carry me downward
into Death's house. I wish he had died in my
    arms, for that way
330   we two, I myself and his mother who bore him
    unhappy,
might so have glutted[22] ourselves with weeping for
    him and mourning."
        So he spoke, in tears, and beside him
        mourned the citizens.
But for the women of Troy Hekabe led out the
    thronging
chant of sorrow: "Child, I am wretched. What
    shall my life be
335   in my sorrows, now you are dead, who by day and
    in the night
were my glory in the town, and to all of the Trojans
and the women of Troy a blessing throughout
    their city. They adored you
as if you were a god, since in truth you were their
    high honor
while you lived. Now death and fate have closed in
    upon you."
340   So she spoke in tears but the wife of Hektor
        had not yet
heard: for no sure messenger had come to her
    and told her
how her husband had held his ground there
    outside the gates;
but she was weaving a web in the inner room of
    the high house,
a red folding robe, and inworking[23] elaborate
    figures.
345   She called out through the house to her lovely-
    haired handmaidens
to set a great cauldron over the fire, so that there
    would be

---

22. glutted (glut′ əd) v. filled; sated.
23. inworking (in′ wər kiŋ) v. sewing into fabric.

hot water for Hektor's bath as he came back out
    of the fighting;
poor innocent, nor knew how, far from waters for
    bathing,
Pallas Athene had cut him down at the hands of
    Achilleus.

350   She heard from the great bastion the noise of
    mourning and sorrow.
Her limbs spun, and the shuttle dropped from her
    hand to the ground.
Then she called aloud to her lovely-haired
    handmaidens: "Come here.
Two of you come with me, so I can see what has
    happened.

355   I heard the voice of Hektor's honored mother;
    within me
my own heart rising beats in my mouth, my limbs
    under me
are frozen. Surely some evil is near for the
    children of Priam.
May what I say come never close to my ear; yet
    dreadfully
I fear that great Achilleus might have cut off bold
    Hektor

360   alone, away from the city, and be driving him into
    the flat land,
might put an end to that bitter pride of courage,
    that always
was on him, since he would never stay back
    where the men were in numbers
but break far out in front, and give way in his
    fury to no man."
        So she spoke, and ran out of the house like
        a raving woman

365   with pulsing heart, and her two handmaidens
    went along with her.
But when she came to the bastion and where the
    men were gathered
she stopped, staring, on the wall; and she saw
    him
being dragged in front of the city, and the running
    horses
dragged him at random toward the hollow ships
    of the Achaians.

370   The darkness of night misted over the eyes of
        Andromache.
    She fell backward, and gasped the life breath
        from her, and far off
    threw from her head the shining gear that ordered
        her headdress,
    the diadem[24] and the cap, and the holding-band
        woven together,
    and the circlet,[25] which Aphrodite the golden once
        had given her
375   on that day when Hektor of the shining helmet
        led her forth
    from the house of Eëtion, and gave numberless
        gifts to win her.
    And about her stood thronging her husband's
        sisters and the wives of his brothers
    and these, in her despair for death, held her up
        among them.
    But she, when she breathed again and the life
        was gathered back into her,
380   lifted her voice among the women of Troy in
        mourning:
    "Hektor, I grieve for you. You and I were born to a
        single
    destiny, you in Troy in the house of Priam, and I
    in Thebe, underneath the timbered[26] mountain of
        Plakos
    in the house of Eëtion, who cared for me when I
        was little,
385   ill-fated he, I ill-starred. I wish he had never
        begotten me.
    Now you go down to the house of Death in the
        secret places
    of the earth, and left me here behind in the
        sorrow of mourning,
    a widow in your house, and the boy is only a baby
    who was born to you and me, the unfortunate.
        You cannot help him,
390   Hektor, any more, since you are dead. Nor can he
        help you.

---

24. diadem (dī ə dem′) *n.* a decorated cloth headband worn as a crown.

25. circlet (sʉr′ klit) *n.* a ring or circular band worn on the head.

26. timbered (tim′ bərd) *adj.* covered with trees.

Though he escape the attack of the Achaians with
all its sorrows,
yet all his days for your sake there will be hard
work for him
and sorrows, for others will take his lands away
from him. The day
of bereavement leaves a child with no agemates to
befriend him.

395 He bows his head before every man, his cheeks
are bewept,[27] he
goes, needy, a boy among his father's
companions,
and tugs at this man by the mantle, that man by
the tunic,
and they pity him, and one gives him a tiny drink
from a goblet,
enough to moisten his lips, not enough to moisten
his palate.

400 But one whose parents are living beats him out of
the banquet
hitting him with his fists and in words also
abuses him:
'Get out, you! Your father is not dining among us.'
And the boy goes away in tears to his widowed
mother,
Astyanax, who in days before on the knees of his
father

405 would eat only the marrow or the flesh of sheep
that was fattest.
And when sleep would come upon him and he
was done with his playing,
he would go to sleep in a bed, in the arms of his
nurse, in a soft
bed, with his heart given all its fill of luxury.
Now, with his dear father gone, he has much to
suffer:

410 he, whom the Trojans have called Astyanax, lord
of the city,
since it was you alone who defended the gates
and the long walls.
But now, beside the curving ships, far away from
your parents,

---

27. **bewept** (bē wept') adj. wet with tears.

the writhing worms will feed, when the dogs have
    had enough of you,
on your naked corpse, though in your house
    there is clothing laid up
415   that is fine-textured and pleasant, wrought by the
    hands of women.
But all of these I will burn up in the fire's blazing,
no use to you, since you will never be laid away in
    them;
but in your honor, from the men of Troy and the
    Trojan women."
        So she spoke, in tears; and the women
        joined in her mourning.

The Wooden Horse

As told by William F. Russell

*One of the most famous wars in ancient history, the Tro-
jan War, was fought over one person—Helen—who was
kidnapped from Greece by the Trojans. In this story about
that war, the Greeks play a famous trick on the Trojans.*

After the death of Achilles,[1] the battles commenced once
again. At times the Trojans would emerge from the gates
to fight the Greeks hand-to-hand out on the plain, but
these occasions were rare. Most days saw the Greeks
gather at the base of the walls of Troy and try to crash
the gates or scale the walls, while the Trojans, safe behind their battlements, killed many Greek warriors with
their arrows and crushed others with huge stones
thrown from the walls above.

After retreating yet again from a day's assault on the
high-walled city, the Greeks held a council and asked advice from the prophet Calchas.[2] Now Calchas would
oftentimes see omens and portents[3] in the activities of
animals and birds, and it happened that on the previous
day he had seen a hawk pursuing a dove, which hid in a
hole in a rocky cliff. For a long while the hawk tried to
find the hole and follow the dove into it, but he could not
reach her. So he flew away for a short distance and hid
himself; then the dove fluttered out into the sunlight,
thinking she was no longer in danger, and the hawk
swooped down on her and made his kill. The Greeks,
said Calchas, ought to learn a lesson from the hawk and
take Troy by cunning, for it was clear that they could not
conquer her by force.

The words of Calchas inspired the wise Ulysses,[4] and
he rose to describe a trick that would allow their warriors
to enter the walled city at last. The Greeks, he said,
ought to make an enormous hollow horse of wood, and
place the bravest men, armed for battle, inside the horse.
Then all the rest of the army should embark in their

---

1. **Achilles** (ə kil' ēz) a Greek hero of the Trojan War.
2. **Calchas** (kal' kəs)
3. **portents** (pôr' tents) *n.* signs.
4. **Ulysses** (yoo lis' ēz)

ships and set sail—not to their homeland—but to a small island that lay but a short distance away. There they could conceal themselves and their ships behind the island, while the Trojans would think they had given up the battle and had sailed for home. The Trojans, he said, would come out of their city, like the dove out of her hole in the rock, and would wander about the Greek camp, and would wonder why the great horse had been made and why it had been left behind. Lest they should set fire to the horse, or smash it open and discover the warriors inside, a cunning Greek, whom the Trojans did not know by sight, should be left in the camp or near it. He would tell the Trojans that the Greeks had given up all hope and had gone home, and he was to say that they feared the anger of Athena,[5] who protected the city from harm. To soothe the goddess and to prevent her from sending violent storms to sink their ships, the Greeks (so the man was to say) had built this wooden horse as an offering to her. The Trojans, believing this story, would surely drag the horse inside the city walls. In the dark of night, then, the army would return from the nearby island, and the horse's belly would quietly issue forth the hidden warriors, who would open the city gates for their waiting comrades. Troy would be theirs at last!

The prophet was much pleased with the plan, and so on the next day, half the army was sent, axes in hand, to cut down trees and to hew thousands of planks that would shape the giant figure. In three days, the horse was finished, and Ulysses asked for brave warriors to hide inside, and for the bravest volunteer of all to stay behind and be captured by the Trojans. Then a young man called Sinon[6] stood up and said that he would risk himself and take the chance that the Trojans might slay him outright or not believe him and burn him alive. Certainly none of the Greeks, throughout the ten years of war, had done anything more courageous, yet Sinon had never been considered a brave man. He had not fought in the front ranks, nor had he distinguished himself in any individual battles, yet there were many brave fighters among the Greeks who would not have dared to do what Sinon undertook.

---

5. **Athena** (ə thē′ nə) the Greek goddess of wisdom, skills, and warfare.
6. **Sinon** (sī′ nən)

The ten or twelve warriors—including the wise Ulysses and Menelaus,[7] the husband of Helen—who climbed into the horse, first embraced their fellows as if for the last time, and then they wrapped themselves and their armor in soft silks so that no sounds would give their presence away. The rest of the army then burned all the huts along the shore and launched their ships, every man hoping that the Trojans would be so foolish as to drag the image into their town and so invite their own destruction.

From the walls the Trojans saw the black smoke go up thick into the sky and the whole fleet of the Greeks sailing out to sea. Never were men so glad, and they armed themselves for fear of an ambush and went cautiously, sending forth scouts in front of them, down to the seashore. Here they found the huts burned down and the camp deserted, and some of the scouts also caught Sinon, who had hidden himself in a place where he was likely to be found. They rushed on him with fierce cries, and bound his hands with a rope, and kicked and dragged him along to the place where Priam[8] and the Trojan generals were staring in wonder at the great wooden horse that had been so mysteriously left along the shore.

One of the leaders said, "It is a very curious thing. Let us drag it into the city that it may be a monument of all that we have suffered for the last ten years." But others said, "Not so; we had better burn it, or drag it out into the sea that the water may cover it, or cut it open to see whether there is anything inside."

Of these, no one was more vehement than Laocoön,[9] one of Priam's sons and the priest of Apollo's temple at Troy. "Take heed what you do, men of Troy," he cried. "Who knows whether the Greeks have really gone away? It may be that there are armed men inside this wooden horse; it may be that it has been made so big so that warriors hidden from our sight may use it to scale our walls. No matter what its purpose may be, I fear the Greeks, even though they bear gifts." And as he spoke, he threw the spear that he had in his hand at the horse

---

7. **Menelaus** (men ə lā′ əs)
8. **Priam** (prī′ əm)
9. **Laocoön** (lā äk′ ō än)

of wood, and struck it on the side. A great rattling sound was heard, and the Trojans, if they had not been so blind and foolish, might have known that there was something wrong.

While the dispute was going on, the scouts arrived with Sinon in tow, and they announced that they had found the Greek hiding not far away. Perhaps he could tell them the meaning of the giant horse of wood. The Trojans crowded around him and began to mock at him, but he cried out in a very piteous voice, "What shall I do? Where shall I go? The Greeks will not let me live, and the Trojans cry out for vengeance upon me." Then they began to pity him, and they bade[10] him say who he was and what he had to tell.

Then the man turned to King Priam and said, "I will speak the truth, whatever may happen to me. My name is Sinon, and I will not deny that I am a Greek. Perhaps you have heard of my cousin, Palamedes,[11] whom the Greeks called a traitor but whose only fault was that he wanted to have peace. Yes, they put him to death, and now that he is gone, they are sorry, but there is nothing they can do to bring him back. It was, in fact, because of the lies that Ulysses told against my cousin that Palamedes was accused and punished, and I swore that someday I would have revenge upon all those who wronged him. So Ulysses was always eager to do me harm, and at last, with the help of the prophet Calchas— but why do I tell you of these things? Doubtless you hold one Greek as bad as another. Kill me, if you will, only remember that my death is the very thing that Ulysses himself would give much money to secure."

Then the Trojans said, "Tell us more."

And he went on. "Many times would the Greeks have gone home, for they were very tired of the war, but the sea was so stormy that they dared not go. Then they made this great horse of wood that you see, but the storms grew worse and worse. Then they prayed to Apollo to guide them in their actions, and Apollo said, 'Men of Greece, when you came here, you first had to sacrifice the beautiful Iphigenia,[12] daughter of Agamemnon,[13] and

---

10. **bade** (bād) *v.* told; commanded.
11. **Palamedes** (pa lə mē′ dēz)
12. **Iphigenia** (if ə jə ni′ ə)
13. **Agamemnon** (az ə mem′ nän)

so appease the winds with blood. You must appease them with blood as you leave or you will never see your homeland again.' All of us trembled at this message, for everyone feared that it might be his blood that would be sacrificed to the winds. After a while, Ulysses brought the prophet Calchas into the assembly and said, 'Tell us now who it is that the gods will have for a victim?' All the Greeks had long respected the prophecies of Calchas, and so no one guessed that he and Ulysses had secretly plotted together to seal my fate. 'Sinon is the man,' said Calchas, and all in the assembly agreed, for now Sinon's doom meant each of them was out of danger. So they fixed a day on which I was to be sacrificed, and everything was made ready. But before that day came, I broke my bonds and escaped, hiding myself in the reeds of a pond, until at last they sailed away. And now I shall never see my own country again—no, nor my wife and children—and doubtless these cruel Greeks will take vengeance on them because I escaped. And now I beseech you, O King, to have pity on me, for I have suffered much, though, indeed, I have not done harm to any man."

Then King Priam had pity on him and bade the Trojans unbind his hands, saying, "Forget your own people; from today you are one of us. But tell us now, why did the Greeks make this great horse of wood that we see?"

Then Sinon lifted up his hands to the sky and said, "O sun and moon and stars, I call you to witness that I have a good right to tell the secrets of my countrymen. Listen, O King. From the beginning, when the Greeks first came to this place, their hope resided in the help of the gods, but after ten long years of battle, they saw that they were no closer to capturing your city and returning fair Helen than they were when they first sailed to your shores. And so Agamemnon called a council of all the chiefs, and there he asked the prophet Calchas to consult the stars and omens and to reveal the will of the gods. And Calchas said to them: 'The gods have allowed us to kill many Trojan princes and to make the people cower behind their city walls, but to capture the city itself, we must go home to Greece before returning here to begin this war anew. Further-more, we must make a horse of wood to be a peace offering to the goddess Athena. We must build it so large that the Trojans cannot take it within their walls, for if they do, Athena will never allow us to conquer the city. Nay, once the gift is within their walls, it has been foretold, the Trojans will soon lay siege to our own cities and kill our wives and children. This the gods have ordained, and also that whoever harms the horse in any way shall perish.' And my countrymen did as Calchas advised; they have gone back to Greece, but they will soon return."

This was the tale that Sinon told, and the Trojans believed it. Nor is this to be wondered at, for even the gods took part in deceiving them. And this is what they did.

While Laocoön, the priest who had thrown his spear at the great horse, was praying that his people would not bring the image into the city, the gods sent two great serpents across the sea from a nearby island. All the Trojans saw them come, with their heads raised high above the water, as is the way of certain snakes when they swim. And when they reached the land, they came on straight to where the Trojans were gathered. Their eyes were red as blood, and blazed like fire, and they made a dreadful hissing with their tongues. The Trojans grew pale with fear, and fled. But the serpents did not turn this way or that, but came straight to the altar at which Laocoön stood, with his two sons by his side. And one serpent laid hold on one of the boys, and the other on the other, and they began to devour them. Then the father picked up a sword, but before he could lash out, the serpents caught hold of him and wound themselves, two times, around his body and his neck, their heads standing in triumph high above his. And still he tried as hard as he could to tear them away with his hands, but to no avail.

And when the serpents had done their work, and both the priest and his sons were dead, then they glided to the hill on which stood the temple of Athena and hid themselves under the feet of her image. And when the Trojans saw this, they said to themselves, "Now Laocoön has suffered the due reward of his deeds, for he threw the spear at the holy thing that belongs to the goddess, and now he is dead and his sons with him."

Then they all cried out together that the horse of wood should be drawn into the citadel.[14] So they opened the

---

14. **citadel** (sit′ ə del) *n.* fortress.

great gate of the city, pulling down part of the wall so that there might be more room, and they put rollers under the feet of the horse, and they fastened ropes to it. Then they drew it into the city, boys and girls laying hold of the ropes, and singing songs with great joy. And everyone thought it a great thing if he could pull on any one of the ropes.

The rejoicing was so complete that no one gave heed to the ample signs of evil to come. Four times did the horse halt as they dragged it, before it passed through the gate, and each time there might have been heard a great clashing of metal sounds within. Also, Cassandra[15] spoke out and prophesied that the horse would bring on the destruction of Troy. But ever since Apollo had punished her by decreeing that no one would believe her predictions again, the people refused to give any heed to her warnings. So the Trojans drew the horse of wood into the city, and that night they held a great and joyous feast to the gods, not knowing the end of their city was now close at hand.

All through the wild festivities that night, the giant wooden horse stood in the courtyard at the very center of the city. The people of Troy danced and drank and sang songs of celebration, and even the guards who had been posted at the gates to the city joined in the revelry and drank wine until they were quite useless as sentinels. All the while, the Greek ships silently made their way from behind the island to the banks of their former camp.

Sometime after midnight, when the celebrants had either fallen asleep from drink or had gone to their homes to enjoy the first night of peace in ten years, Sinon—who had been accepted as a citizen of Troy—carefully opened the secret latch in the belly of the horse, and the Greek warriors let themselves down softly to the ground. Some rushed to the gate, killing the sleeping guards and letting in the army of the Greeks. Others sped with torches to burn the houses of the Trojan princes and to slay those who had killed their friends and brothers during the war. Terrible was the slaughter of men, unarmed and half awake, and loud were the cries of women. All through the city were the sounds of fighting and slaying and dying.

---

15. **Cassandra** (kə san' drə)

When dawn came, Troy lay in ashes, and the women were being driven with spear shafts to the ships, and the men were left unburied, their once-noble bodies now food for wild dogs and birds. All the gold and silver, and the rich embroideries, and the ivory and amber, and the horses and chariots were divided among the army. Agamemnon was given the beautiful Cassandra, daughter of King Priam, as a prize, and lovely Helen, whose capture had begun this war ten long years ago—whose face had "launched a thousand ships and burnt the topless towers of Ilium"[16]—was led in honor to the ship of Menelaus, and eventually back to Sparta, where she and her husband ruled as queen and king.

---

16. **Ilium** (il′ ē əm)

The Sirens

from The Adventures of Ulysses

Retold by Bernard Evslin

In this retelling of a part of Homer's epic Odyssey, *the clever and curious Ulysses expects an easy journey home from the Trojan War. Instead, he is delayed by adventures that test his mind and his spirit.*

In the first light of morning Ulysses awoke and called his crew about him. "Men," he said. "Listen well, for your lives today hang upon what I am about to tell you. That large island to the west is Thrinacia,[1] where we must make a landfall, for our provisions run low. But to get to the island we must pass through a narrow strait.[2] And at the head of this strait is a rocky islet[3] where dwell two sisters called Sirens, whose voices you must not hear. Now I shall guard you against their singing, which would lure you to shipwreck, but first you must bind me to the mast. Tie me tightly, as though I were a dangerous captive. And no matter how I struggle, no matter what signals I make to you, *do not release me*, lest I follow their voices to destruction, taking you with me."

Thereupon Ulysses took a large lump of the beeswax that was used by the sail mender to slick his heavy thread and kneaded it in his powerful hands until it become soft. Then he went to each man of the crew and plugged his ears with soft wax; he caulked[4] their ears so tightly that they could hear nothing but the thin pulsing of their own blood.

Then he stood himself against the mast, and the men bound him about with rawhide, winding it tightly around his body, lashing him to the thick mast.

They had lowered the sail because ships cannot sail through a narrow strait unless there is a following wind, and now each man of the crew took his place at the great

---

1. **Thrinacia** *n.* mythological island that might have been Sicily.
2. **strait** *n.* narrow ocean passage between two pieces of land.
3. **islet** *n.* small island.
4. **caulk** *v.* to stop up and make tight.

oars. The polished blades whipped the sea into a froth of white water and the ship nosed toward the strait.

Ulysses had left his own ears unplugged because he had to remain in command of the ship and had need of his hearing. Every sound means something upon the sea. But when they drew near the rocky islet and he heard the first faint strains[5] of the Sirens' singing, then he wished he, too, had stopped his own ears with wax. All his strength suddenly surged[6] toward the sound of those magical voices. The very hair of his head seemed to be tugging at his scalp, trying to fly away. His eyeballs started out of his head.

For in those voices were the sounds that men love:

Happy sounds like birds railing,[7] sleet hailing, milk pailing. . . .

Sad sounds like rain leaking, trees creaking, wind seeking. . . .

Autumn sounds like leaves tapping, fire snapping, river lapping[8]. . . .

Quiet sounds like snow flaking, spider waking, heart breaking. . . .

It seemed to him then that the sun was burning him to a cinder as he stood. And the voices of the Sirens purled[9] in a cool crystal pool upon their rock past the blue-hot flatness of the sea and its lacings of white-hot spume.[10] It seemed to him he could actually see their voices deepening into a silvery, cool pool and must plunge into that pool or die a flaming death.

He was filled with such a fury of desire that he swelled his mighty muscles, burst the rawhide bonds like thread, and dashed for the rail.

But he had warned two of his strongest men—Perimedes and Eurylochus—to guard him close. They seized him before he could plunge into the water. He swept them aside as if they had been children. But they

---

5. **strain** *n*. tune.
6. **surge** *v*. to rise or swell suddenly.
7. **rail** *v*. to scold.
8. **lap** *v*. to splash in little waves.
9. **purl** *v*. to make a soft murmuring sound like a flowing stream.
10. **spume** *n*. foam.

had held him long enough to give the crew time to swarm about him. He was overpowered—crushed by their numbers—and dragged back to the mast. This time he was bound with the mighty hawser[11] that held the anchor.

The men returned to their rowing seats, unable to hear the voices because of the wax corking their ears. The ship swung about and headed for the strait again.

Louder now, and clearer, the tormenting voices came to Ulysses. Again he was aflame with a fury of desire. But try as he might he could not break the thick anchor line. He strained against it until he bled, but the line held.

The men bent to their oars and rowed more swiftly, for they saw the mast bending like a tall tree in a heavy wind, and they feared that Ulysses, in his fury, might snap it off short and dive, mast and all, into the water to get at the Sirens.

Now they were passing the rock, and Ulysses could see the singers. There were two of them. They sat on a heap of white bones—the bones of shipwrecked sailors—and sang more beautifully than senses could bear. But their appearance did not match their voices, for they were shaped like birds, huge birds, larger than eagles. They had feathers instead of hair, and their hands and feet were claws. But their faces were the faces of young girls.

When Ulysses saw them he was able to forget the sweetness of their voices because their look was so fearsome. He closed his eyes against the terrible sight of these bird-women perched on their heap of bones. But when he closed his eyes he could not see their ugliness, then their voices maddened him once again, and he felt himself straining against the bloody ropes. He forced himself to open his eyes and look upon the monsters, so that the terror of their bodies would blot the beauty of their voices.

But the men, who could only see, not hear the Sirens, were so appalled by their aspect that they swept their oars faster and faster, and the black ship scuttled past the rock. The Sirens' voices sounded fainter and fainter and finally died away.

---

11. **hawser** *n.* a large rope.

When Perimedes and Eurylochus saw their captain's face lose its madness, they unbound him, and he signaled to the men to unstop their ears. For now he heard the whistling gurgle of a whirlpool, and he knew that they were approaching the narrowest part of the strait, and must past between Scylla[12] and Charybdis.[13]

---

12. Scylla *n.* a monster who ate sailors passing through the Straits of Messina between Italy and Sicily.
13. Charybdis *n.* a monster in the form of a deadly whirlpool near Scylla.

Orpheus

Alice Low

In this myth, one man's love for his wife is so great that after her death, he follows her to the underworld to bring her back.

There were nine goddesses called Muses. Born of Zeus and a Titan named Mnemosyne,[1] each Muse presided over a different art or science.

Calliope,[2] one of these sisters, was the inspiration of poets and musicians. She was the mother of Orpheus[3] (a mortal because his father was one) and gave to her son a remarkable talent for music.

Orpheus played his lyre[4] so sweetly that he charmed all things on earth. Men and women forgot their cares when they gathered around him to listen. Wild beasts lay down as if they were tame, entranced by his soothing notes. Even rocks and trees followed him, and the rivers changed their direction to hear him play.

Orpheus loved a young woman named Eurydice,[5] and when they were married, they looked forward to many years of happiness together. But soon after, Eurydice stepped on a poisonous snake and died.

Orpheus roamed the earth, singing sad melodies to try to overcome his grief. But it was no use. He longed for Eurydice so deeply that he decided to follow her to the underworld. He said to himself, "No mortal has ever been there before, but I must try to bring back my beloved Eurydice. I will charm Persephone[6] and Hades[7] with my music and win Eurydice's release."

He climbed into a cave and through a dark passage that led to the underworld. When he reached the river Styx,[8] he plucked his lyre, and Charon, the ferryman, was so charmed that he rowed him across. Then he

---

1. **Mnemosyne** (nē mäs′ i nē) goddess of memory.
2. **Calliope** (kə lī′ ə pē)
3. **Orpheus** (ôr′ fē əs)
4. **lyre** (līr) *n.* a small stringed instrument.
5. **Eurydice** (yoo rid′ i sē)
6. **Persephone** (par sef′ ə nē) wife of Hades.
7. **Hades** (hā′ dēz) the god of the underworld.
8. **Styx** (stiks) *n.* river that flows around Hades.

struck his lyre again, and Cerberus, the fierce three-headed dog who guarded the gates, heard the sweet music and lay still to let him pass.

Orpheus continued to play his lyre tenderly as he made his way through the gloomy underworld. The ghosts cried when they heard his sad music. Sisyphus, who had been condemned to roll a rock uphill forever, stopped his fruitless work to listen. Tantalus, who had been sentenced to stand in a pool of receding water, stopped trying to quench his thirst. And even the wheel to which Ixion was tied as punishment stopped turning for one moment.

At last Orpheus came to the palace of Hades and Persephone, king and queen of the underworld. Before they could order him to leave, he began his gentle song, pleading for Eurydice.

When stern Hades heard Orpheus's song, he began to weep. Cold Persephone was so moved that, for the first time in all her months in the underworld, her heart melted.

"Oh, please, my husband," she said to Hades, "let Eurydice be reunited with Orpheus."

And Hades replied, "I, too, feel the sadness of Orpheus. I cannot refuse him."

They summoned Eurydice, and the two lovers clasped each other and turned to leave.

"Wait!" said Hades to Orpheus. "Eurydice is yours to take back to earth on one condition."

"What is that?" asked Orpheus.

"She must follow you, and you must not look back at her until you are on earth again."

"I understand," said Orpheus. "And I am forever grateful."

Orpheus and Eurydice left the underworld and made their way through the dark passage that led to the upper world. At last they reached the cave through which Orpheus had descended.

"I can see daylight ahead," called Orpheus to Eurydice. "We are almost there." But Eurydice had not heard him, and so she did not answer.

Orpheus turned to make sure that she was still following him. He caught one last glimpse of her with her arms stretched out to him. And then she disappeared, swallowed up by darkness.

"Farewell," he heard her cry as she was carried back to the underworld.

Orpheus tried to follow her, but this time the gods would not allow it. And so he wandered the earth alone. He sang his sad songs to the rocks and the trees and longed for the time when he, too, would die and be reunited with his beloved Eurydice in the underworld.

The Gorgon's Head

Anne Terry White

A number of myths feature an oracle who prophesies, or tells the future, and a human being's ultimately useless efforts to avoid fulfilling the prophecy. In this myth, Acrisius tries to avoid the prophecy that his grandson will kill him.

Acrisius,[1] King of Argos,[2] came home from Delphi with a heavy heart, for he had received a dreadful oracle.

"No sons shall be born to you," the priestess had told him. "But you shall have a grandson, and by his hand you shall die."

Now the king had an only daughter, who was yet a maiden. So in his distress he thought: "I will evade[3] my fate. I will shut Danae[4] up away from a sight of men in a house of bronze all sunk underground." And he carried out his cruel plan.

But Acrisius forgot to take the gods into account. Part of the roof of the house was open to the sky. And one day, as lovely Danae sat sadly looking up at the passing clouds, Zeus[5] beheld the maiden. Changing himself into a shower of gold, he stormed into her chamber.

When afterwards a son was born to Danae, she hid him from her father's sight. Nevertheless, the king discovered the baby and was more than ever filled with fear. He dared not kill the little Perseus[6] directly lest the gods avenge the murder. Instead, he had a great chest built, placed Danae and her boy in it, and set them adrift upon the sea.

All day and all night the chest tossed upon the waves. Danae lulled her child with song, and he slept. But when dawn came, a great wave picked up the chest and carried it close to the tiny island of Seraphos.[7]

It happened that a fisherman, Dictys[8] by name, saw the chest bobbing on the waves close to the shore. He

---

1. **Acrisius** (ə kris′ ē əs)
2. **Argos** (är′ gōs) a city in Greece.
3. **evade** (i vād′) v. avoid; escape.
4. **Danae** (dan′ ä ē) daughter of Acrisius.
5. **Zeus** (zo͞os)
6. **Perseus** (per′ sē us)
7. **Seraphos** (sə ri′ fōs) an island in the Aegean Sea.
8. **Dictys** (dik′ tis)

dragged the box to land and opened it. When he beheld the pitiful mother with the helpless little child, his heart was moved. He took them both to his wife, for Dictys was childless, and there in the kindly fisherfolk's humble home Perseus grew up.

Now Danae had been a beautiful maiden. And when Perseus was grown into a fine tall youth, she was still beautiful. So it was not strange that King Polydectes,[9] who was Dictys' brother, fell in love with her and made her his wife. But the King hated the youth—just because Danae doted on him—and sought some way to be rid of him.

At last Polydectes said to his stepson, "The time has come, Perseus, for you to win glory for yourself in some bold adventure."

Young Perseus thought so, too. But what should the adventure be?

"I think," the wily Polydectes said, "it would be a good idea for you to cut off the Medusa's[10] head. That would bring you the greatest fame."

All unsuspecting, Perseus set off to find the Medusa, not knowing in the least how perilous[11] an adventure he had undertaken. For Medusa was one of the three Gorgons, terrible winged monsters who lived alone on an island. They had teeth like the tusks of a boar, hands of brass, and snakes instead of hair. Perseus did not know where to look for the Gorgons. Nor did he know which of them was Medusa. And this was important, for Medusa was the only one of the three that could be slain.

From place to place the prince went in his quest, getting more and more discouraged. Then one day he beheld a young man of great beauty, wearing winged sandals and a winged cap, and carrying in his hand a wand around which two golden serpents twined. Perseus knew at once that this was Hermes and was overjoyed when the god said:

"Perseus, I approve the high adventure you have in mind. But you must be properly equipped for it. Without the winged sandals, the magic wallet, and the helmet of invisibility which the Nymphs[12] of the North possess, you

---

9. **Polydectes** (päl ē dək′ tēz)
10. **Medusa's** (mə dōō′ säz)
11. **perilous** (per′ el es) *adj.* dangerous.
12. **Nymphs** (nimfz) minor nature goddesses, thought of as beautiful maidens living in rivers, trees, and so on.

can never succeed. Now, I cannot tell you where the Nymphs live, but I will take you to the Gray Women.[13] You can find out from them."

"And will they indeed tell me?" Perseus asked.

"Not willingly," Hermes replied. "But you can make them do it. They have but one eye among the three. Snatch it from them as they pass it from one to another and none can see. And do not give it back till they tell you what you want to know."

With that, Hermes gave Perseus a magnificent curved sword.

"You will need it," he said, "for the Medusa's scales are hard as metal."

Perseus had just taken the sword when there was a sudden brightness in the sky, and he beheld the goddess Athene[14] descending toward them.

"Of what use will be your sword, my brother," she said to Hermes, "when none may look on the Gorgons and live? The sight of them, as you well know, turns men to stone. Take my bright shield, Perseus. Look into it instead of at the monster as you approach to do battle, and you will see the Medusa reflected as in a mirror."

So saying, the goddess disappeared, and the brightness with her.

On and on with his god-companion Perseus journeyed, farther than man had ever been. At last they came to the end of the earth. There the weird Gray Women sat, passing their eye from one to another just as Hermes had said. Danae's son knew what to do. He left the god and crept quietly towards them, waited till one had taken the eye from her forehead, and snatched it away as she passed it to her sister.

The Gray Women raised a fearful clamor when they realized that a stranger had their eye. They howled and they threatened. But without the eye they were helpless, and in the end they grudgingly told Perseus the way to the Nymphs of the North.

So again Perseus went on, this time to find the happy beings who possessed the three priceless things he needed.

---

13. Gray Women also called Graeae (grē′ ē′) three old sisters who act as guards for the Gorgons and have only one eye and one tooth to share among them.
14. Athene (ə thē′ nä) goddess of wisdom, skills, and warfare.

And when the Nymphs heard the reason he wanted them, they were willing to give him the winged shoes, the helmet that would make him invisible, and the magic wallet that would become the right size for whatever he wished to carry.

Fully equipped now, Perseus lightly sped through the air over land and over sea to the fearful island of the Gorgons. As he approached, he could see, scattered in the fields and along the roads, statues of men and beasts whom the sight of the Gorgons had turned to stone. And, at last, from high above, he beheld the monsters themselves reflected in his shield. Their scale-covered bodies glistened in the sun, their great wings were folded, the snakes that were their hair lay hideously coiled and intertwined. The Gorgons were asleep.

But which of the three was Medusa? Perseus could see no difference among them.

Suddenly he heard Athene's voice:

"Descend, Perseus, and strike! The Gorgon nearest the shore is Medusa."

Perseus swept down, and still gazing into the shield, boldly swung his blade. With one stroke he cut off the grisly head. Then, springing into the air, he thrust his prize, all writhing and hissing, into the magic wallet.

Up leaped the Gorgon sisters, for they heard the rattle of Medusa's scales as the severed body thrashed about. They turned their snaky heads and when they saw Perseus, they roared with fury. Flapping their great wings, they set off in pursuit. But they could not outstrip the winged sandals.

Over lands and peoples the hero flew, on and on. He had lost his way now, for Hermes had left him. Below, the Lybian desert stretched endlessly. Perseus did not know what those sands were, nor did he guess that the ruby drops falling from Medusa's head were turning into venomous[15] snakes that would inhabit the desert forever. But now he saw a sight that made his heart beat fast with excitement and wonder.

Fastened by chains to a cliff by the sea was a beautiful maiden. Had it not been that a slight breeze stirred her hair and that tears flowed from her eyes, he would have thought her a statue. Perseus almost forgot to keep his

---

15. venomous (ven′ əm əs) *adj*. poisonous.

winged sandals moving, so struck was he by her rare beauty.

"Lovely maiden, you should not wear such chains as these," he stammered out, "but rather those which bind the hearts of lovers. I pray you, tell me your name and why you are bound like this."

At first the girl made no reply, so abashed[16] was she before the youth. But when he urged her again and again to speak, she told him all her story.

"I am Andromeda,"[17] she said, "daughter of Cepheus,[18] King of the Ethiopians. The beautiful Cassiopeia[19] is my mother. It is her beauty that has chained me here. For the gods are jealous, and in nothing may we mortals surpass them. Woe, woe the day my mother vaunted[20] herself fairer than the daughters of Nereus![21] The sea god has sent a serpent to prey upon our people, and my death alone can appease his anger. So says the oracle."

She had scarcely finished speaking when the loud roaring of the waves announced that the monster was on his way. Andromeda shrieked. At her cry, her frantic father and mother came running. They clung to their daughter and lamented.

"Enough of tears!" Perseus said to them sternly. "I am Perseus, son of Zeus and Danae. Now I will make this contract with you—that Andromeda shall be mine if I save her from the serpent."

"Indeed, indeed, valorous[22] youth, she shall be yours! Only save her from the monster, and you shall have our kingdom as well as our daughter."

The monster was coming on, his breast parting the waves like a swift ship. Suddenly Perseus sprang into the air and shot high up in the clouds. Seeing the youth's shadow upon the sea, the monster attacked it in fury. Then Perseus swooped like an eagle from the sky and buried his sword up to the hilt in the beast's right shoulder. The creature reared upright, then plunged beneath

---

16. **abashed** (ə basht') *adj.* ashamed.
17. **Andromeda** (an dräm' ə dä)
18. **Cepheus** (sē' fē us)
19. **Cassiopeia** (kas ē ō pē' ä)
20. **vaunted** (vänt' əd) *v.* boasted or bragged.
21. **Nereus** (nē' rē us) a god of great kindliness; also called the Old Man of the Sea and Nereus the Truthful, the father of the Nereids, the nymphs of the sea.
22. **valorous** (val' er əs) *adj.* brave.

the water, and turned around and around like some fierce wild boar in the midst of baying hounds.

Nimbly avoiding the snapping jaws, Perseus dealt blow after blow wherever he had the chance to strike. Red blood poured from the monster's mouth. The air was so filled with spray that the hero's winged sandals grew heavy. He dared not trust himself to them longer. Spying a rock over which the waves were breaking, he braced himself against it with his left hand, and four times he drove his sword into the monster's side.

As the creature sank to its death, Perseus heard shouts of joy from the shore. And when he looked, Andromeda already stood free beside her parents.

"I will take this fair maiden without dowry," Perseus said.

And that very day the wedding was celebrated. Torches were tossed in the air, incense was thrown on the flames. Garlands were hung from the palace roof. And everywhere the sound of lyres and pipes and singing was heard.

Now while the marriage feast was at its height, the door of the banquet hall was suddenly flung open, and in burst a mob of shouting, riotous men. Foremost stood Andromeda's uncle, Phineas,[23] javelin in hand.

"Behold, I am here!" he cried. "I have come to avenge the theft of my promised bride."

"What are you doing, brother?" the father cried. "Do you, who stood by and watched while Andromeda was put in chains and did nothing to help her, dare to be indignant because another has snatched the prize? Let the man who rescued her have the reward he was promised! He has not been chosen in preference to you, but in preference to certain death."

Phineas said not a word. He looked from the king to Perseus, undecided at which to aim his weapon, then hurled it at the hero. The spear struck in Perseus' couch. Perseus leaped up from the cushions, wrenched out the spear, and hurled it back at his foe. Had Phineas not taken refuge behind the altar, he would have perished. As it was, one of his followers received the weapon full in his forehead.

---

23. **Phineas** (fin′ ē us)

Then the rioters went wild. Weapons were hurled, and the feast turned into a battle. Thick as hail, javelins sped by Perseus' ears. He set his shoulders against a great stone column and struck down one man after another. But at last he realized that valor could not withstand the numbers against him.

"If I have any friends here, let them hide their faces!" he shouted.

With this he drew Medusa's head out of the wallet. One of the attackers was just preparing to cast his javelin, but before he could cast, he was turned to stone. Another, who was about to thrust his sword through Perseus, stood frozen with it in his hand. A third was turned to stone even as he uttered a taunt. Two hundred men became stony statues before Phineas yielded, crying:

"Put away your horrible weapon. Hide it! Grant me only my life and may the rest be yours!"

"What I can give you, most cowardly Phineas, I will!" Perseus replied. "You shall be a lasting monument here in the palace of my father-in-law."

The unhappy Phineas tried to turn away his eyes, but even as he did so, his flesh turned to stone.

When at the year's end, Perseus sailed home with Andromeda, Polydectes' hatred had in no way lessened. The King was furious that his stepson had returned, and refused to believe that he had actually slain the Medusa. With scornful taunts he upbraided the young man for having come home empty-handed.

It was more than Perseus could bear.

"I shall prove to you that what I say is true!" he cried. "Hide your eyes, all you who are my friends!" And he showed the Gorgon's head to cruel Polydectes.

That was the last time Perseus ever used the horrible head. He gave it most willingly to Athene, who kept it ever after.

Now that Polydectes was dead, Danae yearned to go home again and be reconciled to her father. So Perseus made the fisherman Dictys king of the island and sailed with his mother and Andromeda to Greece.

But it happened that when they came to Argos, King Acrisius was away from home. Games were being held in Larissa, and Perseus, hearing of them, decided to go there and take part. And there at the games it was that the oracle which Acrisius had received at Delphi was strangely fulfilled. For when it came Perseus' turn to throw the discus, he threw it so that it swerved to one side. It landed among the spectators and killed an old man. That old man was King Acrisius, who had gone to such cruel lengths to avoid the fate which the gods had ordained.

Atalanta

Betty Miles

This retelling of an ancient Greek myth features a young woman who is under pressure to be someone that she's not. Think about how it compares to "The Golden Apples," the story that follows.

Once upon a time, not long ago, there lived a princess named Atalanta,[1] who could run as fast as the wind.

She was so bright, and so clever, and could build things and fix things so wonderfully, that many young men wished to marry her.

"What shall I do?" said Atalanta's father, who was a powerful king. "So many young men want to marry you, and I don't know how to choose."

"You don't have to choose, Father," Atalanta said. "I will choose. And I'm not sure that I will choose to marry anyone at all."

"Of course you will," said the king. "Everybody gets married. It is what people do."

"But," Atalanta told him, with a toss of her head, "I intend to go out and see the world. When I come home, perhaps I will marry and perhaps I will not."

The king did not like this at all. He was a very ordinary king; that is, he was powerful and used to having his own way. So he did not answer Atalanta, but simply told her, "I have decided how to choose the young man you will marry. I will hold a great race, and the winner—the swiftest, fleetest young man of all—will win the right to marry you."

Now Atalanta was a clever girl as well as a swift runner. She saw that she might win both the argument and the race—provided that she herself could run in the race, too. "Very well," she said. "But you must let me race along with the others. If I am not the winner, I will accept the wishes of the young man who is."

The king agreed to this. He was pleased; he would have his way, marry off his daughter, and enjoy a fine day of racing as well. So he directed his messengers to

---

1. **Atalanta** (at ə lan′ tə)

travel throughout the kingdom announcing the race with its wonderful prize: the chance to marry the bright Atalanta.

As the day of the race drew near, flags were raised in the streets of the town, and banners were hung near the grassy field where the race would be run. Baskets of ripe plums and peaches, wheels of cheese, ropes of sausages and onions, and loaves of crusty bread were gathered for the crowds.

Meanwhile, Atalanta herself was preparing for the race. Each day at dawn, dressed in soft green trousers and a shirt of yellow silk, she went to the field in secret and ran across it—slowly at first, then fast and faster, until she could run the course more quickly than anyone had ever run it before.

As the day of the race grew nearer, young men began to crowd into the town. Each was sure he could win the prize, except for one; that was Young John, who lived in the town. He saw Atalanta day by day as she bought nails and wood to make a pigeon house, or chose parts for her telescope, or laughed with her friends. Young John saw the princess only from a distance, but near enough to know how bright and clever she was. He wished very much to race with her, to win, and to earn the right to talk with her and become her friend.

"For surely," he said to himself, "it is not right for Atalanta's father to give her away to the winner of the race. Atalanta herself must choose the person she wants to marry, or whether she wishes to marry at all. Still, if I could only win the race, I would be free to speak to her, and to ask for her friendship."

Each evening, after his studies of the stars and the seas, Young John went to the field in secret and practiced running across it. Night after night, he ran fast as the wind across the twilight field, until he could cross it more quickly than anyone had ever crossed it before.

At last, the day of the race arrived.

Trumpets sounded in the early morning, and the young men gathered at the edge of the field, along with Atalanta herself, the prize they sought. The king and his friends sat in soft chairs, and the townspeople stood along the course.

The king rose to address them all. "Good day," he said to the crowds. "Good luck," he said to the young men. To

Atalanta he said, "Good-bye. I must tell you farewell, for tomorrow you will be married."

"I am not so sure of that, Father," Atalanta answered. She was dressed for the race in trousers of crimson and a shirt of silk as blue as the sky, and she laughed as she looked up and down the line of young men.

"Not one of them," she said to herself, "can win the race, for I will run fast as the wind and leave them all behind."

And now a bugle sounded, a flag was dropped, and the runners were off!

The crowds cheered as the young men and Atalanta began to race across the field. At first they ran as a group, but Atalanta soon pulled ahead, with three of the young men close after her. As they neared the halfway point, one young man put on a great burst of speed and seemed to pull ahead for an instant, but then he gasped and fell back. Atalanta shot on.

Soon another young man, tense with the effort, drew near to Atalanta. He reached out as though to touch her sleeve, stumbled for an instant, and lost speed. Atalanta smiled as she ran on. I have almost won, she thought.

But then another young man came near. This was Young John, running like the wind, as steadily and as swiftly as Atalanta herself. Atalanta felt his closeness, and in a sudden burst she dashed ahead.

Young John might have given up at this, but he never stopped running. Nothing at all, thought he, will keep me from winning the chance to speak with Atalanta. And on he ran, swift as the wind, until he ran as her equal, side by side with her, toward the golden ribbon that marked the race's end. Atalanta raced even faster to pull ahead, but Young John was a strong match for her.

Smiling with the pleasure of the race, Atalanta and Young John reached the finish line together, and to-gether they broke through the golden ribbon.

Trumpets blew. The crowd shouted and leaped about. The king rose. "Who is that young man?" he asked.

"It is Young John from the town," the people told him.

"Very well. Young John," said the king, as John and Atalanta stood before him, exhausted and jubilant[2] from their efforts. "You have not won the race, but you have

---

2. **jubilant** (jōō′ bə lənt) *adj.* joyful and successful.

come closer to winning than any man here. And so I give you the prize that was promised—the right to marry my daughter."

Young John smiled at Atalanta, and she smiled back. "Thank you, sir," said John to the king, "but I could not possibly marry your daughter unless she wished to marry me. I have run this race for the chance to talk with Atalanta, and, if she is willing, I am ready to claim my prize."

Atalanta laughed with pleasure. "And I," she said to John, "could not possibly marry before I have seen the world. But I would like nothing better than to spend the afternoon with you."

Then the two of them sat and talked on the grassy field, as the crowds went away. They ate bread and cheese and purple plums. Atalanta told John about her telescopes and her pigeons, and John told Atalanta about his globes and his studies of geography. At the end of the day, they were friends.

On the next day, John sailed off to discover new lands. And Atalanta set off to visit the great cities.

By this time, each of them has had wonderful adventures, and seen marvelous sights. Perhaps some day they will be married, and perhaps they will not. In any case, they are friends. And it is certain that they are both living happily ever after.

The Golden Apples

Retold by Mary Pope Osborne

*Here is a second retelling of the ancient Greek myth fea-
turing a young woman trying to avoid the pressure to
marry. Think about how it compares to "Atalanta," the
story that precedes it.*

Long ago a baby girl named Atalanta[1] was left on a wild
mountainside because her father had wanted a boy instead of a girl. A kind bear discovered the tiny girl and
nursed her and cared for her. And as Atalanta grew up,
she lived as the bears lived: eating wild honey and
berries and hunting in the woods. Finally as a young
woman on her own, she became a follower of Diana, the
goddess of wild things. Preferring to live on her own, Atalanta blissfully roamed the shadowy woods and sunlit
fields.

The god Apollo[2] agreed with Atalanta's choice to be
alone. "You must never marry," he told her one day. "If
you do, you will surely lose your own identity."

In spite of her decision never to marry, Atalanta was
pursued by many suitors. As men watched her run
through the fields and forest, they were struck by her
beauty and grace.

Angry at the men for bothering her, Atalanta figured
out how to keep them away. "I'll race anyone who wants
to marry me!" she announced to the daily throng that
pursued her. "Whoever is so swift that he can outrun me
will receive the prize of my hand in marriage! But
whomever I beat—will die."

Atalanta was certain these harsh conditions would dis-
courage everyone from wanting to marry her. But she
was wrong. Her strength and grace were so compelling
that many men volunteered to race against her—and all
of them lost their lives.

One day, a young stranger, wandering through the
countryside, stopped to join a crowd that was watching a
race between Atalanta and one of her suitors. When

---

1. **Atalanta** (at ə lan′ tə)
2. **Apollo** (ə pöl′ ō) the Greek and Roman god of music, poetry, prophecy, and the
sun.

Hippomenes[3] realized the terms of the contest, he was appalled. "No person could be worth such a risk!" he exclaimed. "Only an idiot would try to win her for his wife!"

But when Atalanta sped by, and Hippomenes saw her wild hair flying back from her ivory shoulders and her strong body moving as gracefully as a gazelle,[4] even he was overwhelmed with the desire to be her husband.

"Forgive me," he said to the panting loser being taken away to his death. "I did not know what a prize she was."

When Atalanta was crowned with the wreath of victory, Hippomenes stepped forward boldly and spoke to her before the crowd. "Why do you race against men so slow?" he asked. "Why not race against me? If I defeat you, you will not be disgraced, for I am the great-grandson of Neptune, god of the seas!"

"And if I beat you?" Atalanta asked.

"If you beat me . . . you will certainly have something to boast about!"

As Atalanta stared at the proud young man, she wondered why the gods would wish one as young and bold as Hippomenes to die. And for the first time, she felt she might rather lose than win. Inexperienced in matters of the heart, she did not realize she was falling in love. "Go, stranger," she said softly. "I'm not worth the loss of your life."

But the crowd, sensing a tremendous race might be about to take place, cheered wildly, urging the two to compete. And since Hippomenes eagerly sought the same, Atalanta was forced to give in. With a heavy heart, she consented to race the young man the next day.

In the pink twilight, alone in the hills, Hippomenes prayed to Venus,[5] the goddess of love and beauty. He asked for help in his race against Atalanta. When Venus heard Hippomenes's prayer, she was only too glad to help him, for she wished to punish the young huntress for despising love.

As if in a dream, Venus led Hippomenes to a mighty tree in the middle of an open field. The tree shimmered

---

3. **Hippomenes** (hi päm' i nēz)
4. **gazelle** (gǝ zel') *n.* a small, swift, graceful antelope.
5. **Venus** (vē' nǝs)

with golden leaves and golden apples. Venus told Hippomenes to pluck three of the apples from the tree, and then she told him how to use the apples in his race against Atalanta.

The crowd roared as Atalanta and Hippomenes crouched at the starting line. Under his tunic,[6] Hippomenes hid his three golden apples. When the trumpets sounded, the two shot forward and ran so fast that their bare feet barely touched the sand. They looked as if they could run over the surface of the sea without getting their feet wet—or skim over fields of corn without even bending the stalks.

The crowd cheered for Hippomenes, but Atalanta rushed ahead of him and stayed in the lead. When Hippomenes began to pant, and his chest felt as if it might burst open, he pulled one of the golden apples out from under his tunic and tossed it toward Atalanta.

The gleaming apple hit the sand and rolled across Atalanta's path. She left her course and chased after the glittering ball, and Hippomenes gained the lead. The crowd screamed with joy; but after Atalanta picked up the golden apple, she quickly made up for her delay and scooted ahead of Hippomenes.

Hippomenes tossed another golden apple. Again, Atalanta left her course, picked up the apple, then overtook Hippomenes.

As Hippomenes pulled out his third golden apple, he realized this was his last chance. He reared back his arm and hurled the apple as far as he could into a field.

Atalanta watched the golden ball fly through the air; and she hesitated, wondering whether or not she should run after it. Just as she decided not to, Venus touched her heart, prompting her to abandon her course and rush after the glittering apple.

Atalanta took off into the field after the golden apple— and Hippomenes sped toward the finish line.

Hippomenes won Atalanta for his bride, but then he made a terrible mistake: He neglected to offer gifts to Venus to thank her for helping him.

---

6. tunic (to͞o′ nik) *n.* a loose, gownlike garment, like an oversized T-shirt, worn by people in ancient Greece and Rome.

Enraged by his ingratitude, the goddess of love and beauty called upon the moon goddess, Diana, and told her to punish Hippomenes and Atalanta.

As the moon goddess studied the two proud lovers hunting in the woods and fields, she admired their strength and valor, and she decided to turn them into the animals they most resembled.

One night as Atalanta and Hippomenes lay side by side under the moonlight, changes began to happen to their bodies. They grew rough amber[7] coats, and stiff, long claws. And when dawn came, they woke and growled at the early light. Then the thick tails of the two mighty lions swept the ground as they began hunting for their breakfast.

From then on, Atalanta and Hippomenes lived together as lions deep in the woods, and only the moon goddess could tame them.

---

7. amber (am' bər) *adj.* brownish yellow in color, like the gemstone amber.

Narcissus

Jay Macpherson

Vanity and pride lead to suffering in this well-known myth.

As beautiful as Adonis[1] was the ill-fated Narcissus,[2] who from his childhood was loved by all who saw him but whose pride would let him love no one in return. At last one of those who had hopelessly courted him turned and cursed him, exclaiming: "May he suffer as we have suffered! May he too love in vain!" The avenging[3] goddess Nemesis[4] heard and approved this prayer.

There was nearby a clear pool, with shining silvery waters. No shepherd had ever come there, nor beast nor bird nor falling branch marred its surface: the grass grew fresh and green around it, and the sheltering woods kept it always cool from the midday sun.

Here once came Narcissus, heated and tired from the chase, and lay down by the pool to drink. As he bent over the water, his eyes met the eyes of another young man, gazing up at him from the depth of the pool. Deluded[5] by his reflection, Narcissus fell in love with the beauty that was his own. Without thought of food or rest he lay beside the pool addressing cries and pleas to the image, whose lips moved as he spoke but whose reply he could never catch. Echo came by, the most constant of his disdained lovers. She was a nymph who had once angered Hera, the wife of Zeus, by talking too much, and in consequence was deprived of the use of her tongue for ordinary conversation: all she could do was repeat the last words of others. Seeing Narcissus lying there, she pleaded with him in his own words. "I will die unless you pity me," cried Narcissus to his beloved. "Pity me," cried Echo as vainly to hers. Narcissus never raised his eyes to her at all, though she remained day after day beside him

---

1. **Adonis** (ə dän′ is) handsome young man loved by Aphrodite, the goddess of love.
2. **Narcissus** (när sis′ əs)
3. **avenging** (ə venj′ iŋ) *adj.* taking revenge for an injury or wrong.
4. **Nemesis** (nem′ ə sis)
5. **deluded** (di lo͞od′ əd) *adj.* fooled; misled.

on the bank, pleading as well as she was able. At last she pined away, withering and wasting with unrequited[6] love, till nothing was left of her but her voice, which the traveler still hears calling unexpectedly in woods and waste places.

As for the cruel Narcissus, he fared no better. The face that looked back at him from the water became pale, thin and haggard,[7] till at last poor Echo caught and repeated his last "Farewell!" But when she came with the other nymphs to lament[8] over his body, it was nowhere to be found. Instead, over the pool bent a new flower, white with a yellow center, which they called by his name. From this flower the Furies, the avengers of guilt, twist garlands to bind their hateful brows.

---

6. unrequited (un ri kwīt′ əd) *adj.* unreturned.
7. haggard (hag′ ərd) *adj.* looking worn from grief or illness.
8. lament (lə ment′) *v.* express deep sorrow for; mourn.

Ancient India
and China

Cities of the Indus Valley

from Lost Cities

Joyce Goldenstern

Cities disappear for many years, and if they can be unearthed centuries later, they reveal valuable information about the culture that built them, as this selection shows.

"The attackers left the dead lying where they fell. In one of the houses sprawled thirteen skeletons—men, women, and children—some wearing bracelets, rings, and beads, and two of them with sword cuts on their skulls. . . . Elsewhere again, yet another skeleton was found in a lane. And all these grim relics lay on the highest and latest level of the city, witness to its last moments."

Sir Mortimer Wheeler, a respected scholar of Indus civilization, described the gruesome scene. He was commenting on the end of a great city that flourished in the Indus Valley from 2500 B.C. to about 1500 B.C. This city, Mohenjo-daro, and its sister city, Harappa, first cradled civilization on the Indian subcontinent. The two cities had prospered for nearly a thousand years. Commerce and river trade helped support the two cities, but they drew their greatest wealth from agriculture. Wheat, barley, dates, field peas, and even cotton prospered on the fertile soil of the Indus river valley. Mohenjo-daro lay near the Indus River in what today is Pakistan. Harappa lay about four hundred miles northeast on the Ravi River—a tributary of the mighty Indus.

Accomplished Artisans The wealth from agriculture supported many crafts. Toolmakers crafted chisels, axes, knives, and other tools from bronze and copper. Potters used wheels to throw pots, and then painted them with red ochre.[1] Weavers wove cotton into garments. Some artisans must have even known how to create statues using molds. Among the ruins, archaeologists found a statue of a pert and pretty dancer cast in bronze.

The inhabitants had had leisure time. They threw dice and played board games. They made toys for their

---

1. **ochre** (ō' kər) *n.* a yellow or reddish brown clay.

children: little birds and tiny carts with wheels—miniatures of real oxcarts that adults used for plowing. The people of these river cities evidently had a strong sense of ownership: Archaeologists found hundreds of seals, used for marking belongings, and decorated with a sunken pattern of an animal—elephants, rhinoceroses, antelopes, crocodiles, even unicorns. Most impressively, though, inscriptions marked each seal. Perhaps the inscriptions were personal names. No one knows for sure, because no one has been able to decipher them. Nonetheless, the inscriptions show that the people of the Indus valley had developed writing. About 1500 B.C., Aryans invaded the Indian subcontinent, and everything started to change.

Fort Destroyers   Until the 1920s, no one in modern times knew about the people of Mohenjo-daro and Harappa. Both cities lay buried and forgotten. It was thought that the warrior Aryans were the first to bring civilization to the Indus Valley. The Aryans, it was thought, had found wandering tribes when they arrived. Yet some scholars wondered: In the Aryan saga *Rig-Veda*, there were references to forts. Indra, chief god of the Aryans, was called *Purmamdara*, which means "fort destroyer." One passage described Indra destroying ninety forts; in another passage, Indra "rends forts as age consumes a garment." Scholars wondered whether this meant that the conquering Aryans had found a settled civilization, rather than a nomadic people.

Excavation   In the 1920s, the Indian Archaeological Survey excavated many sites in the Indus Valley. It was during these excavations that archaeologists unearthed the cities: first Harappa, and then Mohenjo-daro.

Harappa, a city about three miles in circumference, stood on a huge mound. Its most remarkable structure, a citadel[2] about 460 yards long and 215 yards wide, rose high above the city. Bastions[3] projected above the fort, a mighty baked-brick wall surrounded it, and gates prevented enemies from entering. To the north of the fort stood huge granaries. Straight streets ran in a perfect grid.

---

2. **citadel** (sit'ə del) *n.* a fort on a commanding height.
3. **bastions** (bas' chənz) *n.* projections from a fort.

On the streets, modest but spacious houses once stood. They contained bathrooms and latrines. The city had excellent sewer and drainage systems.

Mohenjo-daro, just like its sister city, boasted a towering citadel and huge granaries. The plan of the city followed a design similar to that of Harappa. Sewers and drainage systems were evident. Most impressive was a huge public bath, made watertight with baked bricks. Archaeologists found these structures in even better condition than those at Harappa. The mystery of the forts mentioned in the *Rig-Veda* had evidently been solved.

A Lesson of Ecology The skeletons described by Wheeler testify to many raids on the cities, but scholars do not hold the Aryans completely responsible for the decline of the ancient civilization. Many other factors may have caused its fall. Some anthropologists who specialize in environmental issues speculate that the ecology of the region may have been a factor. The rivers had been a source of wealth for the inhabitants, offering trade routes and soil fertile from flooding. But the rivers could also have contributed to problems.

Some theorize that the inhabitants may have destroyed the forests surrounding the rivers. The Indus and Ravi valley people used huge quantities of baked bricks in their structures. Some anthropologists reason that the inhabitants kept cutting down trees for fuel to bake the bricks. For about a thousand years, structures continually had to be mended and rebuilt. Old cities crumbled, and new ones were built on top of them. As trees were cut down, the bare hills no longer absorbed the water from heavy rains. The rainwater could rush down the hills to the swelling river, and even high dikes might fail. As the people struggled with floods, their resources and energy may have dwindled. When Aryan invaders challenged them, the weakened inhabitants could not defend their magnificent forts.

The Race

Retold by Debjani Chatterjee

*This myth from India has information about Hindu be-
liefs and a competition between brothers that reveals universal ideas.*

This is a story about Ganesh's wisdom, his devotion to
his mother, and the rivalry between him and his younger
brother.

No two brothers could be more different. Kartikeya,
the younger son of Shiva and Parvati, is a most handsome god—and he knows it! Tall, slim, and athletic, Kartikeya is god of War and is accomplished in using all
weapons. Like some young boys he is also rather vain
about his appearance and abilities. Appropriately, his
symbol and pet is the peacock, the most beautiful of all
birds and the national bird of India. Kartikeya enjoyed
energetic games and contests where he could compete
with other gods, especially with his elder brother, and of
course win.

One day Kartikeya was teasing his plump elder brother
and challenged him to a race! Ganesh was used to his
ways, so he smiled but continued reading a book.

"Look mother," Kartikeya appealed, "he does nothing
but poke his trunk in a book all day long. Tell him that
we gods should fly around and patrol the world once in a
while. I'm flying about all the time on my peacock. I am
surely a better god than he is?"

"We shall see," was Parvati's answer. Then she set her
sons a little test. She asked them both to go once
around the universe and whoever returned first would
be the winner. Parvati would give the winner a special
blessing.

Kartikeya leapt up in excitement. "I'll get on my peacock right away and I'll be back in no time at all," he
boasted. The young god laughed to think of Ganesh
riding on his tiny rat. It would take him millions, maybe
billions or even zillions of years to go around the
universe. "You may as well give up right now," said
Kartikeya, "because you haven't a hope of winning!"

Waving a cheery goodbye, Kartikeya was off on his colorful bird. Ganesh just sat and quietly thought for a moment. He joined the palms of his hands together and bowed his head in prayer to the Goddess Parvati. Then he climbed on his rat and very slowly, full of dignity, he began to ride in a circle around his mother.

It took Kartikeya a full day and a night to fly once around the entire universe. So swiftly did he fly that he hardly saw the planets, stars and moons, that went whizzing past. At last, happy and proud, Kartikeya presented himself to his mother, fully expecting to be greeted as the winner.

But, "Kartikeya, it is your brother who was first," were Parvati's astonishing words. The goddess knew that her younger son needed to be taught a lesson if he was to grow up. "Your speed was no match for his wisdom!"

Kartikeya could hardly believe that he had heard correctly. But he knew that his mother always spoke the truth. He turned to Ganesh and asked curiously, "How did you manage it? How can you go around the universe so quickly on your rat?"

"Little brother, our mother who gave us birth and who looks after us, is also the Creator of everything and everyone in the universe. The sun rises in the east, the stars shine at night, the birds sing, the rivers flow, only because our mother wills it. When you see people, animals, trees, mountains, even gods, you are reminded of the great Mother who made all. We are all part of her. She *is* the universe! So I simply went around her," explained Ganesh.

Kartikeya at once understood what his brother was trying to say and felt ashamed of his earlier pride and boasting. He humbly asked Ganesh to pardon him and then bowed to Parvati.

"Mother, will you also forgive me? Because you are so loving and I am young and foolish, I think of you as mine only. I forget that you are the universal Mother."

Parvati stretched out her graceful arms and tenderly called both gods to her.

"My sons, you are both winners," she said. "A mother's love is freely given and there can be no child who fails to win her blessing. You both have my blessings. May you, in turn, be a blessing to all who call to you in their need."

The Major Gods and Goddesses of Hindu Mythology

BRAHMA: The creator of the universe.

VISHNU: The preserver of the universe; Vishnu saves humankind and destroys evil.

SHIVA: The destroyer of the universe; Shiva rides a bull called Nandi.

INDRA: King of the gods and the rain giver.

PARVATI: Shiva's wife and the goddess of motherhood.

GANESH: The elephant-headed god; the Hindu god of wisdom.

KARTIKEYA: The god of war.

The Envious Buffalo

A Jataka Story *from* The Fables of India

Retold by Joseph Gaer

*People around the world have always used stories to
teach important lessons. The Jataka stories from India
teach such lessons. They are part of Buddhism's sacred
writings. Many of the Jataka stories are fables, like this
one. A fable is a brief story with few characters. It teaches
a simple lesson about life called a moral.*

On a small farm in southern India there lived a water
buffalo named Big Red Bubalus with his younger brother
named Little Red Bubalus. These two brothers did all the
hard work on the farm. They plowed and they harrowed;[1]
they seeded; and they brought in the harvest for their
owner. In between the crops they worked the water wheel
which irrigated the farm and the garden; and they turned
the pump to supply water for the house and pigpen.

When the crop was in, Big Red Bubalus and Little Red
Bubalus were harnessed again to turn the grindstone
which milled the flour for the family.

Yet for all their labors they were rarely rewarded. They
were seldom allowed to bathe in the stream, which they
loved to do. And all they were given to eat was grass and
straw, or chaff[2] when the grain was husked.[3]

This same farmer owned a pig who did nothing but eat
and wallow in the water pumped up for him by the buf-
faloes. Yet the hog was fed on rice and millet[4] and was
well taken care of by the farmer and his family.

Little Red Bubalus complained to his brother: "We,
who do all the hard work, are treated shabbily and our
master gives us next to nothing to eat. Most of the time
we have to go out into the pasture to find our own food.
Yet this lazy pig is fed all the time and never does any
work."

---

1. harrow *v.* to break up soil.
2. chaff *n.* the coverings removed from seeds of grain before the grain is ground
into flour.
3. husk *v.* to remove the coverings from seeds of grain.
4. millet (mil'it) *n.* a kind of grain.

"Envy him not, little brother," said Big Red Bubalus (who was the Bodisat[5] in the form of a buffalo). And he would say no more.

Again and again the younger buffalo would complain; and each time the older buffalo merely said:

"Envy not the pig."

One day the farmer's only daughter was engaged to be married. And as the wedding day drew near, the hog was slaughtered and roasted for the wedding feast.

Then Big Red Bubalus said to Little Red Bubalus: "Now do you see why a pig is not to be envied?"

And Little Red Bubalus replied: "Yes, now I understand. It is better to feed on straw and chaff, and to live out our lives, than to be fattened on rice only to end up on a roasting spit."

---

5. Bodisat the Buddha-to-be, who appears in the Jataka stories as a king, teacher, lion, monkey, or other creature.

from The Analects

Confucius

Translated by Arthur Waley

The teachings of Confucius helped shape Chinese society for more than two thousand years. Here is a brief selection of those teachings.

The Master[1] said, To learn and at due times to repeat what one has learnt, is that not after all[2] a pleasure? That friends should come to one from afar, is this not after all delightful? To remain unsoured even though one's merits are unrecognized by others, is that not after all what is expected of a gentleman?

The Master said, A young man's duty is to behave well to his parents at home and to his elders abroad, to be cautious in giving promises and punctual in keeping them, to have kindly feelings towards everyone, but seek the intimacy of the Good. If, when all that is done, he has any energy to spare, then let him study the polite arts.[3]

The Master said, (the good man) does not grieve that other people do not recognize his merits. His only anxiety is lest he should fail to recognize theirs.

The Master said, He who rules by moral force is like the pole-star,[4] which remains in its place while all the lesser stars do homage to it.

The Master said, If out of three hundred Songs[5] I had to take one phrase to cover all my teaching, I would say, "Let there be no evil in your thoughts."

The Master said, Govern the people by regulations, keep order among them by chastisements,[6] and they will flee from you, and lose all self-respect. Govern them by moral force, keep order among them by ritual, and they will keep their self-respect and come to you of their own accord.

---

1. **The Master** Confucius.
2. **after all** even though one does not hold public office.
3. **the polite arts** such activities as reciting from *The Book of Songs*, practicing archery, and learning proper behavior.
4. **pole-star** Polaris, the North Star.
5. **three hundred Songs** poems in *The Book of Songs*.
6. **chastisements** (chas tiz′ mintz) *n.* punishments.

Meng Wu Po[7] asked about the treatment of parents. The Master said, Behave in such a way that your father and mother have no anxiety about you, except concerning your health.

The Master said, A gentleman can see a question from all sides without bias. The small man is biased and can see a question only from one side.

The Master said, Yu[8] shall I teach you what knowledge is? When you know a thing, to recognize that you know it, and when you do not know a thing, to recognize that you do not know it. That is knowledge.

The Master said, High office filled by men of narrow views, ritual performed without reverence, the forms of mourning observed without grief—these are things I cannot bear to see!

The Master said, In the presence of a good man, think all the time how you may learn to equal him. In the presence of a bad man, turn your gaze within!

The Master said, In old days a man kept a hold on his words, fearing the disgrace that would ensue should he himself fail to keep pace with them.

The Master said, A gentleman covets the reputation of being slow in word but prompt in deed.

The Master said, In old days men studied for the sake of self-improvement; nowadays men study in order to impress other people.

The Master said, A gentleman is ashamed to let his words outrun his deeds.

The Master said, He who will not worry about what is far off will soon find something worse than worry close at hand.

The Master said, To demand much from oneself and little from others is the way (for a ruler) to banish discontent.

---

7. **Meng Wu Po** (muŋ wōo bō) the son of one of Confucius' disciples.
8. **Yu** (yoo) Tzu-lu, one of Confucius' disciples.

from the Tao Te Ching

Lao Tzu

Translated by D. C. Lau

This poem from the Tao Te Ching *expresses the Taoist belief that life is a mystery, one that cannot be understood or even described using conventional methods.*

I

The way that can be spoken of
Is not the constant way;
The name that can be named
Is not the constant name,
5   The nameless was the beginning of heaven and
       earth;
The named was the mother of the myriad
       creatures.[1]
Hence always rid yourself of desires in order to
       observe its secrets;
But always allow yourself to have desires in order
       to observe its manifestations.[2]
These two are the same
10   But diverge in name as they issue forth.
Being the same they are called mysteries,
Mystery upon mystery—
The gateway of the manifold[3] secrets.

III

Not to honor men of worth will keep the people
from contention[4]; not to value goods which are
hard to come by will keep them from theft; not
to display what is desirable will keep them from
being unsettled of mind.
15   Therefore in governing the people, the sage
empties their minds but fills their bellies,
weakens their wills but strengthens their bones.

---

1. **myriad** (mir′ ē əd) *adj.* countless.
2. **manifestations** (man ə fes tā′ shənz) *n.* forms in which something is shown or experienced.
3. **manifold** (man′ ə fold′) *adj.* having many forms.
4. **contention** (kən ten′ shən) *n.* disputing; quarreling.

He always keeps them innocent of knowledge
and free from desire, and ensures that the
clever never dare to act.
Do that which consists in taking no action,
and order will prevail.

IX

Rather than fill it to the brim by keeping it
    upright
Better to have stopped in time,[5]
Hammer it to a point
20   And the sharpness cannot be preserved forever:
There may be gold and jade to fill a hall
But there is none who can keep them.
To be overbearing when one has wealth and
    position
Is to bring calamity[6] upon oneself.
25   To retire when the task is accomplished
Is the way of heaven.

The most submissive[7] thing in the world can ride
roughshod over the hardest in the world—that which is
without substance entering that which has no crevices.

    That is why I know the benefit of resorting to no ac-
tion. The teaching that uses no words, the benefit of re-
sorting to no action, these are beyond the understanding
of all but a very few in the world.

---

5. Rather than . . . in time These lines refer to a container that stands in position
when empty but overturns when full.
6. calamity (kə lam′ ə tē) *n.* deep trouble.
7. submissive (sub mis′ iv) *adj.* yielding; giving in.

The Mice That Set Elephants Free

from the Panchatantra

Vishnusharman

Translated by Arthur W. Ryder

This selection is from ancient India's famous "how-to" book, a collection of tales that taught young princes how to rule a kingdom and conduct their lives.

There once was a region where people, houses, and temples had fallen into decay. So the mice, who were old settlers there, occupied the chinks in the floors of stately dwellings with sons, grandsons (both in the male and female line), and further descendants as they were born, until their holes formed a dense tangle. They found uncommon happiness in a variety of festivals, dramatic performances (with plots of their own invention), wedding-feasts, eating-parties, drinking-bouts, and similar diversions. And so the time passed.

But into this scene burst an elephant-king, whose retinue[1] numbered thousands. He, with his herd, had started for the lake upon information that there was water there. As he marched through the mouse community, he crushed faces, eyes, heads, and necks of such mice as he encountered.

Then the survivors held a convention. "We are being killed," they said, "by these lumbering[2] elephants—curse them! If they come this way again, there will not be mice enough for seed.[3] Besides:

> An elephant will kill you, if
> He touch; a serpent if he sniff;
> King's laughter has a deadly sting;
> A rascal kills by honoring.

Therefore let us devise a remedy effective in this crisis."

---

1. **retinue** (ret'n yoo') *n.* a train of followers.
2. **lumbering** (lum'bər iŋ) *adj.* moving heavily and clumsily.
3. **seed** descendants; posterity.

When they had done so, a certain number went to the lake, bowed before the elephant-king, and said respectfully: "O king, not far from here is our community, inherited from a long line of ancestors. There we have prospered through a long succession of sons and grandsons. Now you gentlemen, while coming here to water, have destroyed us by the thousand. Furthermore, if you travel that way again, there will not be enough of us for seed. If then you feel compassion toward us, pray travel another path. Consider the fact that even creatures of our size will some day prove of some service."

And the elephant-king turned over in his mind what he had heard, decided that the statement of the mice was entirely logical, and granted their request.

Now in the course of time a certain king commanded his elephant-trappers to trap elephants. And they constructed a so-called water-trap, caught the king with his herd, three days later dragged him out with a great tackle made of ropes and things, and tied him to stout trees in that very bit of forest.

When the trappers had gone, the elephant-king reflected thus: "In what manner, or through whose assistance, shall I be delivered?" Then it occurred to him: "We have no means of deliverance[4] except those mice."

So the king sent the mice an exact description of his disastrous position in the trap through one of his personal retinue, an elephant-cow[5] who had not ventured into the trap, and who had previous information of the mouse community.

When the mice learned the matter, they gathered by the thousand, eager to return the favor shown them, and visited the elephant herd. And seeing king and herd fettered,[6] they gnawed the guy-ropes[7] where they stood, then swarmed up the branches, and by cutting the ropes aloft, set their friends free.

---

4. **deliverance** (di liv' ər əns) *n.* rescue; release.
5. **elephant-cow** female adult elephant.
6. **fettered** (fet' ərd) *adj.* shackled; tied; chained.
7. **guy-ropes** ropes used to steady, secure, or guide something.

The Brahman, the Thief, and the Ghost

from the Panchatantra

Vishnusharman

Translated by Arthur W. Ryder

Here is another selection from ancient India's famous "how-to" book. This tale features both a thief and a ghost!

There was once a poor Brahman[1] in a certain place. He lived on presents, and always did without such luxuries as fine clothes and ointments and perfumes and garlands and gems and betel-gum.[2] His beard and his nails were long, and so was the hair that covered his head and his body. Heat, cold, rain, and the like had dried him up.

Then someone pitied him and gave him two calves. And the Brahman began when they were little and fed them on butter and oil and fodder[3] and other things that he begged. So he made them very plump.

Then a thief saw them and the idea came to him at once: "I will steal these two cows from this Brahman." So he took a rope and set out at night. But on the way he met a fellow with a row of sharp teeth set far apart, with a high-bridged nose and uneven eyes, with limbs covered with knotty muscles, with hollow cheeks, with beard and body as yellow as a fire with much butter in it.

And when the thief saw him, he started with acute[4] fear and said: "Who are you, sir?"

The other said: "I am a ghost named Truthful. It is now your turn to explain yourself."

The thief said: "I am a thief, and my acts are cruel. I am on my way to steal two cows from a poor Brahman."

Then the ghost felt relieved and said: "My dear sir, I take one meal every three days. So I will just eat this

---

1. Brahman (brä′ mən) *n.* in Hindu culture, a member of the highest caste, or class—that of priests—though not necessarily a member of the richest class.
2. betel-gum (bēt′l gum) *n.* reddish chewing gum made from the nuts and leaves of betel palm trees. This gum is chewed by many people in Asian and Pacific cultures for pleasure, and as a digestive aid.
3. fodder (fäd′ ər) *n.* coarse food, such as cornstalks and hay, used to feed cows and other livestock.
4. acute (ə kyo͞ot′) *adj.* sharp.

Brahman today. It is delightful that you and I are on the same errand."

So together they went there and hid, waiting for the proper moment. And when the Brahman went to sleep, the ghost started forward to eat him. But the thief saw him and said: "My dear sir, this is not right. You are not to eat the Brahman until I have stolen his two cows."

The ghost said: "The racket would most likely wake the Brahman. In that case all my trouble would be in vain."

"But, on the other hand," said the thief, "if any hindrance[5] arises when you start to eat him, then I cannot steal the two cows either. First I will steal the two cows, then you may eat the Brahman."

So they disputed, each crying "Me first! Me first!" And when they became heated, the hubbub[6] waked the Brahman. Then the thief said: "Brahman, this is a ghost who wishes to eat you." And the ghost said: "Brahman, this is a thief who wishes to steal your two cows."

When the Brahman heard this, he stood up and took a good look. And by remembering a prayer to his favorite god, he saved his life from the ghost, then lifted a club and saved his two cows from the thief.

---

5. hindrance (hin′ drəns) *n*. an obstacle.
6. hubbub (hu′ bub) *n*. noise; commotion.

Buddhism

from One World, Many Religions

Mary Pope Osborne

This story of one of the world's major religions begins with a young prince called Siddhartha.

"Be Ye Lamps Unto Yourselves."

—Buddha's Farewell Address, from the *Mahaparinibbana Suttana*

Five hundred years before Jesus was born, a young prince named Siddhartha[1] Gautama was born in the country we now call Nepal.[2] Siddhartha was raised as a Hindu. He read the great writings of Hinduism and practiced Hindu rituals.

Siddhartha had little knowledge of the world outside his luxurious palace. One day when he went out among his people, he was greatly disturbed by four sights: a very old man, a very sick man, a man who had just died, and a wandering monk, or holy man.

The first three sights sorrowed the young prince. He wondered, why do people grow old? Why do they get sick? Why do they suffer and die? Siddhartha decided that he should become a monk himself, so that he could go into the world and search for answers to his questions.

Siddhartha took off his royal garments and put on a faded orange robe. He shaved his hair and his beard. Then he left his palace forever and set out in search of wisdom.

* * *

Siddhartha wandered for six years. Then one night when the moon was full, he stopped to rest under a fig tree. He vowed not to move until he had found answers to his questions.

Siddhartha sat in a cross-legged position. He closed his eyes and began practicing a form of yoga[3] meditation. He concentrated on the great Hindu teachings. He

---

1. **Siddhartha** (sid där′ tə)
2. **Nepal** (nə pâl′) *n.* country in the Himalayas, between India and Tibet.
3. **yoga** (yō gə) *n.* a mystic Hindu discipline that involves intense concentration, deep breathing, and exercise postures.

thought about the endless cycle of death and rebirth. He thought about human pain and suffering.

During his meditation, Siddhartha had a revelation—a sudden divine understanding—that explained everything to him. He understood that people could find an end to suffering. To followers of Buddhism, this new and powerful insight is known as the Enlightenment. When it happened to Siddhartha, he became known as the Buddha.

The Buddha believed that other people could achieve enlightenment as well—but before they did, they had to free themselves from all their worldly desires, such as the desire for riches, for a good job, for a wife or a husband. This special freedom is known as detachment. The Buddha's understanding of suffering and detachment is called dharma.[4] The dharma represents all the teachings of Buddhism.

The basic message of the Buddha's teaching is summed up in the Four Noble Truths. They are clear and simple: All lives are filled with suffering. Suffering comes from a desire for worldly things. Suffering ends when desire ends. People can learn to end desire by following eight rules.

The eight rules, known as the Noble Eightfold Path, are:

Right understanding: Be aware of the Buddha's teachings.
Right intentions: Try to follow these teachings wholeheartedly.
Right speech: Say nothing to harm others.
Right action: Do nothing to harm any living creature.
Right livelihood: Choose a job that hurts no living thing.
Right effort: Strive to become a good person.
Right mindfulness: Learn to control all your thoughts and emotions in order to quiet your mind.
Right concentration: Practice the deepest meditation, which leads to the highest state of enlightenment, known as Nirvana.

Nirvana is something that happens when one is completely released from suffering. It is so different from everyday life that Buddhists believe it cannot be described.

* * *

For forty-five years, the Buddha walked all over the land, teaching people how to find enlightenment. As he taught,

---

4. **dharma** (där′ mə)

a new religion grew around him. This religion was different from Hinduism in several ways. The Buddha taught that following the Noble Eightfold Path could be done without the long fasts and difficult yoga practices of Hindu holy men and women. This less difficult path became known as the Middle Way. Another difference was that the Buddha did not believe in the Hindu caste system. And he did not believe in worshiping the many Hindu gods and goddesses. According to one legend, someone once asked him if he were God.

"No," he said.

"Are you a saint?"

"No."

"What are you then?"

"I am awake," he said.

This is one meaning of the name Buddha: the Awakened One, one who has finally woken up to the truth.

At the age of eighty, the Buddha died from food poisoning. After his death, his followers saved some of his bones and teeth as relics—sacred religious objects—believing that his power still resided in them.

Special structures called stupas[5] were built to house the relics. Today, there are thousands of stupas throughout Asia. Because there are a limited number of relics, most stupas house sacred writings and images instead.

Since the Buddha's death, countless images of him have been erected inside temples and at outdoor shrines. These statues and images give worshipers a sense of the Buddha's loving presence.

* * *

The Buddha organized his followers into a holy community of monks and nuns—men and women who devoted their entire lives to their religion. For centuries after his death, monks and nuns kept Buddhism alive. They inscribed the Buddha's wisdom on palm leaves and stored the leaves in baskets. Eventually, these writings became part of a huge collection of Buddhist scriptures. Buddhist monks and nuns spread the word about the Buddha's teachings, and today there are more than 300 million Buddhists in the world, making Buddhism the world's fourth largest religion.

5. stupa (stoo′ pə)

Confucianism and Taoism

from One World, Many Religions

Mary Pope Osborne

Confucius and Lao Tsu were the original masters of two important religions in China. Here is a description of the major beliefs of each religion.

> *"I am a Transmitter and not a creator. I believe in and have a passion for the Ancients."*

—The Analects of Confucius: VII. I

China is the home of the oldest civilization in the world. Today, the Communist government of China discourages its people from practicing religion. But throughout much of China's history, three religions played an important part in everyday life. They were Buddhism, Confucianism, and Taoism.

Confucianism is based on the ideas of a humble Chinese scholar named Confucius. When the Buddha was teaching in India 2,500 years ago, Confucius was teaching in China. The son of a military officer, Confucius studied music, poetry, and the writing of China's ancient sages, or wise men.

For centuries, the sages had taught the Chinese people how to live a good life. But in Confucius's time, leaders had forgotten the teachings of the past. Society had fallen into chaos, and greed and violence had taken over.

Afraid that China's great civilization might be destroyed forever, Confucius began traveling around his country, teaching the wisdom of the sages.

Confucius taught the old traditions, which were based on goodness and truth. He said that government leaders should stop being so selfish and should start caring for their people the way a loving father cares for his family. He said that people should start respecting their leaders, their parents, and their ancestors; and that rich and poor children alike should get a good education.

Confucius also taught the ancient Chinese belief that everything in the universe is a combination of two forces called yin and yang. Yin is all that is cold, dark, moon-like, and mysterious. Yang is the opposite of yin—everything that is bright, warm, sunlike, and clear. All growth and change come from a combination of these two forces.

Confucius also said that all people should be courteous and kind to one another. One of his best-known sayings is: "Never do to others what you would not like them to do to you." Most major religions teach a version of this saying, which is sometimes called the golden rule.

Confucius thought of his teachings as a guide to wisdom and good behavior rather than as a religion. But after his death, temples were built to honor him, and Confucianism became the official religion of China. Applicants for government jobs had to study the books of Confucianism, and rulers relied on Confucian scholars for help and advice.

Confucius believed his duty was only to remind people of the teachings of the ancient sages. But he brought new meaning to the wisdom of the past. For more than two thousand years, many Chinese have considered him the wisest sage of all. A plaque in a Confucian temple in Taiwan, the main island of the Republic of China, calls Confucius "the great teacher of 10,000 generations."

Taoism began with a man named Lao-tzu, who lived during the time of Confucius. Not much is known about Lao-tzu, whose name means "Old Master." Legend says that when he was a very old man, he grew tired of war and violence and decided to leave China. He drove an ox cart to the border of the country. But a guard there recognized the wise thinker and wouldn't let him pass until he wrote down all his wisdom.

The Old Master quickly wrote his teaching in a short book that later came to be called the *Tao Te Ching*. For many centuries, the *Tao Te Ching* was one of the most important books in China.

The teaching of the *Tao Te Ching* concerns a mysterious force in the universe called the Tao. The word *Tao* means "the way," or "the road." The Tao is the infinite source of all life, and it is impossible to truly name. The more you try to name it, the more it escapes you. The Tao is often described as a flowing stream. Just as you cannot hold flowing water in your hands, you cannot grasp the Tao.

Taoism teaches that in order to live in harmony with the Tao, you should try to live a quiet and simple life close to nature. You should be humble and compassionate. You should do your work without seeking fame or fortune.

Like Confucius, Lao-tzu wasn't interested in creating a religion. But over time, his teachings were combined with Chinese folk religions—the ancient customs and religious practices of ordinary people. Taoism began to include beliefs in gods and goddesses, dragons and magicians, spells and charms. The ancient Chinese religion of ancestor veneration, or respect, also became increasingly important in Taoism.

Folk tradition teaches that the ancestors connect the world of the living to the world of the gods. If people honor their ancestors, the spirits of the ancestors will protect them. During the Chinese New Year celebration, the most important Chinese religious holiday of the year, families gather to feast and honor their ancestors.

After the Chinese Communists took over China in 1949, they discouraged the people of mainland China from following their traditional religions. But in Taiwan, Hong Kong, and other parts of the world, including the United States, many Chinese people still practice a combination of Confucianism, Taoism, folk religion, and Buddhism.

Each religion offers something different. Families might revere the wise Confucius and study his teachings. At the same time, they might keep a shrine to worship a Taoist god, a shrine to honor the Buddha, and a special place to honor their ancestors. For Chinese people, all these ways of worship unite to form one spiritual world.

The Great Wall of China

from Walls: Defenses Throughout History

James Cross Giblin

As this selection shows, the age and the extraordinary length of the Great Wall of China make it one of the engineering marvels of the world.

When Hadrian's Wall[1] was new, another wall already stretched across a vast country on the other side of the world. This rampart is the longest structure ever built. It contains enough building materials to circle the entire globe at the equator with a wall eight feet high and three feet thick. It is the only man-made structure on earth that can be seen with the naked eye from the moon. It is the Great Wall of China.

The Great Wall extends across northern and central China from the Yellow Sea in the east to a point deep in central Asia. There are different estimates of its overall length. Those who count only its distance east to west say it is approximately sixteen hundred miles long. Others claim that, with all of its loops and offshoots included, the wall is more than thirty-six hundred miles long. If straightened, they say, it would cross the United States from New York City to San Francisco, and there would be enough left over to wind back to Salt Lake City.

Construction of the wall spread over almost two thousand years, from 400 B.C., when the first sections were erected, until the 1600s A.D., when it was rebuilt and extended. But most of the wall was built in the ten years between 224 and 214 B.C. by Emperor Shih Huang-ti.

Shih was the first ruler to unify the scattered city states of China into a single nation. He accomplished this by a ruthless use of force. Like Adolf Hitler in the twentieth century, Shih ordered the burning of books he disagreed with, especially the writings of the philosopher Confucius. When some scholars continued to teach from these books, Shih had the scholars buried alive as an example to others who might think of disobeying him.

---

1. Hadrian's Wall a stone wall built across northern England to protect Roman Britain.

So that people and goods could travel easily from one part of China to another, Shih embarked on a vast road- and canal-building program. And to protect his new nation from northern invaders, Shih launched his most ambitious project—the linking of many smaller, older walls into one great defensive wall.

Such a wall was badly needed. For years the Tartars and other nomadic tribes had swept across the loosely defended border and attacked Chinese living in settled communities. The nomads[2] looted Chinese homes, shops, and temples, burned the settlements to the ground, killed most of the men and children, and carried off some of the women as slaves.

The nomads laid siege to larger cities, too. Sometimes the inhabitants managed to hold out for a few weeks behind their city's walls. But unless an army garrison came to relieve them, the city dwellers were usually forced by hunger and disease to surrender. Then the looting, burning, and killing began all over again.

To prevent such terrible raids and bring hope to Chinese living on the border, Emperor Shih made construction of the Great Wall his first priority. He assigned an army of three hundred thousand men under one of his best generals, Meng Tien, to work on the project. Local laborers were recruited to assist the soldiers. Among them were thousands of women, who were hired to weave tents and help to carry loads.

Some of the hardest jobs were given to prisoners who were sent to the construction sites under armed guard. Besides common criminals, these prisoners included many people who had been captured in war or arrested for political reasons.

Historians estimate that all told more than a million people worked on the Great Wall. They labored from dawn to dusk, in freezing winter blizzards and blinding summer sandstorms. Clay for bricks was carried in baskets at the ends of shoulder poles. Building stones often had to be transported for long distances on crude sledges or wagons. In mountainous areas, the stones were sometimes raised into position by teams of specially trained goats.

---

2. nomad (nō′ mad) *n.* a member of a tribe or group having no permanent home but moving around constantly in search of food, pasture, etc.

Most of the workers suffered under harsh living conditions. Food rations frequently ran short and wells dried up. Flimsy tents offered little protection from blazing summer heat or sub-zero winter temperatures. Another problem was surprise attacks by nomadic enemy tribes. Often the soldiers in General Meng's army had to stop work in order to protect the other laborers.

As a result of all this, according to some Chinese historians, more than four hundred thousand men and women died while working on the wall. That was almost half the total work force. Many of the dead were buried within the wall, causing some people to call it "the longest cemetery in the world."

Reports of the human suffering along the wall inspired Chinese storytellers to create myths and legends. One of the best known centered on a princess from a captured city-state whose husband was sent to work on the wall. Like countless others he died and was buried in it.

After overcoming her grief, the princess set out for the wall to find her husband's body. No one could tell her where it was among the thousands of other corpses. The princess was about to give up the search when a spirit suddenly appeared before her.

"Cut your finger and hold it in front of you," the spirit said. "Follow where the blood falls. There you will find your husband's body."

Having spoken, the spirit vanished.

The princess was startled, but she followed the spirit's instructions. After a time the trail of her blood led her, as if by magic, to a gap in the wall where she found her husband's corpse. She took it back to her native city and reburied it with all the proper ceremonies.

At last, after more than ten years, the Great Wall was completed. Its thirty-five-hundred-mile route ran across plains and deserts, bridged ravines and rivers, and climbed over mountains as high as six thousand feet above sea level.

The wall was generally twenty-five feet wide at the base, slanting to seventeen feet at the top. It was between twenty-five and thirty feet high. In eastern China, where rocks were plentiful, the sides were faced with large stones or granite boulders, and the top was paved with bricks. The interior was composed of small stones and earth, cemented with a mortar so hard that nails couldn't be driven into it.

Five-foot-high stone parapets[3] rose on both sides of the wall's flat top. The parapets had openings at regular intervals through which arrows could be shot at attackers. The top itself served as a road, wide enough for eight people to walk abreast, or two horse-drawn chariots to pass each other.

Farther west, the wall crossed barren deserts where stones were scarce. In those sectors it was constructed of earth alone. The builders moistened the earth with water carried from distant wells, and pounded it to make it solid.

Every few hundred yards along the wall, a watchtower rose about twelve feet above the walkway. These towers were manned by small groups of soldiers and served as lookout posts. If the soldiers saw a hostile band approaching the wall, they sent up a signal—smoke during the day, colored lights at night. The lights came from blazing logs that were coated with metal oxides to produce different colors. A red light meant danger, a blue one signified that all was quiet.

There were also many larger *garrison towers*, or forts, along the wall. Each of these could hold between one hundred and two hundred soldiers with their weapons, ammunition, and provisions. When a danger signal sent from a watchtower was seen at one of the garrison towers, the soldiers stationed there raced along the top of the wall to the spot that was threatened.

The entire wall was probably not garrisoned at any given time; that would have required many millions of soldiers. But historians estimate that in the days of Shih Huang-ti an army of perhaps a million men guarded the rampart.

For centuries the Great Wall protected northern China against small-scale attacks. But gradually the number of troops manning it was reduced, and large sections fell into ruin. In 1211 A.D. it proved no barrier to the Mongol leader Genghis Khan. He and his horse soldiers broke through the wall's defenses and conquered much of China.

---

3. parapet (par′ ə pet) *n.* a low wall or railing.

The Mongols were driven out of China in the late 1300s and the wall was rebuilt. Frontier defense forces patrolled its fortifications from Manchuria in the east to Kansu in the west, and kept China largely free of Mongol raiders.

As the military threat from the north lessened, much of the wall was abandoned again. People living nearby started chipping away at it and removing stones to use in building houses and temples. Over time, long stretches of the wall—especially those made of earth—simply crumbled into dust. Other sections remained intact, however. During the war with Japan in the 1930s, Chinese soldiers marched to the northern front along the ancient brick road atop the wall.

After the Chinese Communists took power in 1949, several sections of the wall were restored once more—not as a military fortification but as a historical monument. Today the Communists point to the wall with pride, saying that "it embodies the wisdom and blood and sweat of the Chinese working people." The restored section north of Peking has become a major tourist attraction, visited each year by thousands of people from all over the world.

It takes two hours to reach this restored section by train or bus. Suddenly, craggy mountains loom into view above the plain, and then the wall itself appears, curving over and around the mountains like a giant stone snake.

From the parking lot, steep inclines lead up to watchtowers at both ends of the restored section. It's a hard climb, but the view from the towers is worth the effort. Gazing out at the wall as it winds away across the mountains, one can't help but be amazed at the simple fact that it's there.

Besides its appeal as a tourist attraction, the wall is being used in other ways today. Scientists study it to learn the effects of earthquakes that occurred in the past. Archaeologists dig in and around it in search of tools and other objects from the time when it was built.

And previously unknown sections are still being discovered. In 1983 archaeologists unearthed a sixty-two-mile segment, thus adding to the already incredible length of the Great Wall of China—truly one of the wonders of the world.

To Agni (God of Fire)

from the Rig Veda

translated by P. Lal

This poem from the famous Rig Veda *asks the god of fire to scatter evil with light.*

Scattering evil with light,
Shine on us, Agni, powerfully,
Scattering evil with light;

Our prayers are for rich fields,
For a free road and for wealth
Scattering evil with light;

We have open and excellent minds,
O Agni, thou art open and excellent,
Scattering evil with light;

Thou makest the liberal lords flourish,
Agni, thy blessings give us children,
Scattering evil with light;

O God whose arms embrace the world,
Agni, whose face shines on all sides,
Scattering evil with light;

Ferry us across the hostile waters,
O God whose face shines on all sides,
Scattering evil with light;

Ferry us from sin to goodness,
As a boatman ferries pilgrims over a stream,
Scattering evil with light.

Rama: The Bow That Could Not Be Bent

from The Firebringer and Other Great Stories

Louis Untermeyer

This tale from a major Indian epic dates to 300 B.C. and, like many epics, it tells of the amazing feats of a hero.

Rama is the hero of the *Ramayana*, a major epic of India written about 300 B.C. Like many ancient works, such as the Greek *Odyssey* and the Anglo-Saxon *Beowulf,* the *Ramayana* is full of legends that tell of impossible tasks, dangerous hazards, and wonderful victories.

Rama had been brought up in the court of his father, King Dasaratha. By the time he was sixteen he was more mature than most men. His body had been hardened by countless exercises and preparations for manhood. He was expert in wrestling, running, horsemanship, and swordsmanship. His mind had been developed by studies in philosophy, mathematics, and music. He was ready for whatever life had to offer.

One day an elderly sage entered the court and was given an audience.

"I was once a king," said the sage. "But I gave up the throne for a better way of life. It is for the less worldly life that I make a request."

"As one who is still worldly, I listen," said Dasaratha. "Name your request, and I will try to grant it."

"Let me have your son, Rama, for a while," said the sage. "He seems prepared for any adventure. He is strong in body and sound in mind. But he knows little of the spirit. Let me show him the potency of meditation and the power of prayer."

Dasaratha hesitated. "You ask me to give you the joy of my middle years and the hope of my old age. It is asking a great deal."

"I ask it not only for Rama's sake but also for the sake of the people," said the sage. "Our village has been ruined by a supernatural monster. It is spreading terror through the rest of the country. Only one who combines physical prowess with spiritual strength can defeat it. That is why I ask for Rama."

Before Dasaratha could reply, Rama spoke up. "Father, let me go. I would gladly learn what I lack. Even more gladly would I rid the country of the monster. I beseech you, let me go."

"I cannot deny you your right to learn," said Dasaratha. "And I would not hinder you from employing all your powers, especially in a good cause. So be it. You may go."

The way to the sage's village was long. It took months of travel. On the journey Rama was instructed in prayers, chants, and meditations.

"Your soul is now as pure as your body is perfect," said the sage. "You are religion itself. Now you are ready for whatever may befall."

As though to challenge those words, the air thundered with an earth-shaking roar. A huge elephant-like creature with wicked tusks like ten-foot-long spears and a head like a burning furnace charged upon them. Rama sped arrow after arrow at the monster but, though he wounded it, the monster continued to thrust at them with its death-dealing tusks. Rama uttered a prayer for survival and shot his last arrow. It tore through the air, a fearful shaft of lightning, and lodged in the monster's throat. Black smoke curled from its mouth like a horde of writhing serpents, and its death-cry shattered the trees.

"Evil cannot touch you," said the sage. "Now let us see if your strength of purpose is great enough to bend the bow that has never been bent."

"What bow is that?" inquired Rama.

"In Mithila lives the loveliest, most flowerlike beauty ever born. She is Sita, daughter of King Janaka. Ever since her fifteenth year, princes have come from all over India to woo her. Her father has forbidden anyone to court her who cannot pass one particular test. He must bend the bow—the bow of everlasting power—the bow which cannot be bent."

"I would like to see that bow," said Rama. "And I would also like to look upon the lovely Sita. Let us go to Mithila."

After four days' journeying, they reached the capital at night. It was a superb city, blazing with lights of every conceivable color. Royal banners snapped in the air, bursts of music greeted the visitors. They could not wait for what morning would bring.

A king's son, Rama was used to luxury. But when he stood before King Janaka in the high vaulted throne-room walled in marble set with rubies, sapphires, and emeralds, he knew that he had never seen anything as magnificent. Then, looking at Sita who sat next to her father, he knew he had never seen anything as desirable. She returned his gaze and smiled. He had never seen her before, yet he seemed to recognize her. Perhaps she was some divinity he had worshiped in a dream. Perhaps he had known her in some other life. Perhaps, in that other life, he had been her lover. But it was this life that Rama was now thinking about. He drew in his breath sharply as a herald announced that the ceremonies were about to begin.

First there was music: flute-playing punctuated by the light clashing of finger-cymbals, the low-droning tamboura, and singing accompanied by the sitar, a magically stringed instrument named in honor of the princess. Then there was solemn dancing, the performers weaving to and fro like plumed birds following some slow and half-forgotten ritual. Then there was the hour of meditation. Then six servants brought in the bow.

"As you see," said King Janaka, "it takes six men to carry the bow. It is difficult enough to lift and it has never been bent. There is a prophecy that it can be lifted only by the bravest and that only the purest as well as the strongest can bend it. Does anyone care to attempt the trial?"

The bow was placed upon velvet cushions and a young noble with jewels in his turban came forward. He took hold of the bow, but try as he might, it would not be budged. A second youth, a tall prince from Hindustan, grasped the bow, strained to raise it an inch, and fell on his face. A third, a fourth, and a fifth failed equally. All the contestants drew back in shame, their eyes fixed on the bow as if it were a deadly python.

Sita had shown no interest in the proceedings. Now she looked at Rama. He moved toward the velvet cushions, bowed to the king, and bowed even more deeply to Sita. He clasped his hands, bent his head, and uttered a silent prayer. Then he put his hands on the bow and slowly lifted it to his ankles, then his knees, then his chest, and then, still slowly but without exerting himself, Rama lifted it above his head. The murmur that ran through the room was a mixture of admiration and astonishment. The murmur grew to shouts as Rama took the two ends of the bow in his hands and bent it until the two ends touched. Then, placing the bow across his knee, he snapped it in half as though it were a slender staff. The shouting threatened to crack the marble walls.

Then there was silence as the king left his throne to place a crown on Rama's head. And when Rama looked at Sita, it was she who bowed. It was the bow of a loving wife waiting to serve her lord.

The Peach-Blossom Fountain

T'ao Ch'ien

In this tale, a lost fisherman comes upon a beautiful country that has been mysteriously cut off from the rest of humanity.

Towards the close of the fourth century A.D., a certain fisherman of Wu-ling, who had followed up one of the river branches without taking note whither he was going, came suddenly upon a grove of peach trees in full bloom, extending some distance on each bank, with not a tree of any other kind in sight. The beauty of the scene and the exquisite perfume of the flowers filled the heart of the fisherman with surprise, as he proceeded onwards, anxious to reach the limit of this lovely grove. He found that the peach trees ended where the water began, at the foot of a hill; and there he espied what seemed to be a cave with light issuing from it. So he made fast his boat, and crept in through a narrow entrance, which shortly ushered him into a new world of level country, of fine houses, of rich fields, of fine pools, and of luxuriance of mulberry and bamboo. Highways of traffic ran north and south; sounds of crowing cocks and barking dogs were heard around; the dress of the people who passed along or were at work in the fields was of strange cut; while young and old alike appeared to be happy.

One of the inhabitants, catching sight of the fisherman, was greatly astonished; but, after learning whence he came, insisted on carrying him home, and killed a chicken and placed some wine before him. Before long, all the people of the place had turned out to see the visitor, and they informed him that their ancestors had sought refuge here, with their wives and families, from the troublous time of the house of Ch'in, adding that they had thus become finally cut off from the rest of the human race. They then inquired about the politics of the day, ignorant of the establishment of the Han dynasty, and of course of the later dynasties which had succeeded it. And when the fisherman told them the story, they grieved over the vicissitudes[1] of human affairs.

---

1. **vicissitudes** (vi sis′ ə to͞odz) *n.* unpredictable changes and variations.

Each in turn invited the fisherman to his home and entertained him hospitably, until at length the latter prepared to take his leave. "It will not be worth while to talk about what you have seen to the outside world," said the people of the place to the fisherman, as he bade them farewell and returned to his boat, making mental notes of his route as he proceeded on his homeward voyage.

When he reached home, he at once went and reported what he had seen to the Governor of the district, and the Governor sent off men with him to seek, by the aid of the fisherman's notes, to discover this unknown region. But he was never able to find it again. Subsequently, another desperate attempt was made by a famous adventurer to pierce the mystery; but he also failed, and died soon afterwards of chagrin,[2] from which time forth no further attempts were made.

---

2. chagrin (shə grin') n. a feeling of embarrassment and annoyance because one has failed.

I Built My House Near Where Others Dwell

T'ao Ch'ien

Translated by William Acker

This poem, written almost a thousand years after the death of Lao Tzu, shows the enduring power of the philosophy of the Tao Te Ching.

> I built my house near where others dwell.
> And yet there is no clamor of carriages and
>   horses.
> You ask of me "How can this be so?"
> "When the heart is far the place of itself is
>   distant."
> 5   I pluck chrysanthemums under the eastern
>   hedge,
> And gaze afar towards the southern mountains.
> The mountain air is fine at evening of the day
> And flying birds return together homewards.
> Within these things there is a hint of Truth.
> 10   But when start to tell it, I cannot find the words.

Night Thoughts Aboard a Boat

Tu Fu

Being well-known has always been a mixed blessing. Even in China long ago, the writer of this poem questioned the importance of fame.

A bank of fine grass and light breeze,
A tall-masted solitary night boat.
Stars descend over the vast wild plain;
The moon bobs in the Great River's flow.
Fame: is it ever to be won in literature?
Office: I should give up, old and sick.
Floating, floating, what am I like?
Between earth and sky, a gull alone.

The Friends of Kwan Ming

Paul Yee

In this story, Kwan Ming and his three friends face discrimination as they look for work in North America. When they find jobs, Kwan Ming teaches his unreasonable boss a lesson with the help of his friends.

When his father died, the peasant Kwan Ming was forced to sell his little plot of paddy[1] and the old family house to pay for the burial. After the funeral, Kwan Ming looked around at the banana trees surrounding his village, and saw that he had nothing left to his name—not even one chipped roof tile. He had just enough money to buy a steamship ticket to the New World, where he had heard jobs were plentiful.

"I can start a new life there," he told his mother. "I will send money home."

The voyage lasted six weeks, over rocky waves and through screaming storms. Kwan Ming huddled together with hundreds of other Chinese deep in the ship's hold.[2] There he became fast friends with Chew Lap, Tam Yim and Wong Foon—men from neighboring villages. If one friend took sick, the others fetched him food and water. If one friend had bad luck gambling, the others lent him money to recover his losses. Together the three men ate, told jokes, and shared their dreams for the future.

When they arrived in the New World, everyone scattered throughout the port city to search for work. Kwan Ming hurried to the warehouse district, to the train station, and to the waterfront, but doors slammed in his face because he was Chinese. So he went to every store and laundry in Chinatown, and to every farm outside town. But there was not a job to be found anywhere, for there were too many men looking for work in a country that was still too young.

Every night Kwan Ming trudged back to the inn where he was staying with his three friends. Like him, they, too, had been searching for work but had found nothing.

---

1. **paddy** (pad′ ē) *n.* rice field.
2. **ship's hold** inside of the ship, under the decks, where cargo is usually carried.

Every night, as they ate their meager[3] meal of rice dotted with soya sauce, the friends shared information about the places they had visited and the people they had met. And every night Kwan Ming worried more and more about his mother, and how she was faring.

"If I don't find work soon, I'm going back to China," Chew Lap declared one evening.

"What for, fool?" asked Tam Yim. "Things are worse there!"

"But at least I will be with my family!" retorted Chew Lap.

"Your family needs money for food more than they need your company," Wong Foon commented. "Don't forget that."

Then a knock was heard at the door, and the innkeeper pushed his way into the tiny attic room.

"Good news!" he cried out. "I have found a job for each of you!"

The men leapt eagerly to their feet.

"Three of the jobs are well-paying and decent," announced the innkeeper. "But the fourth job is, well . . ." He coughed sadly.

For the first time since they had met, the four men eyed one another warily, like four hungry cats about to pounce on a bird.

"The biggest bakery in Chinatown needs a worker," said the innkeeper. "You'll always be warm next to the oven. Who will go?"

"You go, Chew Lap," Kwan Ming said firmly. "Your parents are ill and need money for medicine."

"The finest tailor in Chinatown wants an apprentice,"[4] continued the innkeeper. "The man who takes this job will be able to throw away those thin rags you wear."

"That's for you, Tam Yim," declared Kwan Ming. "You have four little ones waiting for food in China."

"The best shoemaker in Chinatown needs an assistant," said the innkeeper. "He pays good wages. Who wants to cut leather and stitch boots?"

"You go, Wong Foon," Kwan Ming stated. "You said the roof of your house in China needs repair. Better get new tiles before the rainy season starts."

---

3. meager (mē′ gər) *adj.* small in quantity; very little.
4. apprentice (ə pren′ tis) *n.* person who agrees to work for a craftsperson for a certain amount of time in exchange for instruction in the craft.

"The last job is for a houseboy."[5]

The innkeeper shook his head. "The pay is low. The boss owns the biggest mansion in town, but he is also the stingiest[6] man around!"

Kwan Ming had no choice but to take this job, for he knew his mother would be desperate for money. So off he went.

The boss was fatter than a cast-iron stove and as cruel as a blizzard at midnight. Kwan Ming's room was next to the furnace, so black soot and coal dust covered his pillow and blankets. It was difficult to save money, and the servants had to fight over the leftovers for their meals.

Every day Kwan Ming swept and washed every floor in the mansion. He moved the heavy oak tables and rolled up the carpets. The house was so big, that when Kwan Ming finally finished cleaning the last room, the first one was dirty all over again.

One afternoon Kwan Ming was mopping the front porch when his boss came running out. In his hurry, he slipped and crashed down the stairs. Kwan Ming ran over to help, but the fat man turned on him.

"You turtle!" he screamed as his neck purpled and swelled. "You lazy oaf! You doorknob! You rock brain! You're fired!"

Kwan Ming stood silently for a long moment. Then he spoke. "Please, sir, give me another chance. I will work even harder if you let me stay."

The boss listened and his eyes narrowed. Then he coughed loudly. "Very well, Kwan Ming, I won't fire you," he said. "But I will have to punish you, for you have ruined this suit and scuffed my boots and made me miss my dinner."

Kwan Ming nodded miserably.

"Then find me the following things in three days' time!" the boss ordered. "Bring me a fine woolen suit that will never tear. Bring me a pair of leather boots that will never wear out. And bring me forty loaves of bread that will never go stale. Otherwise you are finished here, and I will see that you never find another job!"

---

5. **houseboy** *n.* person who cleans and does other tasks for another person. (The word suggests little respect for the person so employed.)
6. **stingiest** (stin' jē əst) *adj.* most unwilling to spend money; cheapest.

Kwan Ming shuddered as he ran off. The old man's demands sounded impossible. Where would he find such items?

In despair, Kwan Ming wandered through the crowded streets of Chinatown. He sat on the raised wooden sidewalk because he had nowhere else to go.

Suddenly, familiar voices surrounded him.

"Kwan Ming, where have you been?"

"Kwan Ming, how is your job?"

"Kwan Ming, why do you never visit us?"

Kwan Ming looked up and saw his three friends smiling down at him. They pulled him up and pulled him off to the teahouse, where they ate and drank. When Kwan Ming told his friends about his predicament, the men clapped him on the shoulder.

"Don't worry!" exclaimed Tam Yim. "I'll make the woolen suit you need."

"I'll make the boots," added Wong Foon.

"And I'll make the bread," exclaimed Chew Lap.

Three days later, Kwan Ming's friends delivered the goods they had promised. An elegant suit of wool hung over a gleaming pair of leather boots, and forty loaves of fresh-baked bread were lined up in neat rows on the dining-room table.

Kwan Ming's boss waddled into the room and his eyes lit up. He put on the suit, and his eyebrows arched in surprise at how well it fit. Then he sat down and tried on the boots, which slid onto his feet as if they had been buttered.

Then the boss sliced into the bread and started eating. The bread was so soft, so sweet, and so moist that he couldn't stop. Faster and faster he chewed. He ate twelve loaves, then thirteen, then twenty.

The boss's stomach swelled like a circus tent, and his feet bloated out like balloons. But the well-sewn suit and sturdy boots held him tight like a gigantic sausage. The man shouted for help. He tried to stand up, but he couldn't even get out of his chair. He kicked his feet about like a baby throwing a tantrum.

But before anyone could do a thing, there was a shattering *Bang!*

Kwan Ming stared at the chair and blinked his eyes in astonishment. For there was nothing left of his boss.

He had exploded into a million little pieces.

Ancient Rome

from The Ancient Romans

Anita Ganeri

Life in a Roman town was very different for adults and children from life as we know it, as this selection shows.

RICH AND POOR

In Rome, people were divided into groups based on their family backgrounds, jobs, and wealth. Citizens could vote in elections and join the army. At first, people were citizens only if they had Roman parents. Later, other people were allowed to become citizens.

The richest citizens were called patricians. They held important government posts. Then came the merchants and farmers. Ordinary citizens were called plebeians.

All the hardest, dirtiest jobs were done by slaves. They were often prisoners of war brought to Rome to be sold at market. Slaves had no freedom and few rights.

LIFE IN A ROMAN TOWN

Life in Roman times was very different for the rich and the poor. Poorer Romans lived in cramped apartment buildings with stores and taverns on the ground floor. The apartments had no kitchens or running water. People ate food from street stalls and carried water from a fountain.

Wealthy Romans had comfortable lives. In town they lived in large, private houses decorated with statues and mosaics. Many houses had their own water supply and central heating. In the summer the family moved to a country estate to escape from the heat and crowds.

GOING TO SCHOOL

Many Roman children did not go to school. They went out to work. Children from wealthier families started school at the age of six or seven. They were taught how to read, write, and do arithmetic. Later, they learned poetry, history, and public speaking. The Romans spoke Latin.

Like children today Roman boys and girls played with toys such as marbles, dolls, and toy animals. They also raced toy chariots.

Early Rome

from The Ancient World: Rome

Sean Sheehan and Pat Levy

How did the great age of Rome—aspects of which still survive today—come into being? This selection gives you some interesting information to answer this question.

In the space of 1,000 years, ancient Rome created the greatest empire that the world has ever seen. It was not only the size of the empire that was so impressive, but also its ability to take on all the best aspects of the cultures that it conquered. Even 1,500 years after the fall of Rome, its legacy survives in the languages, architecture, laws, and thinking of today. Ancient Roman civilization is still regarded as one of the great ages of humankind.

At the time that ancient Rome was beginning to expand its territories, many Mediterranean countries were made up of farming communities. In neighboring Greece there was an advanced culture, but the Greeks wasted a lot of time on civil wars. They had never colonized the other lands around them, apart from some colonies in southern Italy. Other peoples, like the Etruscans, were exploring new lands, settling in the plains of Italy, north and south of the Tiber River. It was Rome, however, that became the most important city in Italy.

Italy is in the center of the Mediterranean; it has a long coastline, making links with Greece, Africa, and Spain possible by sea. This put Italy in a central position to develop trade in the region. Rome itself was in the fertile valley of the Tiber River, in a warm climate. Inland it was easy to defend, with the natural defenses of the seven hills, but at the same time the river gave it access to the sea for war and trading. Much of the rest of Italy is mountainous. All around Rome were other peoples who wanted more land, so at first Rome went to war only to defend its land. Rome first drove other competing cultures out of Italy, made peace with the conquered tribes, and then set out to destroy their competitors farther afield.

Legends and Origins

The story of ancient Rome began around 800 B.C., in a small settlement on one of the seven hills of Rome; but historians do not know how, or exactly when, this first settlement developed.

In one legend, there was a king called Numitor. His sons were killed by his jealous brother, Amulius, who then made Numitor's daughter, Rhea Silvia, become a priestess. After Mars, the god of war, fell in love with her, Rhea had twin sons, Romulus and Remus. When Amulius found out, he threw Rhea and her babies into the Tiber. A female wolf found the twins and brought them up. Years later, a shepherd discovered them and brought them to Numitor, where the whole story was explained.

Amulius was killed in battle, so the twins decided to build a new city to celebrate his death. An oracle told them to build the city on the Palatine Hill; it also said that Romulus was to be the king of the city. Romulus took a plow and plowed a line to show the city's boundaries. Remus, now jealous of his brother, jumped over the furrow to disobey his brother and Romulus killed him. Romulus then became the first king of Rome.

Historians know that the first people to live on the Palatine Hill were Latin peoples from northern Italy. They lived in small oblong huts made of wooden poles, woven around with twigs and branches and filled in with clay. They herded sheep and cattle and kept goats and pigs. Their burial ground was at the foot of the Palatine Hill. Each of the seven hills of Rome was probably a separate village. In the very early history of Rome, these Latin people were invaded by Etruscans from the north, who became their kings. They united the seven hills into one city and brought their skills as builders and artists to this new city.

The Seven Kings

Romulus was said to be the first king of Rome in 753 B.C. He was followed by six more kings until 510 B.C. when Rome became a Republic. These kings began to make Rome an important city. First, they expanded their lands to take in a neighboring city, Alba Longa. Then the sixth king, Servius Tullius, made Rome into a religious center by building a shrine to Diana, the hunter goddess. His son, Tarquinius Superbus, built a huge temple to Jupiter, the king of the gods. Rome soon became an important religious site.

The kings of Rome were very powerful people. They were in charge of war, public buildings, and religion. They also acted as city judges. Everywhere they went, their assistants carried a bundle of rods with an ax in the middle, known as *fasces*,[1] to show that the king had the power to have anyone executed or beaten. Servius Tullius was the first Roman king to have coins made. Before this, cows had been used as money; one cow was equal to ten sheep. Later, for convenience, people began to use bronze bars as money. Finally, a standard bronze coin stamped with a cow's head became the currency.

The kings also commissioned Rome's famous system of sewers. At first people had used the streams that ran between the seven hills of the city to carry waste water away, but then they began to build huge underground sewers.

However, the kings became too ruthless. The last king of all, Tarquinius Superbus, forced the citizens to give up their own work to work for him. A later Roman historian tells the story:

"The poor were set to work in return for a miserable ration of grain: quarrying stone, cutting timber, leading the wagons, or even themselves carrying the materials on their backs. Various craftsmen, coppersmiths, carpenters, and stonemasons were all forcibly removed from their private business to labor for the public good."

A group of noblemen led a rebellion, and Tarquinius, the last Etruscan king of Rome, had to escape from the city with his supporters. The exact year of this event is not known, but it is believed to have been around 510 B.C. The people, having got rid of their kings, set up a republic, meaning "rule by the people," which was headed by two consuls elected each year.

---

1. **fasces** (fas'ēz)

Frontier Fort

from The Eagle of the Ninth

Rosemary Sutcliff

*In this selection, an ambitious young man requests an
assignment that will help him get information about his
long-missing father.*

From the Fosseway westward to Isca Dumnoniorum the
road was simply a British trackway, broadened and
roughly metalled, strengthened by corduroys of logs in
the softest places, but otherwise unchanged from its old
estate, as it wound among the hills, thrusting farther and
farther into the wilderness.

It was a busy road and saw many travellers: traders
with bronze weapons and raw yellow amber in their
ponies' packs; country folk driving shaggy cattle or lean
pigs from village to village; sometimes a band of tawny-
haired tribesmen from farther west; strolling harpers and
quack-oculists, too, or a light-stepping hunter with huge
wolf-hounds at his heel; and from time to time a commis-
sariat wagon going up and down to supply the Roman
frontier post. The road saw them all, and the cohorts[1] of
the Eagles for whom all other travellers must make way.

There was a cohort of leather-clad auxiliaries on the
road today, swinging along at the steady Legion's pace
that had brought them down from Isca Silurium at
twenty miles a day; the new garrison coming to relieve the
old one at Isca Dumnoniorum. On they went, following
the road that now ran out on a causeway between sodden
marsh and empty sky, now plunged into deep boar-
hunted forest, or lifted over bleak uplands where nothing
grew save furze[2] and thorn-scrub. On with never a halt
nor a change of rhythm, marching century by century,
the sun bright on the Standard at their head, and the
rolling dust-cloud kicked up over the pack-train behind.

At the head of the column marched the Pilus Prior Centurion, the cohort Commander, the pride that shone from

---

1. cohort (kō ' hôrt) *n.* an ancient Roman military unit of 300–600 men, constituting
one tenth of a legion.
2. furze (furz) *n.* a prickly evergreen shrub.

him showing clearly that this was his first command. They were, he had long since decided, a command worthy of anyone's pride; six hundred yellow-haired giants recruited from the tribes of Upper Gaul, with the natural fighting power of mountain cats, drilled and hammered into what he firmly believed to be the finest auxiliary cohort ever to serve with the Second Legion. They were a newly joined cohort; many of the men had not yet proved themselves in action, and the spear-shaft of their Standard had no honours on it, no gilded laurel wreath nor victor's crown. The honours were all to win—perhaps during his command.

The Commander was a complete contrast to his men: Roman to his arrogant finger-tips, wiry and dark as they were raw-boned and fair. The olive-skinned face under the curve of his crested helmet had not a soft line in it anywhere—a harsh face it would have been, but that it was winged with laughter lines, and between his level black brows showed a small raised scar that marked him for one who had passed the Raven Degree of Mithras.

Centurion Marcus Flavius Aquila had seen little of the Eagles until a year ago. His first ten years had been lived quietly with his mother on the family farm near Clusium, while his father soldiered in Judaea, in Egypt, and here in Britain. They had been going to join his father in Britain, but before the time came for them to do so, rebellion had flared up among the northern tribes, and the Ninth Hispana, his father's Legion, had marched north to deal with it, and never came marching back.

His mother had died soon afterwards, leaving him to be brought up in Rome by a rather foolish aunt and the plump and purse-proud official who was her husband. Marcus had loathed the official, and the official had loathed Marcus. They saw everything with different eyes. Marcus came of a line of soldiers—one of those Equestrian families who, when the rest of their kind had turned from soldiering to trade and finance, had kept to the old way of life, and remained poor but held their noses high in consequence. The official came of a line of officials, and his code of life was quite other than Marcus's. Neither of them had a shred of understanding for each other's ideas, and they had both been thankful when Marcus was eighteen and could apply for a centurion's commission.

Marcus, his eyes narrowed into the sun as he marched, smiled to himself a little wryly, as he remem-

bered how almost pathetically thankful that plump official had been. (Tramp, tramp, tramp, said the cohort's
feet behind him.)

He had asked to be sent to Britain, though it meant
starting in an auxiliary cohort instead of a line-of-battle
one, partly because his father's elder brother had settled
there when his own years of soldiering were done, but
mostly because of his father. If ever anything became
known of the lost Legion, it would be known first in
Britain, and it might even be that here in Britain he
would find out something for himself.

Marching down the Isca Dumnoniorum road in the
run-honey evening light, he found himself thinking about
his father. He had very vivid memories of a slight, dark
man with laughter lines at the corners of his eyes, who
had come home from time to time, and taught him to
fish, to play 'Flash the Fingers', and throw a javelin. He
remembered vividly that last leave of all. His father had
just been appointed to command the First Cohort of the
Hispana, which meant having charge of the Eagle and
being something very like second-in-command of the Legion beside; and he had been like a jubilant boy about it.
But his mother had been faintly anxious, almost as if she
knew. . . .

'If it was any *other* Legion!' she had said. 'You have
told me yourself that the Hispana has a bad name.'

And his father had replied: 'But I would not have it any
other Legion if I could. I held my first command in the
Hispana, and a man's first Legion is apt to hold chief
place in his heart ever after, be its name good or bad;
and now that I go back to it as First Cohort, we will see
whether there is nothing can be done to better its name.'
He had turned to his small son, laughing. 'Presently it
will be your turn. It has fallen on evil days, but we will
make a Legion of the Hispana yet, you and I.'

Looking back across the years, Marcus remembered
that his father's eyes had been very bright, like the eyes
of a man going into action; and the light had caught suddenly in the great flawed emerald of the signet-ring he always wore, striking from it a spark of clear green fire.
Odd how one remembered things like that: little things
that somehow mattered.

(Tramp, tramp, tramp, came the sound of the cohort's
feet behind him.)

It would be pleasant, he thought, if Uncle Aquila was like his father. He had not met his uncle yet; after learning his foot-drill he had arrived in Britain in the sleety days of late autumn, and been sent straight up to Isca; but he had a rather vague invitation to spend his leave with him at Calleva, when he had any leave to spend. It would be very pleasant if Uncle Aquila was like his father.

Not of course that he and his uncle were likely to have much to do with each other. In a few years' time he would probably be serving in quite a different part of the Empire, since a cohort centurion seldom moved up all the way in the same Legion.

All the way . . . from his present rank right up to his father's rank of First Cohort; and after that? For most of the men who got so far there was nothing after that, but for the outstanding few who went farther—as Marcus intended to go farther—the ways divided there. One could become a camp commandant, as Uncle Aquila had done, or one could go on, by way of the Praetorian Guard, to try for command of a Legion. Legion Commanders were almost always men of Senator's rank, with no experience of soldiering save a year's service as Military Tribune in their youth; but by long custom the two Egyptian Legions were exceptions to the rule. They were commanded by professional soldiers; and an Egyptian Legion had been Marcus's shining goal for as long as he could remember.

But one day, when he had finished with the Eagles, when he had made an honourable name and become Prefect of his Egyptian Legion, he would go home to the Etruscan hills, and perhaps even buy back the old farm, which the plump official had ruthlessly sold to defray expenses. For a moment he remembered almost painfully the sunlit courtyard flickered over with the shadow of pigeons' wings, and the wild olive-tree in the loop of the stream, on a twisted root of which he had once found a kind of gall growing, that was shaped something like a little bird. He had cut it from the root with the new knife his father had given him, and spent much loving care, all one absorbed summer evening, trimming and carving feathers on it. He had that little bird still.

The road topped a gentle rise, and suddenly Isca Dumnoniorum lay before them, with the fortress-crowned Red Mount dark with shadows against the evening sky; and Marcus came back to the present with a jerk. The farm in the Etruscan hills could wait until he was old and tired and famous; in the present was the glory of his first command.

The British town was spread below the southern scarp[3] of the Mount; a sprawling huddle of reed-thatched roofs, every colour from the gold of honey to the black of dried peat, according to the age of the thatch; with the squared, clean lines of the Roman forum and basilica looking oddly rootless in their midst; and the faint haze of wood-smoke lying over all.

The road led straight through the town and up to the cleared slope beyond, to the Praetorian gate of the fort; here and there, crimson or saffron-cloaked men turned to look at the cohort as it swung by, a look that was reserved rather than hostile. Dogs sat scratching in odd corners, lean pigs rooted among the garbage piles, and women with bracelets of gold or copper on very white arms sat in hut doorways, spinning or grinding corn. The blue smoke of many cooking-fires curled up into the quiet air, and the savoury smell of many evening meals mingled with the blue reek of wood-smoke and the sharper tang of horse-droppings, which Marcus had by now come to associate with all British towns. Little that was Roman was here as yet, despite the stone-built forum. One day there would be straight streets, he supposed, and temples and bath-houses and a Roman way of life. But as yet it was a place where two worlds met without mingling: a British town huddled under the dominion of the turf ramparts where once the tribe had had its stronghold and now the Roman sentries paced up and down. He looked about him under the curve of his helmet as he marched, knowing that this place would be part of his life for the next year; then looked up to the turf ramparts, and saw a Roman banner drooping in the still air, and the tall crest of a sentry burning in the sunset, and heard a trumpet-call ring out, as it seemed, from the fiery sky.

.   .   .   .

'You have brought clear skies with you,' said Centurion Quintus Hilarion, lounging in the window of the Commander's quarters, and peering into the night. 'But Hercle! you need not expect it to last.'

---

3. **scarp** (skärp) *n*. a steep slope.

'As bad as that?' said Centurion Marcus Aquila, who was seated on the table.

'Quite as bad as that! It rains always, here in the west, save when Typhon, the father of all ills, brews up a mist to come between a man and his own feet. By the time you have served your year here you will have toadstools sprouting out of your ears, the same as me, *and* not from the damp alone!'

'From what beside?' inquired Marcus with interest.

'Oh, lack of company, for one thing. I am a sociable soul myself; I like my friends around me.' He turned from the window, and folded up on to a low cushioned bench, hugging his knees. 'Ah well, I am off to rub away the blue mould as soon as I have marched the troops back to Isca.'

'Going on leave?'

The other nodded. 'Long leave, lovely leave, among the fleshpots of Durinum.'

'Durinum—that is your home?' asked Marcus.

'Yes. My father retired and settled there a few years ago. There is a surprisingly good circus, and plenty of people—pretty girls too. A pleasant enough place to get back to, out of the wilds.' An idea seemed to strike him. 'What shall you do when *your* leave falls due? I suppose, coming out from home, you have no one here to go to?'

'I have an uncle at Calleva, though I have not yet met him,' Marcus said, 'and certainly there is no one at home I should want to spend my leave with.'

'Father and mother both dead?' inquired Hilarion with friendly interest.

'Yes. My father went with the Ninth Legion.'

'Pericol! You mean when they—'

'Disappeared. Yes.'

'So. That is bad!' said Hilarion, wagging his head. 'A deal of ugly stories, there were—still are, for that matter; and of course, they did lose the Eagle.'

Instantly Marcus was up in arms to defend his father and his father's Legion. 'Since not a man of the Legion came back, it is scarcely a matter for wonder that neither did the Eagle,' he flashed.

'Surely not,' agreed Hilarion amicably. 'I was not blowing on your father's honour, so you can keep your feathers on, my Marcus.' He looked up at the other with a wide, friendly grin, and suddenly Marcus, who had been ready to quarrel with him the instant before, found himself grinning back.

It was several hours since Marcus had marched his cohort across the hollow-ringing bridge, answering the sentry's challenge, 'Fourth Gaulish Auxiliaries of the Second Legion, come to relieve this garrison.' Dinner was over, in the officers' mess, with the Quartermaster, the Surgeon, and the double complement of ranker centurions. Marcus had taken charge of the pay-chest keys—in a garrison as small as this there was no pay-master; and for the past hour, here in the Commander's quarters in the Praetorium, he and Hilarion had been going through the office work of the frontier fort. Now, crested helmets and embossed breastplates laid aside, the two of them were taking their ease.

Through the doorless opening Marcus could see almost the whole of the sleeping-cell, the narrow cot piled with gay native rugs, the polished oaken chest, the lamp-bracket high on the bare wall, and nothing more. The outer room held the battered writing-table on which Marcus was sitting, a cross-legged camp-stool, the cushioned bench to represent comfort, another chest for the record rolls, and a bronze pedestal lamp of peculiarly hideous design.

In the little silence that had fallen between them, Marcus looked round him at the austere room in the yellow flood of lamplight, and to him it seemed beautiful. But though it would be his tomorrow, for this one night he was a guest here, and he looked back to his host with a quick smile of apology for having looked too soon at his surroundings with the eye of mastery.

Hilarion grinned. 'You will not be feeling like that this day next year.'

'I wonder,' said Marcus, swinging one sandalled foot and idly watching the swing of it. 'What does one do here, beside growing toadstools? Is there good hunting?'

'Good enough; it is the one thing to be said for this particular corner of the Empire. Boar and wolf in the winter, and the forest swarms with deer. There are several hunters below in the town, who will take you out for the price of the day's work. Unwise to go alone, of course.'

Marcus nodded. 'Have you any advice for me? I am new to this country.'

The other considered. 'No, I think not.' Then he sat up with a jerk. 'Yes, I have, if no one has warned you already. But it has nothing to do with the hunting. It is the priest-kind—the wandering Druids. If one of them appears in the district, or you get the least idea that there is one about, look to your weapons. Good advice, that is.'

'The Druids?' Marcus was surprised and puzzled. 'But surely Suetonius Paulinus dealt with them once and for all, sixty years ago?'

'As an organized priesthood, maybe; but as easily hold off these heathen mists with a palm-leaf umbrella as end the Druids, by destroying their stronghold. They spring up still, from time to time, and wherever they do spring up, there is likely to be trouble for the Eagles. They were the heart and soul of British resistance in the early days, and even now, when there is any sign of unrest among the tribes, you can wager your sandals there is a holy man at the bottom of it.'

'Go on,' Marcus prodded, as the other seemed to have finished. 'This becomes interesting.'

'Well, the thing is this. They can preach holy war, and that is ever the most deadly kind, for it recks[4] nothing of consequences.' Hilarion spoke slowly, as though he was thinking the thing out as he went along. 'The frontier tribes are not like those of the south coast, who were half Romanized before ever we landed; they are a wild lot, and superbly brave; but even they have mostly come to think that we are not fiends of darkness, and they have enough sense to see that destroying the local garrison will only mean a punitive[5] expedition and their homes and standing crops burned, and a stronger garrison with a heavier hand thereafter. But let one of their holy men lay hold of them, and all that goes whistling down the wind. They cease to think whether there can be any good come of their rising, cease to think at all. They are keeping faith with their gods by smoking out a nest of the unbelievers, and what happens after is no concern of theirs, for they are going West of the Sunset by the warriors' road. And when you get men into that state there is apt to be trouble coming.'

Outside in the quiet darkness the trumpets sounded for the second watch of the night. Hilarion uncurled himself and stood up. 'We had best do Late Rounds together tonight,' he said, and reached for his sword, slip-

---

4. recks (rekz) *n.* cares; is concerned about.
5. punitive (pyōō′ ni tiv) *adj.* inflicting punishment.

ping the baldrick[6] over his head. 'I am native born,' he added as though in explanation. 'That is how I come to have some understanding of these matters.'

'I imagined that you must be.' Marcus tested a buckle of his own equipment. 'You have had no holy man round here, I suppose?'

'No, but my predecessor had a certain amount of trouble just before I took over, and the trouble-maker slipped through his fingers and disappeared. We lived a month or two on Vesuvius—all the more so as the harvest was bad for the second year running—but it never erupted.'

Footsteps sounded outside, and a red light glimmered at the window; and they went out together to the Duty Centurion, who stood outside with a flaring torch. The clashing Roman salute was exchanged, and they set out on their tour of the darkened fort, from sentry-post to sentry-post along the rampart walk, from guard-point to guard-point, with the low exchange of the password; lastly to the small lighted room in the Praetorium where the pay-chest was kept and the Standard stood against the wall, and between rounds the Duty Centurion sat with his drawn sword on the table before him, through the night.

Marcus thought: 'After tonight it will be for me alone to follow the centurion's torch from guard-post to guard-post, from barrack block to horse-lines, seeing that all is well with the frontier of the Empire.'

Next morning, after the formal take-over ceremony in the forum, the old garrison marched out. Marcus watched them go, out across the ditch and downhill between the crowding hovels of the native town whose reed-thatched roofs were gold-dusted by the morning sun. Century after Century, marching away up the long road that led to Isca; and at their head the glint of gold and crimson that was the cohort Standard. He narrowed his eyes into the piercing light, and watched that coloured glint till it disappeared into the brightness of the morning. The last driver of the baggage-train dropped out of sight beyond the lift of the road, the rhythmic tramp-tramp-tramp of heavily sandalled feet ceased to pulse through the sunlit air, and Marcus was alone with his first command.

---

6. baldrick (bôl′ drik) *n.* a belt worn over one shoulder and across the chest to support a sword, a bugle, etc.

from Gladiator

Richard Watkins

This selection depicts the strange gladiatorial games in Rome as a political tool as well as a thrilling spectacle.

THE FIRST GLADIATORS

The first known gladiatorial combat in Rome took place at the funeral of a nobleman named Junius Brutus in 264 B.C. His sons Marcus and Decimus revived an ancient Etruscan custom of having slaves fight at the funeral of a great leader in the belief that such a sacrifice would please the gods. During the ceremony, which took place in the Forum Boarium, or cattle market, three pairs of slaves were forced to fight to the death. This strange custom grew in popularity as more rich and powerful men presented these displays as part of the ceremonies to honor their dead.

In 216 B.C., twenty-two pairs of slaves fought at the funeral of a man named Marcus Lepidus. Sixty pairs fought when Publicus Licinius died in 183 B.C. These slave fighters were now known as *bustiarii*, funeral men. As Rome's taste for slave fights grew, so did the occasions that required them. If a family's reputation could be enhanced by these displays, then so could a politician's chance of election or a general's popularity. It became clear that an ambitious Roman could buy a crowd's attention, ensure his social standing, and demonstrate his power over life and death.

By the time of Julius Caesar, any direct association with funerals and religion was gone, and these fighters, now known as *gladiators*, meaning swordsmen, were a powerful force in Roman politics. Caesar's genius at entertaining the masses with extravagant gladiatorial displays equaled his skills as a general and a politician. He bought the affection of the people with magnificent banquets and spectacles that were open and free to the public. He showered his political supporters and his *legionaries* (soldiers) with gold. All this gave Caesar unlimited power and established the precedent of keeping the populace occupied with triumphal processions, chariot races, and gladiator shows. The bigger the event, the more impressed the people were. In 46 B.C. Caesar staged a battle between two armies, each with 500 men, 30 cavalrymen, and 20 battle elephants. He topped that with a naval battle with 1,000 sailors and 2,000 oarsman, staged on a huge artificial lake dug just for that purpose.

These gladiatorial combats affirmed Julius Caesar's power and, to him, the cost in gold and human lives was worth it. Augustus Caesar, in 22 B.C., brought all games in Rome under his direct control, making them a state monopoly. He realized that the games were too important a political tool to be exploited by anyone else.

WHO WERE THE GLADIATORS?

Of the thousands of men who ended up in the arena, the vast majority were either prisoners of war, criminals, or slaves. As the Roman Empire grew through constant wars of conquest, soldiers of the defeated armies found themselves on the way to Rome, roped neck to neck with their arms tied behind their backs. Among them were Samnites, Thracians, and Gauls from territories conquered early in Rome's history, followed by Britons, Germans, Moors, and Africans, captives from virtually every land that became part of the empire. These human trains were whipped and beaten as they marched, or were packed into the dark and dirty holds of cargo ships bound for Rome. Captives ended up in Rome's slave markets to be auctioned off. Many of the biggest and strongest were bought for the gladiator schools to be trained for combat in the arena.

Criminals were another major source of gladiators. Originally, those convicted of murder, robbery, arson, or sacrilege were sent to the arena to be killed by an executioner with a sword (*damnati ad gladium*) or thrown to the beasts (*damnati ad bestius*), in the belief that this would act as a deterrent for would-be criminals. As the games grew in popularity and entertainment became more important than deterrence, more criminals were sentenced to train in gladiator schools (*damnati in ludum*). The amount of instruction they received varied. In general, a sentence to the schools meant three years of training and combat in the arena followed by two years teaching in the schools (anyone who survived three years as a gladiator made an excellent teacher). Some of these convicted criminals turned gladiators learned their new profession well and became heroes of the arena, winning fame, fortune, and, possibly, freedom from further combat. Occasionally, though, large-scale shows demanded so many gladiators that any criminal, regardless of his crime, could find himself holding a sword and fighting for his life with little or no instruction whatsoever.

Ordinary slaves were the other major source of gladiators. Owners could dispose of their slaves any way they wanted, just like other property. A slave who tried to run away or was accused of theft or simply bored his master could be sent to the arena. It wasn't until the second century A.D. that owners were prohibited from sending a slave into the arena without just cause.

Obviously, prisoners of war, criminals, and slaves had no choice but to fight, so it is incredible to think that there were men who actually volunteered to be gladiators. At the height of the Roman Empire, more than half of all gladiators were in this deadly profession by their own choice. Most were simply poor and desperate, and the life of a gladiator, however short, offered regular meals and the dream of glory.

Champion gladiators who showed exceptional skill and bravery in the arena were sometimes presented with a wooden baton, the *rudius*, that awarded the champion honorable retirement from further combat. Many continued to fight, even after winning the *rudius*, knowing they could command a high price to enter the arena again, this time as a volunteer. The great Syrian gladiator Flamma (the Flame) earned four *rudi*, only to keep on fighting. The emperor Tiberius offered one thousand pieces of gold per performance to entice retired gladiators back to the arena. Many accepted, not only for the money, but to hear again the roar of the crowd and experience the thrill of combat.

Occasionally a nobleman would dare to be a gladiator. An appearance by one of these wealthy thrill-seekers would send the audience into a frenzy. To see an aristocrat fighting among the slaves and criminals thrilled the mob of *plebeians*, or common people, in the stands. The demand for them was so great at times that some emperors, Augustus and Tiberius in particular, tried to stop them, but there were always some noblemen ready to risk their lives in the arena. Sometimes, though, these privileged gladiators could fight without fearing for their lives. Their status would entitle them to special consideration, allowing them to fight not to the death, but only as a special exhibition between the regular fights. As popular as these blue-blooded gladiators were with the mob at the amphitheater, they were an embarrassment to their peers in the upper class.

The lure of the arena was so strong that even some emperors played at being gladiators, among them Caligula and Hadrian. The emperor Commodus did more than play. He claimed to have fought more than one thousand fights and paid himself one million *sesterces*[1] for each. By comparison, a laborer in Rome might earn one thousand *sesterces* a year.

Because every level of Roman society had representatives in the arena, emperors and slaves, senators and criminals, it is not surprising that women also appeared as gladiators. They were considered a novelty, but a carving found in Halicarnassus in Asia Minor (what is now Turkey) shows a pair, one appropriately called Amazon, fighting with the same equipment and, apparently, the same intensity as men. The carving says they were honorably discharged. In one way, these women gladiators succeeded where men failed; they managed to offend Roman sensibilities enough to be banned in A.D. 200.

---

1. sesterce (ses' tərs) *n.* an old Roman coin, originally silver but later brass or copper.

Famous Women: Scholars and Artists
from Women in Ancient Rome

Fiona Macdonald

Women made a substantial but little-known contribution to art, literature, medicine, and mathematics in Ancient Rome, as this selection explains.

SCHOLARS AND ARTISTS

Roman women from wealthy families were educated in literature, music and philosophy, so that they would be more attractive to their husbands, and good companions. They were not expected to use these skills to earn a living. But some women did give money to help support male scholars, writers, musicians and artists. And a few women managed to break society's rules and win fame for their own wisdom, learning and skill.

Hypatia (c. A.D. 370–415)
Hypatia lived in Alexandria, the most important city in Roman Egypt and a great center of learning. Her father was a mathematician, and he sent her to study with the greatest scholars of the day. She taught math and philosophy at the University of Alexandria, and wrote books on math and science. These were praised when they appeared, but have not survived for us to read today. Although Hypatia was a respected teacher, her scientific views were criticized by the leader of the Christian Church in Alexandria. He encouraged a mob of men to attack and kill her.

Doctor Fabiola (died in A.D. 399)
Fabiola was born into a noble family in Rome, and was married, unhappily, while still a teenager. She became a Christian, and later married again, but her husband died. She decided to spend the rest of her life working in medicine and charity. In A.D. 390, with two friends, she founded a hospital in the port of Ostia, near Rome. She was a skilled surgeon, and admired for the loving care she gave to patients. Another medical woman, who worked alongside her doctor husband (c. A.D. 100), was

called Panthia. After her death, he wrote, "Though you were a woman, you were not behind me in skill."

Iaia of Cyzicus (c. 100 B.C.)

We know of only eight women who worked as artists during Roman times. Most were the daughters of male artists, and their fathers taught them how to paint. This was the only way they could train professionally. Iaia was described as the daughter and student of her father. She carved ivory, and painted pictures on plaster and wood. She mainly painted women but, unlike many male artists, did not always choose young, rich or beautiful people as her subjects. Her most famous work was of an old woman, but it has not survived. Her work was highly praised, and she was able to ask higher prices for her pictures than many male artists.

Sulpicia (c. 30 B.C.)

Although we know that several Roman women wrote poems and letters, very little women's writing has survived. Sulpicia's poetry was kept almost by accident, because it was collected together with the works of a famous male poet, who was one of her friends. Sulpicia came from a wealthy family that gave money to support male writers. She met many of them at her home and learned a great deal about poetry. But her own poems are unlike anything else written at the time. She experimented with using words in different ways—with double meanings and unusual rhythms and rhymes. She wrote passionately about falling in love, and insisted that women's feelings were as strong and important as men's.

The Ship of State

Horace

*In this poem, the government becomes a ship in danger
from storms, rocks, and rough waters.*

Ship of State, beware!
Hold fast the port. Cling to the friendly shore
Lest sudden storms and whirling eddies[1] bear
Thy shattered hull to faithless seas once more.

5   See how the rower faints upon his oar!
    Hark to the groaning of the mast,
    Sore stricken by the Libyan blast!
    Thy shrouds are burst; thy sails are torn;
    And through thy gaping ribs forlorn
10   The floods remorseless pour.

Dare not to call for aid on powers divine;
    Dishonored once, they hear no more:
    Nor boast, majestic pine,
Daughter of Pontic forests, thy great name,
15   Old lineage, well-earned fame,
    The honors of this sculptured prow—
Sport of the mocking winds, nor feared nor
    trusted now.

Alas! my country, long my anxious care,
Source now of bitter pain and fond regret!
20   Thy stars obscured, thy course beset
    By rocks unseen, beware!
Trust not soft winds and treacherous seas
Or the false glitter of the Cyclades.

---

1. eddies (ed′ ēz) *n.* little whirlpools or whirlwinds.

Julius Caesar: The Ides of March

from The Firebringer and Other Great Stories

Louis Untermeyer

Even a hugely popular ruler can be brought down by jealous and ambitious politicians, as this tale shows.

In his mid-fifties Julius Caesar was at the height of his glory. As a warrior he was adored by his soldiers. As a general he had won victory after victory. He had driven back two tribes of German invaders across the Rhine.[1] He had spent nine years fighting in Gaul until all western Europe was subject to Rome. He had extended Roman rule by invading Britain and establishing an army there. He had crossed the Rubicon[2] and was master of all Italy.

As a ruler he was beloved by the people. He never tired of doing things for them. He spent much of his income on festivals and food for the hungry. In return, the citizens offered him the crown. When he refused it, they named him "Father of his Country" and made him dictator for life. He was literally idolized. Statues of Caesar were placed in temples; his face appeared on all sorts of coins; the seventh month of the year was called Julius (or July) in his honor.

He was, in short, worshiped by everyone except the politicians. They feared and envied him. Cassius was the most evil-minded of these. He was wildly jealous of Caesar. They had been schoolmates, and he had always considered himself Caesar's equal if not his superior. Now things were different. He complained (in Shakespeare's words): "This man is now become a god, and Cassius is a wretched creature and must bend his body if Caesar carelessly but nod at him."

Cassius organized a conspiracy. He knew that he could not show personal hatred; there had to be a cause. He had little trouble convincing several others that Caesar was a tyrant and that, for the good of Rome, they would have to get rid of him. Hardest to convince was Caesar's friend, Brutus. Brutus was a noble being, an

---

1. **Rhine** (rīn) *n.* river in Western Europe.
2. **Rubicon** (roō′ bi kön) *n.* small river in northern Italy.

would have to get rid of him. Hardest to convince was Caesar's friend, Brutus. Brutus was a noble being, an idealist, a dedicated lover of Rome. He found it difficult to hate. Yet he, a loyal citizen, a believer in democracy, hated dictatorship. What Cassius suggested—nothing less than Caesar's assassination—was abhorrent to him. Deeply troubled, he could not sleep. Finally he came to an unhappy decision. He decided that it would be better to destroy a despot[3] than let a despot destroy the government. Caesar was his friend, but friendship must not stand in the way of saving Rome from tyranny. He remembered what Cassius had said:

> "Why, man, he doth bestride the narrow world
> Like a Colossus, and we petty men
> Walk under his huge legs."

Caesar was unaware of any conspiracy. One morning, as he was walking, attended by a devoted crowd, a soothsayer, who foretold the future, warned him. "Caesar!" he called. "Beware the ides of March!"

Caesar shrugged. "He is a dreamer. Why should the fifteenth of March disturb me more than any other day? Let us leave him—pass."

A few weeks later Caesar was on his way to the Capitol. Passing the soothsayer he could not help but tease him. "Today is the fifteenth," he said. "The ides of March have come."

"So they have," softly answered the soothsayer. "But they are not yet past."

Caesar smiled, but inwardly he was troubled. The night before, there had been a violent storm and his wife had waked in terror.

"It is not the storm that woke me," she told Caesar, trembling. "It was a dream, a terrible dream. I dreamed that lightning had struck the house, that the roof had caved in, and that—I can see it still!—you had been slain and were lying in my arms. Do not leave me. Do not, I beg you, go out of doors today."

Caesar shook his head. "Do not let a dream alarm you. My time has not yet come, and when it comes I will meet it without fear.

---

3. **despot** (des' pə) *n.* an absolute ruler; a tyrant.

"Cowards die many times before their deaths,
The valiant never taste of death but once."

Not to be deterred, Caesar went to the Capitol. He was
stopped on the way by Artemidorus, a teacher, who knew
some of Cassius' confederates and had found out their
plan. He handed Caesar a roll of paper.

"Read it," said Artemidorus. "Read it at once. It concerns you greatly."

Caesar took the paper, but thinking it was merely an
appeal for aid, did not unroll it. So many people thronged
to shake his hand or wish him well that he never had a
chance to see what was written. Had he glanced at even
the first line his life would have been saved.

When he entered the Capitol, the entire Senate stood
up to honor him. As he seated himself, many flocked
about him, including the conspirators. One of them presented a petition for the return of a brother who had
been banished from Rome. When Caesar refused, they
pressed closer, and suddenly Caesar was struck on the
shoulder. This was the signal. Before he could stand, the
conspirators drew their daggers and stabbed Caesar
again and again. He did not succumb until he saw his
friend Brutus with a bloody weapon in his hand.

"And you, too, Brutus?" he said. "Then fall, Caesar."
With these words he died.

from The Kingfisher Book of the Ancient World

Hazel Mary Martell

Here is an account of life in the Roman empire—from its rise to its decline.

LIFE IN THE ROMAN EMPIRE
27 B.C.–A.D. 250

The Romans took their civilization to all the countries that they added to their empire. They tried not to upset the local way of life too much, however, as they wanted to live in peace with the people they had conquered. So long as these people were prepared to respect Roman gods and Roman laws, they were allowed to keep many of their own traditions.

The situation was made easier by the fact that many of the conquered peoples already knew about the Roman way of life through trading contacts. Some of them were only too pleased to become Romanized and accept what the empire had to offer.

The Romans built a system of good paved roads between major cities. They were built mainly for military use, to allow the army to travel quickly in times of trouble, but were also used by people traveling for trade or for pleasure.

New Towns Military camps and permanent forts for the army were built along the new roads, and towns often developed near or around these. Other towns grew up where two roads crossed or joined each other.

The towns were well-planned, with many public buildings and open spaces, as well as houses, apartment blocks, workshops, food stores, taverns, and restaurants where families could eat out. Not all Roman houses had cooking facilities.

The public buildings included a theater and an amphitheater, and at least one bath house, which usually had a *palaestra*, or open courtyard, where people could exercise. There were also government buildings and a *basilica*, or large hall, where meetings were held.

Judges sat inside the basilica to consider different legal cases, relating to the state and to individuals. Next door to it was a building called the *curia*. This was where the councilors met to pass local laws and to arrange how taxes would be collected. Above them were two magistrates, called *duoviri*, who held office for a year and governed the town.

All business in the town stopped around noon, and in the hottest weather people took a rest. The poor went back to work later, and the rich had the rest of the day off.

The Forum Most of the government buildings in a town, and also many of the temples, were grouped around the *forum*, an open area with covered pavements where people could meet and talk in all kinds of weather. Each temple was dedicated to a different god or goddess. Many of the Roman deities were the same as the Greek ones, but with different names. For example, the Roman goddess Diana was the same as the Greek goddess Artemis. Jupiter was the same as Zeus and Neptune the same as Poseidon.

People thought of a temple as a house for the particular god or goddess whose statue was kept there. Priests and priestesses carried out ceremonies and made animal sacrifices to the deity. Ordinary people made promises to different gods in exchange for their help.

The Romans also thought that their emperors became gods when they died, so temples were dedicated to them, too.

Children in towns were able to go to school from the age of seven. They learned to read, write, and do arithmetic before moving on to study history, geometry, and literature at the age of 11.

Schools were usually set up in private houses, and parents had to pay a fee for their children to attend. Many more boys than girls went to school, but evidence from letters and wax tablets shows that some women could read and write.

A Life of Luxury Life in the Roman Empire was luxurious for the rich. Their town houses were large, private, and well furnished, and they had many slaves to help with the work. Many wealthy people also had a country villa or an estate where they could go for relaxation.

Wealthy women wore makeup and perfume and dressed in clothes made from silk and fine linen. They probably helped choose the decorations for their houses. These included frescoes and mosaics.

Not everyone was pleased to be part of the Roman Empire. Many people wanted to keep their independence and live by their own laws. Rebellions broke out at various times in Spain, Gaul, Britain, and Judea. The Romans always crushed the rebels, often with great loss of life on both sides. For example, during the main British rebellion against the Romans in A.D. 61, up to 60,000 people died, and the Roman towns of Colchester and London were badly damaged.

THE DECLINE OF
THE ROMAN EMPIRE
A.D. 250–500

The decline of the Roman Empire began during the A.D. 200s. Central government weakened as a series of emperors were assassinated or removed from power by the army. Crippling taxes were demanded to pay for stronger defenses and more soldiers as frontiers came under attack.

In A.D. 286 the emperor Diocletian decided that the empire was too big for one man to rule by himself. He appointed a co-emperor to rule the western half while he ruled the east. He reorganized and expanded the army and imposed a system of taxation to help to pay for it.

Diocletian also subdivided the provinces to make them easier to rule. On a personal level, he persecuted people who did not believe that the emperor possessed divine authority and became a god when he died. He viewed such people as a threat to the security of the empire.

Constantine
Constantine the Great was emperor from A.D. 306 to A.D. 337. During his reign he reversed many of Diocletian's policies.

After his victory in an important battle, he became a Christian and encouraged the spread of this religion throughout the empire. He reunited the empire, made Byzantium in the east his capital, and renamed it Constantinople. Soon it became as grand as Rome itself.

The western half of the empire became weaker in the 400s, and parts were overrun by people the Romans called Barbarians. They set up their own kingdoms within the empire, and in A.D. 410 they attacked the city of Rome.

Soon after this the western half of the Roman Empire finally collapsed, but that in the east continued and became known as the Byzantine Empire.

from The Bronze Bow

Elizabeth George Speare

Here, an exiled boy meets some friends from a former life and tells them a little about his current life.

A boy stood on the path of the mountain overlooking the sea. He was a tall boy, with little trace of youth in his lean, hard body. At eighteen Daniel bar Jamin was unmistakably a Galilean, with the bold features of his countrymen, the sun-browned skin, and the brilliant dark eyes that could light with fierce patriotism and blacken with swift anger. A proud race, the Galileans, violent and restless, unreconciled that Palestine was a conquered nation, refusing to acknowledge as their lord the Emperor Tiberius in far-off Rome.

Looking down into the valley, the boy could see the silver-gray terraces of olive trees splashed with burgeoning thickets of oleander.[1] He remembered that in the brown, mud-roofed town every clump of earth, every cranny in a stone wall, would have burst into springtime flower. Remembering, he scowled up against the hot noonday sun.

He was waiting for two figures to reappear among the boulders that tumbled on either side of the path just above him. He was puzzled and uneasy, at odds with himself. Who were these two who had been so foolhardy as to climb the mountain? He was resentful that they had reminded him of the village, fearful that they might look back and discover him, yet unwilling to let them out of his sight. Why was he so bent on following them, when all he had wanted for five years was to forget that other world in the valley?

He glimpsed the boy again, some distance up, then the girl. Some memory nagged at him. Brother and sister, that was evident. They moved alike, with a sort of free, swinging ease. They had the same high cheekbones and dark ruddy complexions. Their voices were sharp in the clean air. Daniel could see the girl clearly. She had stopped to snatch a cluster of pink flax blossoms and she

---

1. oleander (ō′ lē an dər) *n.* a poisonous evergreen shrub with white, pink, or red flowers.

stood now, poised on a rock, her face lifted, her yellow head covering slipped back off her dark hair.

"Look, Joel!" she cried, her voice coming down to him distinctly. "How blue the lake is! You can see the tetrarch's palace in Tiberias."

Daniel's black brows drew together fiercely. Now he recognized the boy. He was Joel bar Hezron, the red-cheeked boy who used to come to the synagogue school, the scribe's son, the one the rabbi held up for an example, the one they used to tease because his twin sister always waited outside to walk home with him. She had an odd name—Malthace. Five years ago that was, and Daniel could still feel the hurt of seeing her waiting there outside the school, while his own sister—

"We're almost there!" the boy's voice rang out. The girl sprang down from the rock. The two flicked out of sight, sending a quick hail of pebbles bounding down the path. Daniel moved forward with the caution of an animal stalking its prey.

He reached the top just as the girl, flushed and out of breath, flung herself down on the patch of grass where Joel waited. She snatched the head covering clear off, letting the wind pull at her hair. Daniel could see them pointing out to each other the landmarks below.

From where he crouched he could not see the valley, but he knew the sight of it well enough. How many times had he sat where those two sat now, looking down on the village of Ketzah that had been his home? Not so often these last years, but at first, before he had got used to life in the cave. Sometimes he had climbed up and sat here till dark, straining his eyes to catch the specks of light, picturing Leah and his grandmother at their evening meal, wondering if he would ever see them again. He never had, and he had stopped remembering and wondering—until today.

Now that Joel and his sister were no longer shouting, the wind hid their voices. He stared at them, disappointed and baffled. He had to hear them. More than that, he was fighting back a longing to speak to them. His own people—after five years! He looked down at his bare calloused feet, at the goatskin tunic bound with a thong around his waist. What would they think of him, those two in their clean robes and leather sandals? Suppose he should risk his freedom for nothing? But he could not help himself. Like an animal lured out of hiding, he edged slowly from behind the rock.

Instantly the boy was on his feet, the girl swiftly up beside him. He might have known they would be off at the sight of him. To his astonishment, they stood still. He saw Joel's hands clench; the boy was no coward. Daniel stood on the trail, his heart pounding. If they ran from him now he could not bear it. He fumbled for the remembered greeting.

"Peace be with you," he said.

Joel did not relax his guard. "Peace," he said shortly; then, "What do you want?"

"No harm, Joel bar Hezron," said Daniel.

"How do you know me?"

"I heard your sister call you. I am Daniel bar Jamin."

Joel stared, remembrance suddenly livening his face. "The apprentice who ran away from the blacksmith?"

Daniel scowled.

"No one blamed you," said Joel quickly. "Everyone knows how Amalek treats his boys."

"I care nothing for Amalek," Daniel said. "Can you tell me about my grandmother and my sister?"

Joel frowned and shook his head. "I'm afraid I can't. Do you know them, Thace?"

The girl had been frightened, and her breath was still uneven, but she spoke with a frankness like Joel's.

"There is an old woman who comes to the well in the morning," she said. "She lives in a house behind the Street of the Cheesemakers."

"Yes," Daniel said hungrily.

The girl hesitated. "They say she has a little girl who never goes out of the house."

Still? He had thought perhaps in all this time—"That is my sister Leah," he said. He wished he had not asked. It had been better not knowing.

"No one has ever seen her," the girl went on. "But I know that she's there. I'm sorry. I wish I could tell you more."

Daniel hesitated, embarrassed, but unwilling to give up.

"There was a boy named Simon," he said. "Six or seven years older. He was bound to Amalek too."

"You must mean Simon the Zealot," said Joel.

"You know him?"

"I've heard of him. He has his own shop now. They say he gets more business than Amalek."

"He used to help me," said Daniel.

"He has a reputation for being a good man—and a good patriot."

"Would you give him a message for me? Would you tell him I'm up here? I'd like him to know."

Joel looked surprised. "You mean you live up here?"

"Yes."

"Alone? Is it safe? I mean—they say the mountain is full of robbers."

Daniel said nothing.

"Aren't you lonely?"

"I don't live alone," said Daniel.

"Oh." Joel was baffled. "Don't you ever come back to the village?"

"I'd just get dragged back to Amalek's shop."

"I suppose so. Yes, I'll tell Simon, of course. How long since you ran away?"

"Five years, about. Simon will remember me, though."

The girl spoke, in a straightforward voice that matched the look in her eyes. "Five years! Do you mean your grand-mother hasn't known where you were in all this time?"

Daniel looked at the ground, his lips tightening.

"Tomorrow, when she comes to the well, can I tell her I've seen you?"

Daniel looked back at her with resentment. He had long since managed to quiet his conscience, and he did not like having it stirred up again. "If you like," he said. He felt angry at himself now, and disappointed. Why had he given himself away after all these years? What had he expected? There was nothing more to stay for.

"You'd better go back," he said, turning away. "You shouldn't have come up here?"

"Why not?" asked Joel, looking not at all alarmed.

"I'm warning you. After this, stay in the village." He walked away from them.

"Wait," called Joel. He looked at his sister with a swift question, and she nodded. "We—we brought our lunch. Will you eat it with us?"

The blood rushed up into Daniel's face. He had not asked for their charity.

"It's not much," Joel said. "But we'd like to talk to you some more."

Was it possible this boy had made the offer in friend-ship? Slowly, like a wary animal, Daniel took a few steps back and let himself down on the grass. From the pocket of the wide striped girdle that bound her waist, the girl pulled a neatly wrapped bundle. Joel produced a small flask which he handed to his sister, then sat down and solemnly held out his hands. With astonishment Daniel watched the girl pour a little stream of water over her brother's hands. Hand-washing before a meal—he hadn't given a thought to it for five years. He wouldn't have imagined that even a scribe's son would carry water all the way up the mountain just to observe the law. Then the girl turned toward him. He saw the question in her eyes and the slight shrinking, and a stubborn pride stiffened him. He was a Jew, wasn't he? He held out his hands, and watched the drops trickle over his blackened knuckles, embarrassed, thinking how the men in the cave would hoot if they could see him.

The girl unwrapped the bundle and made three small piles, equal piles, he noticed, not skimping herself the way his mother used to do. Then Joel spoke a blessing and they handed Daniel his share, a few olives, a flat little loaf of wheat bread, and a small honey cake whose taste his tongue suddenly remembered from childhood. For the first time Daniel felt his tight muscles begin to relax. His eyes met Joel's, and the two boys studied each other without hostility.

"Why did you come up here?" Joel asked, wiping the last crumbs of cake off his chin.

In some way the food had made it easier to speak. "I knew there were caves up here," Daniel answered. "All I wanted was a place to hide where Amalek couldn't catch me. But I couldn't find any caves, and I wandered around for three days, and then—a man found me."

He thought of how Rosh had found him lying flat on his face, starving, half frozen, his back still raw from the last flogging. How could he tell this boy what that night had been like? He remembered the terrible moment when he had seen the man bending over him, and how Rosh had reached out a hand, not to strike him but to help him to his feet, and then, when he had flopped over, how Rosh had picked him up and carried him like a baby all the way to the cave.

"A robber?" Joel questioned.

"A good man," said Daniel fiercely. "He took me to live with him."

"What's it like up here? What do you do all the time?"

"Hunt. Wolves and jackals, even panthers. Sometimes we hunt as far north as Merom. I work at my trade too. I made a forge to work on."

Joel looked impressed. Even the girl was listening with dark eyes as lively as her brother's. Daniel looked at the other boy with curiosity. He had been trying to find a distinguishing mark about Joel. "What is your trade?" he asked.

"I'm still at school," said Joel. "I'm going to go on to be a rabbi, probably. But I studied sandal-making too. I could earn my living at it, but I'm sorry for the man who has to wear my sandals."

Daniel nodded. Of course Joel would be a rabbi. He had always been the smartest boy in the school. But even a rabbi must learn a trade, like any other man.

"Why did you come today?" he asked. "No one comes up here from the village."

The girl laughed. "We'll be skinned alive if anyone finds out we've come," she said.

"We always planned to," Joel explained. "Ever since we were children. We weren't allowed to because it's supposed to be dangerous. Today's a holiday, and we just decided to come without telling anyone. It was our last chance. We're leaving the village and going to live in Capernaum."

His sister frowned at him. "I don't see why you always have to sound so dismal about it," she protested. "I think Capernaum is going to be wonderful."

Joel's face looked suddenly closed. His fingers snapped the tops off the red blossoms, one after another. It was plain to Daniel that this was an old argument between them.

"What more do you want?" she demanded, forgetting Daniel in her insistence. "A big house to live in, shops, and people, and a school with the best teachers in Galilee!"

Joel went on snipping the blossoms savagely. "Father doesn't want to go," he said. "He's only going to please Mother."

"Well," she answered, "Mother left it all to please him once. It hasn't been easy for her, living in Ketzah. Why shouldn't she go back, now that Grandfather's left his house to her? It doesn't really matter to Father where he is, so long as he has his books."

Daniel listened, shut out again from the clean, safe world that they shared. But all at once his attention was diverted. Far down the mountain, on the narrow ribbon of road, he spotted a moving line that threw off reddish flashes of metal in the sunlight. Legionaries.[2] At the sight, black hatred churned up in him. Out of habit he spat violently. The shocked attention of the two jerked back to him, and they followed his savage gaze, leaning to peer at the moving line.

"Romans!" snorted Joel. Daniel liked the way he said the word. He spat again for good measure.

"You hate them too," said Joel, his voice low.

Daniel closed his teeth on a familiar oath. "I curse the air they breathe," he muttered.

"I envy you," said Joel. "Up here you're free."

"No one is free," said Daniel. "So long as the land is cursed by the Romans."

"No. But at least you don't have to look at them. There's a fortress at Capernaum. I'll have to watch them all the time, strutting around the streets."

"Oh, Joel!" the girl protested. "Do they have to bother us?"

"Bother us? Bother—!" The boy's voice broke. "I should think even a girl could see—"

"Of course I see!" She was stung almost to tears by her brother's contempt. "But what use is it to be always making yourself miserable? The Romans won't be here forever. We know that deliverance will come."

"You're talking like Father!"

"But he's right! The Jews have been worse off before. There have always been conquerors—and there was always deliverance, Joel."

Joel was not listening. He had caught Daniel's eye, and the two boys were studying each other, each asking a silent question.

Malthace sprang to her feet, recognizing well enough that this time it was she who was shut out. "I'm not going to have my holiday spoiled by those soldiers," she said, with the trace of a childish pout. "We've climbed all the way up here and you've scarcely looked at the things we came to see."

Joel turned back to her good-naturedly. "We've seen something we didn't expect," he said. "Daniel."

---

2. **legionaries** Roman soldiers.

She tossed her head. "What about the places we used to talk about? The plain where Joshua marched out against the heathen kings?"

Joel shaded his eyes, taking his bearings. Just below them the village clung to the rocky slope, the dark block of the synagogue showing clearly among the clustering flat-roofed houses. Around it circled the gray-green olive orchards and the fresh, clear green fields of grain, banded by purple iris and shining yellow daffodils. To the south lay the lake, intensely blue. To the north, beyond the line of hills, through the shimmering, misty green of the valley, the silver thread of the Jordan wound up to the shining little jewel that was the Lake of Merom. Suddenly bold, Daniel got to his feet.

"There," he pointed out. "On that plain. Horses and chariots drawn up against him, and a great host of men like the sands of the shore. And Joshua fell on them and drove them as far as the Great Sea."

He saw surprise on their faces. They thought he was an ignorant savage. The girl did, anyway. This was something he knew. Five years ago, that first morning, when he was warm and fed and slept out, Rosh had brought him up here, and stood with an arm across his shoulders, and pointed to the plain in the distance, and told him how a few brave men had dared to go out against a great army, and how they had won a great victory for Israel. Up here, in the clean sunlight, Daniel bar Jamin, orphan, runaway slave, had found something to live for.

"All the mighty ones," he said, remembering Rosh's very words. "Joshua, Gideon, David, all of them fought on the soil of Galilee. No one could stand against them. It will be so again."

"Yes," breathed Joel. "It will be so again. God will send us another David." His eyes glistened, as though he too could see the shadow of a vast army moving on the distant plain.

"You mean the Messiah!" Malthace cried. "Oh Joel, do you remember? We always thought that up here we'd see him."

"I was sure," said Joel. "I knew that if we could only climb up here, that would be the day he would come. I believed it so hard, it seemed to me I could *make* it happen."

"So did I. And we would be the ones to rush down the mountain and tell them. And all the people in the village would drop their work and follow him. Do all children have such wild imaginations?"

Joel was instantly sober. "The Messiah is not imagination. It's the truth. It is promised."

"But straining our eyes at every cloud in the distance, and thinking we would be the first ones—"

"I still want to be!" cried Joel, so passionately that the other two were startled. "Call it childish if you like. That's why I don't want to go to Capernaum."

"But it may be years!"

"No. It must be soon. Not the way we imagined it, Thacia. I used to think he would come with a great host of angels. Now I know it must be men, real men, trained and armed and ready—" He checked himself.

"There are such men," said Daniel, keeping his eyes on the distant hills. Without looking, he felt the other boy's muscles tighten.

"I know," Joel answered. Excitement leaped from one boy to the other. The question had been answered.

Malthace looked at her brother, puzzled by something she could not understand. "We should start back now," she said. "We must be home for supper."

"I'll walk a way with you," Daniel offered. He was thinking that he would like to see them safely onto the main road.

They started down the steep slope of the mountain. Once they left the summit behind, the breeze died down, the golden sun hung close above them, and not a leaf moved beside the path. They did not talk now. Daniel could see that Joel was still seething with hidden thoughts. He suspected that for the girl this holiday had not turned out as she had hoped. As for himself, he was already beginning to wish that they had never come. He had been satisfied up here, not thinking too much, shutting out the things he didn't want to remember—working for Rosh, and waiting, nursing his hatred, for the hour that would come. He had never had a friend of his own, and he had never thought about wanting one. Why hadn't he let well enough alone?

Malthace was impatient now. Probably her conscience was beginning to trouble her. But Joel lingered, trying deliberately to fall behind. When his sister was distracted by a clump of myrrh blossoms just ahead, he spoke half under his breath.

"There was something else I hoped for when I came up here," he said. "I've heard that Rosh the outlaw lives on the mountain. I hoped I might be lucky enough to see him."

"Why?"

"He's a hero to every boy at school. But no one has ever seen him. Have you?"

Daniel hesitated. "Yes," he said.

Joel stopped in the pathway, forgetting his caution. "What I'd give—! Are the things they say about him true?"

"What do they say?"

"That he fought beside the great leader Judas when they rebelled against the Romans at Sepphoris, and that when the others were crucified, he escaped and hid in the hills. Some men say he's nothing but a bandit who robs even his fellow Jews. But others say he takes the money from the rich and gives it to the poor. Do you know him? What is he really like?"

No caution in the world could hide the fierce pride that rushed over Daniel. "He's the bravest man in the world! Let them say what they like. Some day every man in Israel will know his name!"

"Then it's true!" cried Joel. "He's raising an army to fight against Rome! That's what you meant up there, isn't it? And you—you are one of them. I knew it!"

"Rosh is the man I told you about, the one who found me. I've been with him ever since."

"I envy you! I've dreamed of joining Rosh."

"Then come. No one could find you up here."

Malthace had stopped and turned back, waiting. Joel looked down at her and made a small helpless gesture. "It's not so simple as all that," he said. "My father—"

"Oh Joel, why are you so slow? What are you talking about?" The girl stood in the pathway, her arms full of crimson blossoms, her dark hair, still uncovered, falling about her shoulders, her cheeks flushed with the sun.

If he were Joel would he run away? Daniel wondered suddenly. Suppose his father and mother waited, with the lamps lighted and a good supper laid out? Suppose he had a sister who could run to the top of the mountain with him and be scarcely winded?

Then abruptly he stopped wondering. Just below Malthace he caught sight of another figure. In the middle of the trail, blocking their way, stood one of Rosh's sentries, Ebol, waiting for them to come down.

from The Burning of Rome

from the Annals

Tacitus

Translated by Michael Grant

*The ancient historian Tacitus makes this account of the
great fire of Rome come alive with vivid descriptions of
burning buildings and terrified people.*

Now started the most terrible and destructive fire which
Rome had ever experienced. It began in the Circus,[1]
where it adjoins the Palatine and Caelian hills.[2] Breaking
out in shops selling inflammable goods, and fanned by
the wind, the conflagration[3] instantly grew and swept the
whole length of the Circus. There were no walled mansions or temples, or any other obstructions, which could
arrest it. First, the fire swept violently over the level
spaces. Then it climbed the hills—but returned to ravage
the lower ground again. It outstripped every counter-
measure. The ancient city's narrow winding streets and
irregular blocks encouraged its progress.

Terrified, shrieking women, helpless old and young,
people intent on their own safety, people unselfishly sup-
porting invalids or waiting for them, fugitives and linger-
ers alike—all heightened the confusion. When people
looked back, menacing flames sprang up before them or
outflanked them. When they escaped to a neighboring
quarter, the fire followed—even districts believed remote
proved to be involved. Finally, with no idea where or what
to flee they crowded onto the country roads or lay in the
fields. Some who had lost everything—even their food for
the day—could have escaped, but preferred to die. So did
others, who had failed to rescue their loved ones. Nobody
dared fight the flames. Attempts to do so were prevented
by menacing gangs. Torches, too, were openly thrown in,
by men crying that they acted under orders. Perhaps

---

1. **Circus** (sur′ kəs) *n.* In ancient Rome, games and chariot races were held in the
Circus, an oval arena surrounded by tiers of seats.
2. **Palatine and Caelian** (pal′ ə tīn′ and kē′ lē ən) **hills** where Nero's imperial
palaces were located.
3. **conflagration** (kän′ flə grā shən) *n.* a large fire.

they had received orders. Or they may just have wanted to plunder unhampered.[4]

Nero was at Antium.[5] He only returned to the city when the fire was approaching the mansion he had built to link the Gardens of Maecenas to the Palatine. The flames could not be prevented from overwhelming the whole of the Palatine, including his palace. Nevertheless, for the relief of the homeless, fugitive masses he threw open the Field of Mars, including Agrippa's public buildings, and even his own Gardens. Nero also constructed emergency accommodation for the destitute[6] multitude. Food was brought from Ostia[7] and neighboring towns, and the price of corn was cut to less than ¼ sesterce[8] a pound. Yet these measures, for all their popular character, earned no gratitude. For a rumor had spread that, while the city was burning, Nero had gone on his private stage and, comparing modern calamities with ancient, had sung of the destruction of Troy.

By the sixth day enormous demolitions had confronted the raging flames with bare ground and open sky, and the fire was finally stamped out at the foot of the Esquiline Hill. But before panic had subsided, or hope revived, flames broke out again in the more open regions of the city. Here there were fewer casualties; but the destruction of temples and pleasure arcades was even worse. This new conflagration caused additional ill-feeling because it started on Tigellinus' estate[9] in the Aemilian district. For people believed that Nero was ambitious to found a new city to be called after himself.

Of Rome's fourteen districts only four remained intact. Three were leveled to the ground. The other seven were reduced to a few scorched and mangled ruins. To count the mansions, blocks, and temples destroyed would be difficult. They included shrines of remote antiquity,[10] such as Servius Tullius' temple of the Moon, the Great Altar and holy place dedicated by Evander to Hercules,

---

4. unhampered (un ham′ pərd) v. not hindered or impeded; free of burdens or other constraints.

5. Antium (an′ tē əm) n. town in central Italy where Nero was born.

6. destitute (des′ tə to͞ot′) adj. not having; lacking; poor.

7. Ostia (äs′ tē ə) n. Roman port at the mouth of the Tiber River.

8. sesterce (ses′ tərs) n. Roman coin, equal in value to two and a half cents.

9. Tigellinus' estate (to jel ē′ nəs) land belonging to Tigellinus, second to Nero in power.

10. antiquity (an tik′ wə tē) n. the early period of history.

the temple vowed by Romulus to Jupiter the Stayer, Numa's sacred residence, and Vesta's shrine containing Rome's household gods. Among the losses, too, were the precious spoils of countless victories, Greek artistic masterpieces, and authentic records of old Roman genius. All the splendor of the rebuilt city did not prevent the older generation from remembering these irreplaceable objects. It was noted that the fire had started on July 19th, the day on which the Senonian Gauls[11] had captured and burnt the city. Others elaborately calculated that the two fires were separated by the same number of years, months, and days.[12]

But Nero profited by his country's ruin to build a new palace. Its wonders were not so much customary and commonplace luxuries like gold and jewels, but lawns and lakes and faked rusticity—woods here, open spaces and views there. With their cunning, impudent[13] artificialities, Nero's architects and engineers, Severus and Celer, did not balk at effects which Nature herself had ruled out as impossible.

They also fooled away an emperor's riches. For they promised to dig a navigable canal from Lake Avernus to the Tiber estuary,[14] over the stony shore and mountain barriers. The only water to feed the canal was in the Pontine marshes. Elsewhere, all was precipitous[15] or waterless. Moreover, even if a passage could have been forced, the labor would have been unendurable and unjustified. But Nero was eager to perform the incredible; so he attempted to excavate the hills adjoining Lake Avernus. Traces of his frustrated hopes are visible today.

In parts of Rome unfilled by Nero's palace, construction was not—as after the burning by the Gauls—without plan or demarcation.[16] Street-fronts were of regulated alignment, streets were broad, and houses built round courtyards. Their height was restricted, and their

---

11. Senonian Gauls (sə nō′ nē ən gôlz) barbarians from Gaul, an ancient region in western Europe; they burned Rome in 390 B.C.
12. the same number of years, months, and days 418 years, months, and days.
13. impudent (im′ pyoo dənt) *adj.* shamelessly bold and disrespectful; saucy.
14. Tiber estuary (tī bər es′ choo wer ē) the wide mouth of the Tiber, a river in central Italy that flows south through Rome.
15. precipitous (prē sip′ ə təs) *adj.* steep.
16. demarcation (dē mär kā′ shən) *n.* boundary.

frontages protected by colonnades. Nero undertook to erect these at his own expense, and also to clear debris from building-sites before transferring them to their owners. He announced bonuses, in proportion to rank and resources, for the completion of houses and blocks before a given date. Rubbish was to be dumped in the Ostian marshes by corn-ships returning down the Tiber.

A fixed proportion of every building had to be massive, unlimbered stone from Gabii[17] or Alba[18] (these stones being fireproof). Furthermore, guards were to ensure a more abundant and extensive public water supply, hitherto diminished by irregular private enterprise. Householders were obliged to keep fire-fighting apparatus in an accessible place; and semidetached houses were forbidden—they must have their own walls. These measures were welcomed for their practicality, and they beautified the new city. Some, however, believed that the old town's configuration had been healthier, since its narrow streets and high houses had provided protection against the burning sun, whereas now the shadowless open spaces radiated a fiercer heat.

So much for human precautions. Next came attempts to appease heaven. After consultation of the Sibylline Books,[19] prayers were addressed to Vulcan, Ceres, and Proserpina. Juno, too, was propitiated.[20] Women who had been married were responsible for the rites—first on the Capitol, then at the nearest sea-board, where water was taken to sprinkle her temple and statue. Women with husbands living also celebrated ritual banquets and vigils.

But neither human resources, nor imperial munificence,[21] nor appeasement of the gods, eliminated sinister suspicions that the fire had been instigated. To suppress this rumor, Nero fabricated scapegoats—and punished

---

17. Gabii (gäb′ ē ē) *n.* ancient Roman town where Romulus, legendary founder of Rome, was reared. Gabii supposedly resisted a siege and was an important city until it was overshadowed by Rome.
18. Alba (äl′ bə) *n.* Alba Longa, a powerful ancient Roman city; legendary birthplace of Romulus and Remus.
19. Sibylline (sib′ əl in) **Books** books of prophecies by Sibyl, Apollo's priestess at Cumae, a city in southwest Italy near Naples.
20. propitiated (prō pish′ ē āt′ əd) *v.* appeased.
21. munificence (myōō nif′ ə səns) *n.* generosity.

with every refinement the notoriously depraved Christians (as they were popularly called). Their originator, Christ, had been executed in Tiberius' reign[22] by the governor of Judaea,[23] Pontius Pilatus. But in spite of this temporary setback the deadly superstition had broken out afresh, not only in Judaea (where the mischief had started) but even in Rome. All degraded and shameful practices collect and flourish in the capital.

First, Nero had self-acknowledged Christians arrested. Then, on their information, large numbers of others were condemned—not so much for incendiarism[24] as for their antisocial tendencies. Their deaths were made farcical. Dressed in wild animals' skins, they were torn to pieces by dogs, or crucified, or made into torches to be ignited after dark as substitutes for daylight. Nero provided his Gardens for the spectacle, and exhibited displays in the Circus, at which he mingled with the crowd—or stood in a chariot, dressed as a charioteer. Despite their guilt as Christians, and the ruthless punishment it deserved, the victims were pitied. For it was felt that they were being sacrificed to one man's brutality rather than to the national interest.

Meanwhile Italy was ransacked for funds, and the provinces were ruined—unprivileged and privileged communities alike. Even the gods were included in the looting. Temples at Rome were robbed, and emptied of the gold dedicated for the triumphs and vows, the ambitions and fears, of generations of Romans. Plunder from Asia and Greece included not only offerings but actual statues of the gods. Two agents were sent to these provinces. One, Acratus, was an ex-slave, capable of any depravity. The other, Secundus Carrinas, professed Greek culture, but no virtue from it percolated to his heart.

Seneca,[25] rumor went, sought to avoid the odium of this sacrilege by asking leave to retire to a distant country retreat, and then—permission being refused—feigning a muscular complaint and keeping to his bedroom. According to some accounts one of his former slaves, Cleonicus by name, acting on Nero's orders intended to poison

---

22. **Tiberius'** (tī bir′ ē əs) **reign** Tiberius was emperor of Rome A.D. 14–37.
23. **Judaea** (jōō dē′ ə) *n.* ancient region of South Palestine.
24. **incendiarism** (in sen′ dē ə riz′m) *n.* willful destruction of property by fire.
25. **Seneca** (sen′ ə kə) *n.* philosopher and minister of Nero.

Seneca but he escaped—either because the man confessed or because Seneca's own fears caused him to live very simply on plain fruit, quenching his thirst with running water.

At this juncture there was an attempted breakout by gladiators at Praeneste.[26] Their army guards overpowered them. But the Roman public, as always terrified (or fascinated) by revolution, were already talking of ancient calamities such as the rising of Spartacus.[27] Soon afterwards a naval disaster occurred. This was not on active service; never had there been such profound peace. But Nero had ordered the fleet to return to Campania by a fixed date regardless of weather. So, despite heavy seas the steersmen started from Formiae. But when they tried to round Cape Misenum a southwesterly gale drove them ashore near Cumae and destroyed numerous warships and smaller craft.

---

26. Praeneste (prī nest′) a town in central Italy.
27. Spartacus (spärt′ ə kəs) *n.* ancient Thracian slave and gladiator who led a slave revolt.

Biographical Notes

William Acker (1910–1974) Acker was a professor of Chinese language and culture who edited and translated a number of Chinese texts.

Daisy Aldan (b. 1923) Aldan, who has travelled in Europe, Central America, India, and the Far East, has taught creative writing, English, literature, film studies, and speech in New York City, England, and Switzerland. An award-winning poet, she has received the DeWitt American Lyric Poetry Award of the Poetry Society of America and the National Endowment of the Arts Poetry Prize. In 1978 her book of poems, *Between High Tides,* was nominated for a Pulitzer Prize.

Bernarda Bryson A writer and an illustrator, Bryson did research for many years before writing the text for *Gilgamesh.* She lives in New Jersey.

Debjani Chatterjee (b. 1953) Chatterjee was born in India and now lives in Sheffield, England. Of the Hindu myths she retells, Chatterjee says, "They contain voices from hundreds of years ago. . . . These stories come from ancient India, but they belong to children everywhere and in every age."

Shirley Climo (b. 1928) Climo remembers being rocked in a carriage while her mother, an author of children's books, recited stories to her. She was telling stories to herself and anyone else who would listen before she could read. She uses her own experience, including her childhood in Cleveland, Ohio, as sources for her writing. In fact, each new addition to her life brings additional storytelling materials.

Confucius (551?–449? B.C.) The ideas of Confucius, a scholar from the Shantung province in northeast China, have influenced the pattern of Chinese life for more than two thousand years. Confucius lived at a time when corruption and civil strife raged in China. He taught that if people followed tradition and authority with the proper spirit of reverence, the country's health could be restored.

James M. Deem Born in Wheeling, West Virginia, Deem has also lived in Arizona, Kansas, Michigan, and New York. He has a bachelor's degree from the University of Kansas and a doctorate from the University of Michigan, and he has written more than ten books for young people.

Justin Denzel Early in his career, Denzel worked at the American Museum of Natural History, where he studied prehistoric life. During World War II, he wrote for *Nature* magazine and for *Stars and Stripes*. When the war ended, he became a research librarian for a pharmaceutical company in New Jersey, where he now lives and writes full-time for young readers.

Bernard Evslin (1922–1993) Evslin was born in Philadelphia and attended Rutgers University. He wrote more than thirty books for young people, many of them dealing with Greek mythology and history.

John L. Foster (b. 1930) Foster, who was born in Chicago, studied at Kalamazoo College, Harvard University, and the University of Michigan. He has been on the faculty of the University of Connecticut in Storrs, Wisconsin State University, and Roosevelt University in Chicago. In 1971 he received a fellowship from the National Endowment for the Humanities for translating ancient Egyptian literature.

Joseph Gaer (1897–1969) Gaer was born in Russia and came to the United States in 1917, becoming a citizen in 1926. He was a prolific writer, publishing short stories, articles, plays, poetry, novels, and histories.

Anita Ganeri Born in Calcutta, India, Ganeri attended secondary school and college in England. She has published more than one hundred books and has been made a Fellow of The Royal Geographical Society. She lives in West Yorkshire, England.

James Cross Giblin (b. 1933) Giblin, an editor and writer of children's books, thought of writing about walls when he went to China in 1975 and climbed a section of the Great Wall. Several of his books for young people have received the ALA Notable Book award.

Joyce Goldenstern A teacher and a freelance textbook writer, Goldenstern is also a writer of nonfiction and screenplays.

Michael Grant (b. 1914) Grant was born in London and now lives in Italy. He is a well-known writer of the history of the ancient Mediterranean. He has a particular interest in Roman coins.

Homer (c. 800–750 B.C.) Little is known about the life of Homer, the blind ancient Greek poet. He probably lived in Asia Minor (now Turkey) or on an island in the eastern Mediterranean, and he is thought to have been a wandering poet who recited his poems at royal courts in exchange for food and lodging. In the *Iliad* and the *Odyssey*, Homer first set down in writing legends that had been recited by generations of poets before him.

Horace (65–8 B.C.) Horace's father had once been a slave, but by the time Horace was born, his father could afford to give him the best available education. After the murder of Julius Caesar, Horace fought with Brutus' army and was defeated at Philippi. He went to Rome, where he wrote poetry and prose, particularly satire.

Elaine Landau Landau, who lives in Miami, has written over 185 nonfiction books on subjects such as the supernatural, planets, dinosaurs, and ancient civilizations. Her husband works with her on many of her books, and she says that she often writes under a palm tree while drinking lemonade.

Lao Tzu (c. fifth or fourth century B.C.) Lao Tzu, which means "Old Master," is the author of the *Tao Te Ching*, or *The Way and Its Power*, one of the basic texts of Taoist philosophy. According to legend, Lao Tzu, who was unhappy with the political situation of his day, tried to leave China through a mountain pass in the west. The gatekeeper of the pass recognized him as a wise and learned man and refused to let him through until he wrote down some words of wisdom. Lao Tzu then wrote the *Tao Te Ching* and was allowed to leave the country.

Patricia Lauber (b. 1924) Lauber, who loves mysteries and puzzles, has written more than eighty books of fiction and nonfiction dealing with such subjects as the Ice Age, volcanoes, the Loch Ness monster—and runaway fleas!

Alice Low (b. 1926) As a girl, Low enjoyed making puppets and performing in plays. As an adult, she has written a musical play and many articles for magazines, and she is famous for her retellings of myths and folk tales.

Jay Macpherson (b. 1931) Macpherson is best known for her poetry, which celebrates the power of imagination. Because her poems feature many symbols from myths and legends, it's no surprise that Macpherson has also written a retelling of the Greek myth *Narcissus*. Although she was born in England, Macpherson has lived most of her life in Canada.

Geraldine McCaughrean (b. 1951) Born in Enfield, Middlesex, England, McCaughrean says she was shy as a child and can't remember a time when she wasn't writing stories. She also says that if she hadn't been a writer, she would have been miserable.

Betty Miles (b. 1928) Miles says that she gets the ideas for her books "from the same places everyone else does: from things that happen to me and to people I know, from places I go to, from what I read. . . . I get ideas from the things I observe or overhear, and, of course, from memory . . . Often, my story ideas come when I ask 'What if?' . . . . I always hope, when my ideas have become a book, that my readers will enjoy sharing experiences and feelings with my characters—and with me."

Mary Pope Osborne (b. 1949) Osborne, who earned a degree in religion from the University of North Carolina, has written a number of outstanding novels for young adults. She lives in New York City.

Leontyne Price (b. 1927) Known as one of the world's great divas (leading women singers, especially in grand opera), Price is famous for her portrayal of the Ethiopian princess in the opera version of *Aïda*. In fact she retired in 1985 with her final performance of *Aïda*, a performance that was televised live and viewed by millions.

William F. Russell (b. 1945) Russell not only enjoys writing about ancient myths, he encourages children and adults to enjoy listening to myths that are read aloud. He has written books about reading myths and classic stories aloud. He earned a Ph.D. in education by studying ways in which parents influence the achievements of their children.

Arthur W. Ryder (1877–1938) "Ten men like him would make a civilization." Such was the praise a colleague gave to Ryder, a brilliant Sanskrit scholar. The first professor of Sanskrit at the University of California at Berkeley, Ryder completed his translation of the *Panchatantra* in 1924.

Tiphaine Samoyault (b. 1968) Samoyault, who lives in Paris, has written a series of books using art to explain classical literary texts to children. She is a professor of literature, a novelist, and a literary critic.

Sean Sheehan and Pat Levy Both Sheehan and Levy have studied ancient Roman literature and have written a number of books for young readers. They are both very interested in the ancient world, especially ancient Greece and Rome.

Elizabeth George Speare (1908–1994) Speare was born in Melrose, Massachusetts, and started writing as a child. After she married, she moved to Connecticut, and when her children were young, she didn't have much time to write. When her children were in junior high school, she began to write articles for magazines and eventually began to write novels. Two of her books, *The Witch of Blackbird Pond* and *The Bronze Bow*, were awarded the Newbery Medal.

Rosemary Sutcliff (1920–1992) Sutcliff was born in England, but, as a child, she lived in Malta, where her father was an officer in the Royal Navy. She was home-schooled by her mother and introduced to Celtic and Saxon legends. Of the forty-six novels that she wrote for young people, several have been placed on the ALA Notable Books list and the Horn Book Honor List.

T'ao Ch'ien (365–427) T'ao Ch'ien was born into a family of government officials in China. When he was thirty-five, he resigned from his government position and settled on a rural farm. There he lived quietly with his family and wrote poetry that expressed his philosophy of living a tranquil life.

Publius Cornelius Tacitus (c. A.D. 55–117) Tacitus was a master of several kinds of prose writing on a variety of subjects. His major works, the *Annals* and the *Histories*, give a year-by-year account of the first eighty years of the Roman Empire. In all his works, Tacitus shows a gift for drama, as well as a genius for concise, convincing psychological portraits.

Tu Fu (712–770) Tu Fu, who travelled extensively as a young man and met the great poet Li Po, is considered by many to be the greatest Chinese poet. He had a difficult life filled with hardships, including the death of several of his children from starvation. His poetry celebrates the beauty of the natural world, regrets the passage of time, and speaks against the senselessness of war.

Louis Untermeyer (1885–1977) Born in New York City, Untermeyer was a poet, a critic, and a biographer, but he is best known for his many anthologies. He published more than eighty books.

Richard Watkins Watkins, who is a toy designer, loves monster movies and toys from the sixties. His parents contributed to his interest in gladiators by travelling to Italy and bringing him back a book with stories and pictures of ancient Rome.

Anne Terry White (1896–1980) Born in Russia, White worked as a teacher, a social worker, and a translator of Russian literature. The subjects of her writing are as varied as her interests were: stars, rocks, rivers, mountains, American history, and ancient civilizations. She has become most famous, however, as an authority on ancient Greece.

Leonard Wibberley (1915–1983) An author and a journalist, Wibberley wrote over fifty books for children. He was a native of Ireland but lived in California for many years.

Geraldine Woods A teacher of English and director of the independent study program at Horace Mann School in New York City, Woods has written more than thirty-five books for young people, many co-authored with her husband Harold.

Paul Yee (b. 1956) Born in Saskatchewan, Canada, Yee grew up in Vancouver and now lives in Toronto. The source of much of his award-winning writing is Vancouver's Chinatown.

Acknowledgments continued from copyright page

Macmillan Publishing Co., A Division of Simon & Schuster, Inc. "Orpheus" by Alice Low from *Greek Gods and Heroes*. Copyright © 1985 by Macmillan Publishing Company. **Jay Macpherson** "Narcissus" by Jay Macpherson from *Four Ages of Man: The Classical Myths*. Copyright © 1962 by Jay Macpherson. **Margaret K. McElderry Books, Simon & Schuster Children's Publishing Division** "The Great Flood" by Geraldine McCaughrean from *God's People: Stories from The Old Testament*. Copyright © 1997 by Geraldine McGaughrean. **Oxford University Press, Inc.** "The Race" by Debjani Chatterjee from *The Elephant-headed God and Other Hindu Tales*. Copyright © 1989 by Debjani Chatterjee. **Oxford University Press, Inc.** "Scarlet on the Loom" by Rosemary Sutcliff from *Warrior Scarlet*. Copyright © 1958 Oxford University Press. **Oxford University Press, UK** From *The Eagle of the Ninth* by Rosemary Sutcliff. Copyright © 1954 by Oxford University Press, England & Henry Z. Walck, Inc. **Penguin Books Inc.** From *Tao Te Ching (or The Way and Its Power)* by Lao Tzu. Copyright ©1963 by D.C. Lau. From "The Burning of Rome" by Tacitus from *The Annals of Imperial Rome*. Copyright © Michael Grant Publications Ltd., 1956, 1959, 1971. **Penguin Putnam, Inc., A Pearson Company** From *The Boy of the Painted Cave* by Justin Denzel. Copyright © 1988 by Justin Denzel. **Peter Bedrick Books Inc.** "Famous Women: Scholars and Artists" by Fiona Macdonald from *Women in Ancient Rome*. Copyright © 2000 by Fiona Macdonald. **Raintree/Steck-Vaughn Publishers, Division of Steck-Vaughn Company** From *The Ancient Romans* by Anita Ganeri. Copyright © 2000 by Steck-Vaughn Company. "Early Rome" by Sean Sheehan and Pat Levy from *The Ancient World: Rome*. Copyright © 1999 by Steck-Vaughn Company. **Random House, Inc.** "The Wooden Horse" by William Russell from *Classical Myths to Read Aloud*. Copyright © 1988 by William F. Russell. Used by permission of Crown Publishers, a division of Random House, Inc. **Scholastic, Inc.** "The Golden Apples" by Mary Pope Osborne from *Favorite Greek Myths*. Copyright © 1989 by Mary Pope Osborne. "The Sirens: A Greek Myth" by Bernard Evslin from *The Adventures of Ulysses*. © 1969 Scholastic, Inc.

Scott, Foresman and Company, a division of Pearson Education "Night Thoughts Aboard a Boat" by Tu Fu, "Ship of State" by Horace, "The Peach-Blossom Fountain" by T'ao Ch'ien from *Scott Foresman Database*. **Simon & Schuster, Inc.** "Deborah" by Carol Armstrong from *Women of the Bible*. Copyright © 1998 by Carol Armstrong. **The Atlantic Monthly Press, an imprint of Grove/Atlantic** "I Built My House Near Where Others Dwell" by T'ao Ch'ien from *Anthology of Chinese Literature*. Copyright © 1965 by Grove Press Inc. **The Estate of Arthur Waley, c/o John Robinson** From *The Analects of Confucius*, translated and annotated by Arthur Waley. Copyright © 1938 by George Allen and Unwin Ltd. **The Estate of Louis & Norma Untermeyer** "Rama: The Bow That Could Not Be Bent," "Julius Caesar: The Ides of March," and "The Firebringer: Prometheus" by Louis Untermeyer from *The Firebringer and Other Great Stories*. Copyright © 1968 by Louis Untermeyer. **The Millbrook Press Inc.** "In the Beginning" and "Babylonia" by Elaine Landau from *The Babylonians: The Cradle of Civilization*. Copyright © 1997 by Elaine Landau. **University of Chicago Press** "The Mice That Set Elephants Free" and "The Brahman, The Thief, and the Ghost" by Arthur W. Ryder (translator) from the *Panchatantra*. Copyright 1952 by The University of Chicago; copyright renewed 1953 by Mary E. Ryder and Winifred Ryder. "The Death of Hektor" from Book XXII of the *Iliad* by Homer, from *Iliad of Homer*, translated by Richmond Lattimore. Copyright 1951, The University of Chicago. **University of Texas Press** "I Love a Girl, But She Lives Over There" by John L. Foster from *Love Songs of the NEW Kingdom*. Copyright © 1969, 1970, 1971, 1972, 1973, 1974 by John L. Foster. **Viking Penguin, Inc., a division of Penguin Putnam, Inc.** "Writing and Alphabets: Why Did People Begin Writing?" by Tiphaine Samoyault from *Alphabetical Order: How The Alphabet Began*. Copyright © 1996 Circonflexe. Translation copyright © Penguin Books USA Inc. 1998.

Note: Every effort has been made to locate the copyright owner of material reprinted in this book. Omissions brought to our attention will be corrected in subsequent printings.